CW01432352

THE WINDSOR LEGACY

THE WINDSOR LEGACY

A Royal Dynasty of Secrets, Scandal and Survival

ROBERT JOBSON

First published in the UK in 2025 by Blink Publishing
An imprint of Bonnier Books UK
5th Floor, HYLO, 105 Bunhill Row,
London, EC1Y 8LZ

A CIP catalogue record for this book is available from the British Library.

Hardback ISBN: 9781789468762
Trade Paperback ISBN: 9781789468779

Also available as an ebook and an audiobook

1 3 5 7 9 10 8 6 4 2

Design and Typeset by Envy Design Ltd
Printed and bound by CPI (UK) Ltd, Croydon CR0 4YY

The authorised representative in the EEA is
Bonnier Books UK (Ireland) Limited.
Registered office address: Floor 3, Block 3, Miesian Plaza,
Dublin 2, D02 Y754, Ireland
compliance@bonnierbooks.ie

www.bonnierbooks.co.uk

For my mother, Jean Edith Jobson.
An inspiration, forever in my heart.

It will keep its tradition of compromise and of respect for a law that is above the State, and it will be tolerant of dissent, as well as of religion – although it will nonetheless leave anachronisms and loose ends everywhere, including, perhaps, the monarchy...

GEORGE ORWELL, *THE LION AND THE UNICORN: SOCIALISM AND THE ENGLISH GENIUS*, 1941

CONTENTS

Introduction: A Dynasty Reborn 1

1. LILIBET AND GRANDPA ENGLAND 13
2. THE 'LITTLE MAN' AND 'THAT WOMAN' 21
3. THIS GHASTLY VOID 37
4. FOR VALOUR 53
5. TROUBLE IN PARADISE 71
6. FORBIDDEN BONDS 79
7. A BURIED FILE 93
8. FAIR GAME 103
9. THE CAMILLA DILEMMA 117
10. A LAMB TO THE SLAUGHTER 129
11. SEPARATE LIVES 141
12. SPECIAL FRIENDS 149

13. THE PEOPLE'S PRINCESS 157
14. THE PROUD MEDDLER 173
15. SACRED VOWS 187
16. THE EPSTEIN CONNECTION 199
17. TIME'S UP 211
18. THE FALLOUT 229
19. THE FLIGHTS OF ANGELS 243
20. VIVAT REX CAROLUS! 257
21. WORRYINGLY DECREPIT 267
22. ROYALLY MINTED 279
23. THE SILENT THREAT 293

ACKNOWLEDGEMENTS 309
SELECT BIBLIOGRAPHY 315
SOURCE NOTES 321

INTRODUCTION:

A DYNASTY REBORN

I may be uninspiring, but I'll be damned if I am going to be an alien.

KING GEORGE V, 1917

Today the British monarchy stands firm – symbolic, steady and above the political fray. King Charles III holds no power, yet he leads. He listens, advises and warns – but he does not rule or ride into battle at the head of his troops, as his forebears once did.[1] Modern monarchs, after all, reign not rule – overstep, and the Crown risks collapse.

Magna Carta in 1215 symbolised the start of the gradual constitutional curb on monarchy, but kings and queens regnant effectively lost any real authority with the 1689 Bill of Rights, which started a century long process of handing control of laws, taxation and the military to Parliament. In the eighteenth century, George I and his Hanoverian successors increasingly leaned on ministers – clearing the path for Britain's first de facto prime minister, Sir Robert Walpole, who served from 1721–42.[2]

By Queen Victoria's reign, the monarchy was largely symbolic.

Power lay with the Prime Minister and Cabinet – hired, fired, and steered by the leader, dubbed 'first among equals'.[3] Between them, they set the agenda; MPs vote it through Parliament. The monarch in turn rubber-stamps these decisions, giving Royal Assent, but it is a formality; the last refusal was in 1708.[4]

Prime Ministers come and go – three already under King Charles: Truss, Sunak, now Starmer. The Crown stays put. His mother, Queen Elizabeth II, saw fifteen of them 'serve at her pleasure' over her seventy-year reign.

There is currently no overwhelming push to abolish the British monarchy – polls show only about a quarter of the public express half-hearted support for doing so – but there is no great enthusiasm for system change. Sentiment alone would not be enough anyway. As an integral part of our democracy, the Crown is woven into the fabric of the UK's parliamentary democracy and dismantling it would require a fundamental overhaul of the entire system as well as our culture and national identity.

Scrapping the monarchy would take a public mandate – likely a referendum – and a legal overhaul of epic scale. Parliament would need to unravel centuries of law: the Acts of Settlement, Union, and Royal Succession. The Crown would vanish from state machinery – no more 'Crown in Parliament', Royal Assent, or oaths to the sovereign. A written constitution would be needed to reboot the system with a new head of state. Monumental, but history has shown that even the mightiest monarchies fall when the people shift.[5]

England was once a republic, born in blood when Charles I lost his head for defying Parliament. Obsessed with divine right, he tried to rule alone. His bungled attempt to arrest five MPs in 1642 triggered civil war. Defeated by Oliver Cromwell and Sir Thomas Fairfax's New Model Army at the decisive battles of Marston Moor (1644) and Naseby (1645), he fled, was captured by the Scots and handed over, tried, and executed in 1649. His final word said to be – 'Remember' – still haunts, its meaning a mystery.[6]

The monarchy was abolished and replaced by Cromwell's republic; first the Commonwealth, then the Protectorate. But after Cromwell's death in 1658, it quickly fell apart. His son Richard failed to lead, and by 1660 the monarchy was back with Charles II. The Interregnum lasted just eleven years but changed everything. The new king, son of Charles I, faced limits: no money without Parliament, no standing army, tighter laws, and rising pushback. Absolute rule was gone – future kings or queens regnant would now have to govern with consent.

Critics of monarchy have long warned that hereditary rule risks disaster, placing power in the hands of individuals chosen by birth, not ability. At least Anglo-Saxon England had a safeguard: the Witan, a council that chose kings based on merit, not blood. That restraint vanished with the Norman Conquest, replaced by William the Conqueror's unchecked authority. It marked the dawn of feudal absolutism, with the king supreme over land, law, and loyalty. Claiming power 'by the sword', William ruled on the belief that all land was held by the Crown, and he established monarchy *jure hereditario* – by right of inheritance – entrenching dynastic succession over election or consent.

Charles I was not the only disaster – history has laid bare the flaws of dynastic succession. Edward II was weak, pliable, and ousted – likely murdered. Richard II was vain, autocratic, and deaf to advice; revolt cost him his crown. Henry VI, unfit to rule, lost control and plunged England into civil war. James II clung to Catholic absolutism and was booted out and fled in the Glorious Revolution. Edward VIII ditched duty for infatuation, then disgraced the Crown with Nazi sympathies. The long list of royal missteps shows that who ends up on the throne matters – but it is more luck than judgement. Imagine modern Britain accepting King Harry (with Meghan as Queen Consort) or King Andrew – highly unlikely, yet both are still in the line of succession.

Today's royal dynasty, the House of Windsor, was born in the flames of the Great War. It owes its name to King George V's gut instinct for survival. As the battles against the Germans raged, author H.G. Wells infamously slammed his own royal court in an article in the *Daily Herald*. Furious, and quoting Wells, the King retorted, 'I may be "uninspiring", but I'll be damned if I'm an "alien!"' In that moment, the King, stung, knew at once he could not let it slide and moved to shed the monarchy's Germanic links, becoming a new British-sounding dynasty; rebuilt on resilience and reinvention.

In 1917, anti-German rage swept the streets. Riots had torn through London two years earlier after the sinking of the ocean-going liner RMS *Lusitania*; sunk by a German U-boat on 7 May 1915 when it was torpedoed off the coast of Ireland, resulting in the deaths of 1,197 passengers and crew. Mobs had smashed German shops, bakeries and pubs in response.

As their sons fell at Passchendaele (the Third Battle of Ypres) from July to November 1917, mowed down by machine-gun fire as they climbed from the trenches 'over the top' towards enemy lines, back home tensions rose again. In Liverpool, windows were shattered, and fires raged in neighbourhoods known for German families. Streets such as Berlin Road were renamed for fear of reprisals; becoming Albany Road, scrubbed clean of ties to the 'Hun'.[7]

It was the same story across the country, largely fuelled by wartime propaganda. There were witch-hunts and spy scares.

Rallies were held to denounce Germans. Families with any German links faced being terrorised and many changed their names – Schmidt to Smith, Müller to Miller – fearing a backlash from angry mobs. Businesses hid any Germanic roots, rebranding to survive. Thousands of foreign nationals living in the UK were arrested, deported or imprisoned on the orders of the British government as 'enemy aliens', suspected of spying, despite there being no proof. Fear ruled the streets.

King George V, fifty-two at the time, was experienced enough to know he could not risk the monarchy becoming a target. It reached crisis point in 1917, when there was genuine concern that Germany might win the war. His private secretary, Lord Stamfordham, a hardened veteran of the Anglo-Zulu War, had his finger firmly on the nation's pulse, as did the Liberal prime minister, Lloyd George. Both urged swift action; the King agreed and nodded the changes through. With the enemy Gotha bombers over London's skies, George V and his family, mostly of German descent, reclaimed their British identity. The dynasty name of Saxe-Coburg-Gotha was discarded and replaced by the new House of Windsor; a name drawn from the ancient Berkshire castle, a royal residence, as enduring and English as its stone.

At a Privy Council meeting on 17 July 1917, the King proclaimed that 'all descendants in the male line of Queen Victoria, who are subjects of these realms, other than female descendants who marry or who have married, shall bear the name of Windsor.' It was a decisive move, a public relations masterstroke, but a timely and vital one. The *Manchester Guardian* hailed it as 'wise', strengthening the monarchy's bond with the people. *The Times* echoed the sentiment, calling it a 'timely act of patriotism'.

The German Emperor, Kaiser Wilhem II, the King's first cousin and Queen Victoria's grandson, mocked George's rebrand. He sarcastically referred to the renaming by joking that a famous William Shakespeare play should be retitled *The Merry Wives of Saxe-Coburg and Gotha*, instead of *The Merry Wives of Windsor* – a pointed jab at the monarchy's efforts to obscure its German heritage.[8]

British princes had for years traditionally married foreign princesses – many of German heritage – to forge political alliances and because they were royal and related. King George also issued Letters Patent limiting the use of royal titles. While it did not specifically address the subject of marriage to non-royals, it marked a giant step towards modernising the monarchy and its customs, leading the way for royals being able to wed so-called commoners.

Just a few years later, on 20 May 1910, King George V, only two weeks into his reign after the death of Edward VII on 6 May, was photographed with eight other leading European royals at his father's funeral. The group included Haakon VII of Norway, Ferdinand I of Bulgaria, Manuel II of Portugal, Wilhelm II, German Emperor, George I of Greece, Albert I of Belgium, Alfonso XIII of Spain, and Frederick VIII of Denmark. Dubbed the 'Nine Kings' photograph, it captured a rare assembly of European royalty on the eve of what would be a seismic change; within months Manuel II was deposed in the Portuguese revolution, and others would later be swept from their thrones by war and political upheaval.

The assassination in 1914 of Archduke Franz Ferdinand, heir-presumptive to the Austro-Hungarian throne, was the starting gun that triggered the First World War, as a web of alliances, nationalism, and imperial tensions escalated rapidly. Suddenly, Europe was engulfed in the chaos of war. It threatened to upend everything. By 1918 the conflict had claimed the lives of nine million soldiers. Those who returned home and those who mourned their dead loved ones demanded change, and more; they wanted their voice heard. The old ways were as dead as their fallen comrades.

Four empires fell: Russia, Germany, Austro-Hungary, and the Ottomans. Republics rose from the ruins. The royal tapestry unravelled. The people demanded leaders from their ranks, or at the very least kings who bent to their will. George V bent to survive. Others broke. In November 1918, under pressure from German military leaders and revolutionaries as Germany faced defeat, Wilhelm II was forced to abdicate and was exiled to the Netherlands. The Weimar Republic was established. Ferdinand resigned. Spain's throne wobbled. Portugal's crown went too.

Russia's autocratic ruler, Tsar Nicholas II, was also toppled. Blamed for Russia's disastrous failures in the war, poor leadership and domestic unrest, he abdicated in March 1917 following mass protests and the February Revolution. Nicholas and George, first cousins, had been wartime allies, and were close. After he was overthrown, the Tsar and his family were exiled to Siberia, later moved to Yekaterinburg, under house arrest.

Nicholas begged King George V for refuge in Britain through personal letters and diplomatic channels. At first George agreed, then reneged, warned off by senior aides such as Lord Stamfordham, who advised that Alexandra, the German-born Tsarina, was too toxic, and Nicholas was seen as a despot with blood on his hands. Fearing for his own crown, George did nothing. The trapped Romanovs hoped for a rescue by British secret services, but none came. On 17 July 1918, the Bolshevik guards executed them all – the Tsar, his wife Alexandra Feodorovna, and their five children Olga, Tatiana, Maria, Anastasia, and Alexei. King George carried the guilt for years.

The Romanovs' murders were a stark warning: adapt or perish. George V again read the runes. He cut royal funding to the wider family, toured front lines, embraced austerity, and linked the Crown to public sacrifice through creating Remembrance Day. Duty became the royal creed, blending tradition with service and spectacle.

In 1924, despite his staunch opposition to socialism, which he saw as a threat to the monarchy and social order, George V pragmatically invited Ramsay MacDonald to form Britain's first Labour government. Labour had won 191 seats in the 1923 election, trailing the Conservatives' 258, but Baldwin's government collapsed after losing a vote of confidence. Backed by the Liberals, MacDonald led a short-lived minority government, brought down less than a year later by the Campbell Case scandal (August-October 1924) and the forged Zinoviev Letter in October 1924, which stirred fears of socialist revolution. The King's pragmatism cemented the monarchy's survival as a politically neutral, stabilising force.[9]

On 21 April 1926, Princess Elizabeth of York was born to Prince Albert (Bertie) and Elizabeth, the Duke and Duchess of York. Third in line to the throne, few imagined this charming baby girl would ever reign. Her uncle, Edward, the Prince of Wales, was after all the direct heir to the throne and still expected to marry a suitable bride and have children.

Fate had other plans. Baby Elizabeth grew to become the sixth undisputed queen regnant of England and Great Britain, the longest-serving and oldest monarch in British history, and a symbol of the Windsor dynasty's enduring leadership.

At the time of Elizabeth's birth, the British Empire ruled over a quarter of the world's population and land, the largest empire in history on which the sun never set. In the century since her birth, the House of Windsor has shed its imperial crown but survived wars, scandals, divorces, betrayals, a devastating fire, and a global pandemic.

Each Windsor monarch has left their mark on the ever-evolving institution: George V steadied the Empire, Edward VIII forced it to modernise before abandoning it, George VI led through war, and Elizabeth II upheld stability for over seventy years. On 8 September 2022, her eldest son, Charles III, became the oldest person ever to accede to the British throne, after also serving the longest apprenticeship as Elizabeth's heir.

Over a century since Elizabeth's birth, the Crown has proved resilient. It has learned from the mistakes of European royalty, weathered scandal and embraced change as the nation transformed politically, socially and culturally. From the rise of fascism and communism across Europe to technological revolutions across the world, the British monarchy has evolved to align with societal changes. As the British empire dissolved, the nation turned inward, and the Commonwealth, a legacy of the Empire, was reimagined for a modern age.

The Second World War left Britain battered: bombed cities in ruins, 450,700 dead, including military personnel and civilians, and an economy in tatters. But from the chaos rose the Welfare State, a lifeline for all. By the late 1950s, recovery was visible. Jobs were plentiful, more homes were constructed for working families, and markets boomed. Conservative prime minister Harold Macmillan famously said, 'Most of our people have never had it so good.'

Under Elizabeth II's stewardship, Britain transformed. The class system crumbled. Aristocrats faded, women demanded equality, and the middle and working classes rose. The old world fell, and a new Britain emerged. Post-war, her people wanted more.

Homes were filled with gadgets, youth roared to Merseybeat and the Beatles, and Swinging London buzzed in the Sixties. Then came Margaret Thatcher, 'The Iron Lady' and Britain's first female prime minister. She sold industries, crushed unions, and rewired the economy as the UK splintered with the miners' strikes and the Poll Tax. She was criticised as divisive and damaging. Later as churches emptied, gay marriage became legal in the UK, industry shifted to tech, and Brexit marked the UK leaving the EU.

Meanwhile, amid failed royal marriages and scandals, the monarchy faltered too. Respect lingers, but to many young people it is seen as a relic; apathy, not rebellion, is a serious threat. Elizabeth II, skilled in subtle influence, watched on uneasily. Ahead of Scotland's 2014 independence vote, while chatting to crowds at Balmoral, she expressed her hope that Scots would 'think very carefully about the future' before voting. This subtle remark was seen as the Queen's concern over the potential breakup of the UK, a rare nudge from the monarch. When the vote stayed with the union, she reportedly 'purred down the line', a small victory for a Sovereign who valued her unified kingdom.[10]

Queen Elizabeth II's death in 2022 was much more than a turning point – it was a reckoning. The monarchy now stands at a crossroads, its future uncertain. In fifty years, the UK will be a very different place. It could splinter: an independent Scotland, a united Ireland, even Wales breaking away. England might once more stand alone. British identity is shifting, shaped by diversity. Tradition will clash with change. The Crown may survive as a symbol – or may vanish into history.

King William V or King George VII, if they choose those regnal names, face a bumpy ride ahead. Reverence for royalty, which has ebbed and flowed for years, may wane even further. The Crown, passed by birth and adorned with colonial spoils, feels to many like a vestige of a bygone era. Critics argue that wisdom is not in the DNA of kings, and modern democracy has no room for hereditary power. Those voices are no longer alone in the dark.

For *The Windsor Legacy*, published in time to mark Queen Elizabeth II's centenary in early 2026, my aim is clear: to tell the true story of the House of Windsor from the date of her birth to the present day – how it became the world's most enduring royal dynasty, survived scandal and crisis, and stood the test of time. I also set out to ask a pressing question: can an unelected institution still justify its place in a modern democracy?

With over thirty-five years reporting experience on the royal beat, I have covered defining royal moments at home and across the globe – from Charles and Diana's divorce and her tragic 1997 death to Andrew's Epstein scandal; in 2005 I broke the world exclusive on Charles's engagement to Camilla, earning Scoop of the Year, and I had a front-row seat to Harry and Meghan's 2020 royal exit. The Queen's Platinum Jubilee and her 2022 death closed one chapter; Charles III's coronation and a new generation of heirs began the next.

CHAPTER 1

LILIBET AND GRANDPA ENGLAND

A character with an air of authority and reflectiveness astonishing in an infant.

CHURCHILL'S REFLECTIONS ON PRINCESS ELIZABETH, AGED TWO, AFTER THEIR FIRST ENCOUNTER

It was April 1926 and London had been shrouded in gloom for a week, as the country teetered on the brink of a fiscal meltdown. The threat of a general strike cast a long shadow.[11] Outside 17 Bruton Street in Mayfair, beneath a bleak sky, reporters clustered together in the chill. They nursed steaming cups of tea and devoured sandwiches graciously provided by the aristocratic homeowners. Stories and gossip flowed as they waited for something – anything – worth printing.

The headlines kept rolling in. On 21 April, Italian dictator Benito Mussolini narrowly escaped an assassin's bullet. Weeks earlier, in Riga, Latvia, negotiators from both sides signed a treaty to end the Polish Soviet war, establishing a border between the two countries. For the reporters in London, bundled in trench coats and tipped hats, their assignment may have felt trivial by comparison.

Yet within the walls of the white Palladian fronted house with Corinthian columns on either side, a different vibe prevailed, one of pure, undiluted joy. It was there, in the early hours of 21 April 1926, at precisely 2.40 a.m., that Princess Elizabeth, the Duke and Duchess of York's firstborn child, and King George V and Queen Mary's first grandchild, came into the world; a beacon of new life amid a gathering storm.

The Duchess, Elizabeth, had been in labour for hours. Sir Henry Stratton, the surgeon, eventually made the call for a caesarean section. It went well and the baby girl was healthy, weighing 6 pounds (around 2.73 kg). She stood third in line to the throne at birth, behind her uncle, the Prince of Wales, and her father, the Duke of York. No one realistically expected then that her father would become king or that she would eventually accede to the throne.

As the reporters kicked their heels outside, news of her birth remained private for a few hours. The first to be told were Their Majesties the King and Queen, who were at Windsor Castle. They drove to London that afternoon to see the newborn child. 'A little darling with a lovely complexion and pretty fair hair,' Queen Mary later wrote in her diary. The Duke of York also penned a letter to his mother, saying, 'You don't know what a tremendous joy it is to Elizabeth & me to have our little girl.'

Despite their royal rank, the Duke and Duchess, Albert and Elizabeth, were regarded as attentive parents for the time. Elizabeth wrote to her mother on 28 October from Sandringham, 'My Darling Mother . . . The baby is very well and now spending the entire day taking her shoes off & sucking her toes!' They hired Clara Knight, known as 'Allah', as a nanny, who handled the nurturing care, almost serving as a surrogate mother. The little princess was baptised eight months later at Buckingham

Palace by the Archbishop of Canterbury, the aloof Scot, Dr Cosmo Gordon Lang. She was named Elizabeth Alexandra Mary.

This was a moment of joy after what had been a turbulent time. Through the war and after, the King had stood as a symbol of grit and royal resilience. At home, strikes and Irish uprisings simmered, but reforms and Labour's rise kept revolt at bay. Fear of Bolshevism held people to the steady ground.

King George sidestepped politics, preferring instead to embrace spectacle. At the 1924 Empire Exhibition, crowds came, drawn to the royalty's power on full display. In public, he was the king and a family man, an image carefully crafted. But in private, he lived relatively simply at York Cottage, far from royal splendour. He had a fierce temper, and his bond with his children was at best strained.

His stern parenting style had lasting consequences for his children. He was gruff – gruff voice, gruff manner. Not cruel by intent, but cruel by effect. When he barked, everyone around him jumped. He famously told his friend Edward Stanley, 17th Earl of Derby, 'I was afraid of my father, my father was afraid of his mother, and I'm going to make damn sure my children are afraid of me!' His dark humour cut deep. Once, young Edward asked about babies and where they came from; George replied eerily that they flew in, wings chopped off. The young Prince Edward was haunted by the image for weeks.

The royal children's austere upbringing left lasting scars. Prince Edward, the eldest, known as 'David' to his family, became anxious and restless, later confessing his fears to his biographer Hector Bolitho who wrote, 'The prince has a horror of his father.' Bertie, the second son, likely developed his stammer from the age of eight from being under his father's stringency. His strict upbringing included corporal punishment, and painful leg splints to treat his knock knees. He was also forced to switch from left- to right-handed writing.

Only the third son, Prince Henry, found stability in military discipline, while his younger sister, Princess Mary, embraced a steady life of service.[12] George, the fifth child, sought escape in drugs, masking inner turmoil with charm; while Prince John, the youngest, was born into a world that rejected him. His seizures and likely autism isolated him, and the King had no tolerance for frailty.

As John's health declined, he was tucked away at Wood Farm, cared for by his loyal nanny, Lala Bill, and left to fade from memory before his death in 1919, aged thirteen. The King's diary called him 'a worry', and mourning for him was muted. It was as if the prince had never lived. Critics saw neglect, a family more concerned with appearances than compassion. His brief, hidden life revealed a harsher truth about the House of Windsor; its willingness to turn away from perceived imperfection to preserve the Crown.

Prince George was trouble, too. Like Prince Edward, the Prince of Wales, he gave his father headaches. But as the fourth son, he was free of the crown's weight. He went through Osborne and Dartmouth colleges, where the boys' Royal Navy careers were shaped, but George was made for other things. He was the ultimate party prince.

In his twenties, George lived fast and recklessly. Morphine and cocaine were his companions, and Kiki Preston, the 'Girl with the Silver Syringe', was his match. A Vanderbilt by blood and a wild beauty by reputation, Kiki thrived in Paris's jazz-fuelled nightlife, where she and George collided. Recently dismissed from the Royal Navy for what was described as unseemly behaviour, the prince embraced Parisian freedom with abandon.

Married but hedonistic, Kiki was a magnet for trouble. Her fiery affair with the prince ended when King George V intervened, exiling her and sending George away to recover. She later disappeared into Kenya's scandalous Happy Valley, deeper in drugs and whispers of a secret child; a boy born in 1926 and adopted in America, leaving behind a trail of intrigue.

Rumours swirled around George, claiming he fathered Princess Diana's stepmother Raine Spencer with Barbara Cartland – another unsubstantiated tale. His secrets lay tangled in beds and nightclubs, with alleged lovers spanning society heiress Poppy Baring, cabaret star Florence Mills, singer Jessie Matthews, and Margaret, Duchess of Argyll. A bisexual, there were male lovers too, reportedly including Noël Coward, writer Cecil Roberts, and Jorge Ferrara, son of the Argentine ambassador. One story alleged he was arrested for an affair but released when his identity emerged. His marriage to Princess Marina of Greece and Denmark, on 29 November 1934, brought George V relief and momentarily hushed the gossip in society circles.

By the time Princess Elizabeth was born, the King had perhaps learned his lesson. His children, long used to his brusque nature, were surprised at the warmth and affection he bestowed on the little princess. He became a doting grandfather. In 1927, at his request, the Yorks embarked on a six-month tour of the colonies, leaving their baby in the care of her no-nonsense nanny, Clara Knight. The Duchess dreaded the separation, noting in her diary on 6 January 1927: 'Feel very miserable at leaving the baby. I drank some champagne & tried not to weep . . .'

Elizabeth brightened the days of her grandparents, King George and Queen Mary. As a toddler, she could not say 'Elizabeth', so she said 'Lilibet' instead, and it stuck. Her father would later say, 'Lilibet is my pride. Margaret is my joy.'

When the King became seriously ill in December 1928, he asked for her to go with him to Bognor to recuperate by the sea. Before returning, he is famously said to have roared, 'Oh, bugger Bognor,' when the town council asked if they could rename the place Bognor Regis in honour of his convalescence there. His private secretary politely granted the request, and in 1929 the town added 'Regis' to its name.

As the King's health crisis unfolded, the nation anxiously followed the daily updates. His errant heir, Prince Edward, the Prince of Wales, however, showed little interest in the grim news. While touring Kenya, he received an urgent telegram from Prime Minister Stanley Baldwin recalling him to London. He dismissed it nonchalantly as a ploy by 'silly old Baldwin' and called it 'an electoral dodge'.

Even when his assistant private secretary, Alan 'Tommy' Lascelles, implored him to take it seriously, saying, 'The King of England is dying,' the prince shrugged, went out and continued seducing the wife of a colonial official. The next morning, Lascelles resigned in disgust at the prince's behaviour. (He later agreed to return.) Prince Edward's attitude, however, confirmed the King's fears and those of senior courtiers and politicians that his immaturity and reckless behaviour meant he was unfit for the throne.

Oblivious, Princess Elizabeth's early years were full of joy at the York's family home, 145 Piccadilly. Her paternal grandfather adored her, often inviting her to the palace so they could play together. When apart, he would call the nursery at her nearby home and watch her wave through binoculars. By 1930, the York family moved to Royal Lodge in Windsor. Her beloved Grandpa England gave her a Shetland pony, igniting her lifelong passion for horses. Her mother taught her to read at home, keeping the family close. On 21 August 1930, her sister Margaret Rose was born. Elizabeth called her 'Bud', saying, 'She's not a rose yet, is she? Just a bud.'

If Margaret had been a boy, Elizabeth's significance in terms of her constitutional position would have faded. The law of male preference primogeniture, in place until 2013 when Parliament changed it during her long reign, at that time dictated that a younger brother would outrank an older sister in the line of succession. Margaret's birth kept the focus on the York family, which her father fondly called 'we four'.

The little princesses were too young to grasp how the clash between their beloved grandpa and their uncle 'David' would shape their world. To them, he was not a troubled heir but a playful, dashing figure who brought the tales of 'Winnie the Pooh' to life when he read to them aloud. In their eyes, he was sheer enchantment.

CHAPTER 2

THE 'LITTLE MAN' AND 'THAT WOMAN'

I have found it impossible to carry the heavy burden of responsibility and to discharge my duties as King as I would wish to do without the help and support of the woman I love.

KING EDWARD VIII'S ABDICATION SPEECH, 1 DECEMBER 1936

The Abdication Crisis of 1936 rocked the monarchy and British society. A frail George V saw it coming, warning Prime Minister Stanley Baldwin, 'After I am dead, the boy will ruin himself in twelve months.' This prediction proved astonishingly accurate. Baldwin, who viewed Edward as 'half-child, half-genius', also believed he was reckless and unfit to reign. As King Edward VIII, he defied his government, seemingly blind to the constitutional peril he created. His aides, exasperated by his abandonment of duty for hedonistic escapes, watched on helplessly as he spiralled into personal and political ruin, his wilful action placing his public role in jeopardy.

He had started his public life with such promise. Edward's postwar tours as the Prince of Wales kept the monarchy in the spotlight while many of Europe's royal dynasties crumbled. Charismatic and golden-haired, he had the allure of a movie star and a rare magic that captivated the public. But his obsession with his image raised eyebrows. He famously carried a mirror everywhere, confessing, 'I never seem to get tired of looking at myself.' Buoyed by his fame and blinded by ego, Edward was oblivious to the warning signs as powerful enemies circled.

His brand was an elaborate façade built on artifice and illusion – a masterclass in reinvention, crafted from public hopes and shielded by the old guard. People chose to see only what they wished, conveniently overlooking the real picture. With socialism and fascism sweeping across Europe, the British establishment – aristocrats, courtiers and politicians – closed ranks by doing their best to preserve the monarchy, fearing their own demise if it fell. Meanwhile, George V, though stern and rooted in Edwardian traditions, adapted just enough to personify British values: prudence, loyalty and discipline. By the time of his death in 1936, he would have gained the nation's love and the respect of the majority, standing as a steadfast patriarch in turbulent times.

The King may have lacked charm, but Edward had it in spades. Yet, behind his polished exterior lay a frail prince consumed by inner turmoil, grappling with mental health issues, duty, and his desire for personal freedom. To the public, he was a royal superstar; privately, he was unravelling. 'A hopelessly lost feeling has come over me,' he confided to his assistant private secretary, Alan Lascelles. 'I think I'm going mad . . . I long to die.'[13]

Edward's empathy for the working classes won him admiration and the widespread support of the masses. His outspoken concerns, however, put him at odds with the government. Touring the Empire, he became a beacon of hope for a post-war generation, drawing massive crowds with his charisma. Meanwhile, George V stayed home, content with his stamp collection and blasting pheasants on his Norfolk estate. One king stood for the old guard: the other was an enigmatic symbol of a changing world.

Father and son, who were never close, drifted even further apart. Edward's affairs with married women, such as Freda Dudley Ward, repelled the King, who longed for his heir to settle down with a suitable royal or aristocratic bride and produce his own heir. Princess Elisabeth of Romania, Princess Olga of Greece and Denmark, Lady Rosemary Leveson-Gower, a debutante with impeccable lineage, and Lady Rachel Cavendish, daughter of the Duke of Devonshire, were all considered ideal matches. Edward, however, resisted such unions, infuriating the King even more. George's disapproval left lasting scars.[14]

The King rarely praised his eldest son, even when he deserved it. When Edward's 1920 Australian tour drew adoring crowds and bolstered Empire ties, the King brushed off his significant achievement, focusing instead on petty details that his son may have got wrong, such as his choice of spurs for an event, and downplaying the significance of his overall success.

When the Great Depression hit (1930–33), George V invited the Labour prime minister Ramsay MacDonald to form a national coalition government to address the crisis. While legal, it skewed Parliament and left the nation without meaningful opposition. Working-class voters felt blindsided and feared the King had effectively engineered a one-party state, dubbed 'The King's Party'.

Amid turmoil, George sought unity, launching the royal Christmas broadcast in 1932. Encouraged by forward-thinking Prime Minister MacDonald, he turned to radio, speaking from a modest box room at Sandringham; its simplicity hidden to preserve royal grandeur. His address was penned by the master wordsmith Rudyard Kipling, a first cousin of three-time Stanley

Baldwin, which reached 20 million listeners. George's gravelly voice struck a chord. His heartbeat with England.[15]

Edward was restless. He craved change and yearned to break free from his father's outdated world of rigid traditions. Determined to modernise the monarchy, he clashed with George V's fixation on the past. Years later, Edward criticised his father in a BBC interview, recounting his frustration with George's nostalgic refrain: 'Those were the good old times.' The King often admonished his sons with a booming, 'Remember who you are.' But Edward, already riddled with self-doubt, sometimes felt he had no idea. His father's animosity and constant criticism only deepened his inner conflict, leaving himself to question, 'Who am I?'

A diminutive figure, standing around 5 feet 7 inches tall, Edward was known as the 'little man' by his many mistresses. Before Wallis Simpson, there was Lady Thelma Furness. She calmed his inner storms and offered solace, but fate was not on her side. Thelma, a married American heiress and identical twin sister to Gloria Vanderbilt Morgan, found her husband Viscount Furness, a British shipping magnate, dull and began a passionate affair with Edward in 1930. By 1934, it was over.

Before leaving on a transatlantic crossing for the US, Thelma entrusted Wallis, another American, to 'look after the little man'. If she had designs on keeping him for herself, it was a mistake. The enigmatic Wallis, twice married and fiercely ambitious, immediately set about seducing Edward and eclipsing Thelma. Reflecting after his abdication, Thelma said, 'I thought I'd be Queen of England. Instead, I'm just the forgotten mistress.'

By now King George, not in the best of health, weary and frustrated, had lost all faith in Edward. He shifted his focus to Bertie and Elizabeth, finding in them the monarchy's reliable future. The couple had met in June 1920 at a London dance. Instantly smitten, Bertie had no idea she was besotted with his equerry, James Stuart. Over two years and three rejected proposals, Bertie persisted, encouraged by his mother, Queen Mary, who quietly steered events in his favour. The then Lady Elizabeth Bowes Lyon recorded her thoughts in her diaries, revealing a mix of hesitation, affection and independence. Finally, after twelve days of deliberation in January 1923, she accepted Bertie's final proposal, setting the stage for a marriage that would later stabilise the monarchy in crisis.

Their love story, chronicled in Sally Bedell Smith's *George VI and Elizabeth: The Marriage That Saved the Monarchy*,[16] revealed how devotion overcame doubt. What began as a shy prince's unshakable affection became a royal partnership that would reshape the House of Windsor. The King had initially struggled to show admiration for his second son, leaving Bertie burdened by doubt. Yet despite his stammer and insecurity, the young prince threw himself into his duty, serving his father with quiet devotion. With Elizabeth by his side, everything changed – George V softened, embracing the couple and recognising their daughters as the monarchy's future.

Edward, the dashing rebel, and Bertie, the quiet stalwart, epitomised sibling contrasts. The older brother dominated the younger, often overshadowing him with his own confidence and charm. Despite this, they were not always at odds in the early days. As family tensions rose, however, the King saw how important Bertie's role would be. Charming photographs of the princesses by the talented society photographer Marcus Adams were distributed to the press, captivating the public, and casting Elizabeth as the Windsor dynasty's beacon of hope. His 1934 photo of eight-year-old Princess Elizabeth became the portrait on Canada's 1935 $20 bill: not just a colonial currency, but a symbol of continuity, securing the House of Windsor's legacy.

There is strong evidence that George V harboured doubts about his eldest son Edward and towards the end of his life preferred Bertie as his successor. While there is no concrete record of King George explicitly telling Queen Mary he wanted Bertie to succeed him, his disapproval of Edward's conduct and his admiration for Bertie's sense of duty were well known. Queen Mary, ever dutiful and reserved, remained publicly loyal to Edward until his abdication. He was the direct heir, and parental favour was not enough to change that.

On 6 May 1935, the King marked his Silver Jubilee with a grand procession from the palace to St Paul's Cathedral accompanied by Queen Mary, smiling and waving to cheering crowds. Touched by their affection, he later addressed the nation on the radio, saying, 'I know that in some homes today, the rejoicing is overshadowed by anxiety and sorrow. I would ask them to remember that they are in our thoughts and prayers.' His heartfelt words of gratitude and service struck a deep chord with the people.

Privately, however, the King was furious. Edward's reckless behaviour, including openly flaunting his affair with Wallis Simpson, caused constant embarrassment at court. At the Jubilee Ball, the prince stormed off with Wallis after Queen Mary, exasperated by her son's audacity in bringing his mistress to the palace, asked, 'Who is this woman?' Family tensions reached breaking point as the King, increasingly unwell, faced the inevitability of Edward's reign.

By the end of his Silver Jubilee year, the King's health was failing rapidly. Dependent on an oxygen mask to breathe through the night, he grew weaker daily. In January 1936, his condition declined sharply and bulletins from Sandringham were posted on Buckingham Palace gates, charting his deterioration. First, they reported a cold, then, by 17 January, the Palace acknowledged his condition as 'heart weakness'. With the end nearing, the Royal Family gathered at the royal estate of Sandringham in Norfolk, bracing themselves for the inevitable.

Eventually, the King's personal physician, Lord Dawson of Penn, took matters into his own hands for the sake of 'royal dignity'. To prevent prolonged suffering for both the monarch and his family, he personally administered lethal doses of morphine and cocaine around 11 p.m. on 20 January, but only after a nurse had bluntly refused to carry out his earlier instructions.

Dawson timed the death carefully, ensuring the monarch's passing could be reported in the morning edition of *The Times*, avoiding what he saw as the 'lesser' afternoon press such as the *Evening Standard, Evening News* and the *Star*. An hour and a half earlier, Dawson had issued his now-infamous bulletin: 'The King's life is moving peacefully toward its close.' He even called his wife Minnie Ethel, Lady Dawson, to make a call to ensure *The Times* held back publication, orchestrating the King's death to fit media schedules.

The King's final coherent words were reported as 'How's the Empire?' – but this is likely to have been romanticised. In his private memoirs, Dawson noted that the King's actual last words, spoken to his nurse, were reportedly 'God damn you!' in frustration after being given a sedative. The nation mourned, oblivious of Dawson's shocking secret act of euthanasia, which remained secret for fifty years and was only revealed in 1986 when his private papers became public.

With George V dead, the crown fell heavily on Edward's shoulders. At the funeral, just eight days later, the new king looked hollowed out, burdened by his new role. A modern monarch – first to pilot a plane, racing past tradition, and a snappy dresser – but not the one the establishment had hoped for. He ruffled feathers on purpose, even flipping his stamp portrait to show his 'better side'. Already doubtful of his suitability for the role, the Prime Minister, the Cabinet and senior courtiers grew increasingly uneasy.

More troubling was Edward's admiration for the fascist regimes led by Benito Mussolini in Italy and Adolf Hitler in Germany. While he privately admired the efficiency of authoritarian leaders, he was careful not to make his thoughts public. Nazi Germany held answers, the new king believed, but tired old England did not. Prime Minister Baldwin saw the danger: Edward's fixation on Wallis Simpson and dalliance with fascism went too far. He was the king they could not control or tolerate.

In political and society circles rumours swirled about the King. Secret documents whispered of Edward's meddling with foreign policy. He wanted to meet with Hitler, it appeared. But Baldwin could not trust him and refused. The King would not be told either. Behind closed doors, ministers fretted.

MI5 and British intelligence closely monitored Wallis Simpson, suspecting her of leaking sensitive information to Joachim von Ribbentrop, Germany's ambassador to the UK. Ribbentrop, sent to London in 1936 with Hitler's backing, worked to ingratiate himself with Edward and Wallis. Reports suggested an affair, reinforced by claims that he sent her carnations daily, each symbolising an alleged intimate encounter. British officials grew alarmed as Ribbentrop seemed to acquire inside knowledge of British affairs far too quickly, leading them to believe Wallis was the source.

Leading Liberal politician and diplomat Walter Runciman[17]

grew wary when Nazi leaks surfaced. His son, historian Sir Steven Runciman, later recalled his father describing a Cabinet meeting – only for Ribbentrop to repeat its secrets at a reception the same evening. The suspected source? Edward, through Wallis, to Ribbentrop. The government was alarmed enough to tap her phones, but Baldwin knew the scandal had to be contained quietly.[18]

Hitler had heard enough from von Ribbentrop to act. Cunning as a fox, he sensed an opportunity to strike at the heart of the British establishment. He dispatched to England Edward's cousin, the mercurial Charles Edward, the Duke of Saxe-Coburg, a grandson of Queen Victoria and a passionate Nazi. An absurd character, Saxe-Coburg attended George V's funeral wearing a British army uniform, his presence as a Nazi party member sparked controversy. Hitler saw Edward VIII as a potential British dictator, a monarch with powers the likes of which had not been seen since George II. The Duke of Saxe-Coburg met Edward in private and reported back to the Führer.

During the meeting, Edward, defiant, spoke of his being disgruntled by Baldwin's interference, and insisted that meeting Hitler was his decision alone as head of state. He told his German cousin, 'Who is King here, Baldwin or I? I wish to speak to Hitler, and I will, here or in Germany.' Was Edward now playing both sides, hedging his bets? If he was, Hitler took the bait. He saw the King as useful to his cause and countering the threat of communism.

Hitler regarded Saxe-Coburg as a useful idiot, but in the end a liability. Born into privilege in Surrey he was raised as an English prince. He moved to Germany aged fifteen and acceded to the ducal throne in 1900, ruling until deposed like other German princes in 1918. During the 1920s, he financed violent far right paramilitary groups and joined the Nazi party in 1933. He became leader of the German Red Cross and an unofficial Nazi diplomat handling secret missions. From 1935 to 1939, he became a Nazi link in London, and used his connections that included his sister, Alice, Countess of Athlone, to foster relationships with British society and the royal family. Intelligence archives later revealed his push for an Anglo-German alliance with Edward VIII. By 1945, Hitler wanted Saxe-Coburg killed, with Bletchley Park intercepting a telegram ordering his death. After the Second World War, he faced denazification, was fined, lost his property, and died broke and disgraced in 1954.[19]

When Baldwin learned of Edward's treachery, he was deeply troubled, but again kept his concerns private. Viewing the King as disingenuous and dangerously unpredictable, Baldwin grew uneasy, especially after Hitler reoccupied the Rhineland. Edward stunned his government by urging no action, a breach of his constitutional role. Rumours of the overt Nazi sympathies shared by Edward and Wallis swirled in Whitehall. Baldwin acted decisively, ordering Home Secretary Sir John Simon to have MI5 bug their phones.[20]

Edward, reckless in love and politics, drifted further. The establishment watched warily while the public stayed oblivious. Now openly with Wallis, still married, he chartered the yacht *Nahlin* for a carefree Mediterranean cruise, strolling through Greek and Turkish ports as if the throne were an afterthought. Edward believed he could live two lives – 'be kingly' when needed, then switch off – fooling himself that the crown's weight could be shed like a coat. His assistant private secretary, Lascelles, recognised Edward's foolishness and later gave the diarist Harold Nicolson a peek behind the curtain, saying, 'They're like two children together.' Edward, always detached, would say after the trip, 'Back to striped trousers and coats again, back to school.' Edward hated the role and even then, he seemed ready to leave it behind.[21]

Upon his return, Edward shirked royal duties, sending Bertie to open a hospital in Aberdeen while he whisked Wallis away to Balmoral. The British media, led by powerful press barons such as Lord Rothermere of the *Daily Mail* and Lord Beaverbrook of the *Daily Express*, kept a self-imposed blackout, shielding the affair from the UK public even as the wider world watched, engrossed in the scandal. Across the Atlantic, American journalist H.L. Mencken, dubbed 'The Voice of the Jazz Age', called it 'the biggest story since the Resurrection'. Foreign newspapers exposed the affair, while British editions carefully excised snippets to keep their readers in the dark.

Years later, in his 1966 memoir, *The Abdication of King Edward VIII*, Lord Beaverbrook described Baldwin's mounting frustration as the crisis dragged on. Baldwin viewed Edward's insistence on marrying Wallis Simpson as a direct threat to the stability of both the monarchy and the government. Petulant and determined, Edward clumsily tried to force Wallis into his public world, even hoping to win over Queen Mary, a futile move.

Her rejection only fuelled his defiance. He showered Wallis with jewels, slashing servants' pay to fund his extravagance, spending a third of his fortune on gifts, which included a tiara from Van Cleef & Arpels in 1937. Undeterred by whispers in Whitehall or disapproving stares, he flaunted his mistress in public, on ski trips, at lavish dinners and by his side, as if she were already his Queen Consort.

The affair could no longer be hidden from the British public. Wallis filed for divorce from her second husband, Ernest Simpson. The decree nisi was granted on 27 October at Ipswich Assizes,

Suffolk, citing *his* adultery, and the news was reported in the British press. It was a pivotal moment, escalating the crisis and deepening Baldwin's fears about Edward's intention to marry her. Wallis's divorce would be completed on 3 May 1937 only nine days before George VI's coronation.

For Baldwin and his Cabinet, the scandal had already escalated into a constitutional crisis. As Supreme Governor of the Church of England, it was unthinkable at that time for the King to marry a divorced woman; he risked alienating the clergy and his people. The stakes were now clear: the throne or Wallis. The clock was ticking on his reign.[22]

On 13 November, the King's private secretary, Alec Hardinge, 2nd Baron Hardinge of Penshurst, delivered a stark warning to his boss: 'The silence in the British press about Your Majesty's friendship with Mrs Simpson is not going to be maintained. Judging by the letters from British subjects abroad, the effect will be calamitous.' The letter made clear that the scandal would soon explode into public view. Calm was over; chaos was coming.

On 16 November 1936, the King summoned Baldwin and declared his intention to marry Wallis. Baldwin, adamantly opposed to the union, stood firm: it would not be accepted by him, his government or the wider public, he said. 'The Queen becomes the Queen of the country. Therefore, in the choice of a Queen, the voice of the people must be heard.' Baldwin's stance was echoed by Stanley Bruce, the Australian High Commissioner and formerly Australia's eighth prime minister, who was appalled at the prospect of such a marriage.

That evening, Edward went to see his mother and again begged Queen Mary to meet Wallis, but the respected royal matriarch flatly refused, dismissing her as 'an adventuress'. Edward had backed himself into a corner. He knew then there was no escape.

While the British press had shielded the affair, the Royal Family and Cabinet had long grappled with the mounting crisis. Behind closed doors, the prospect of an abdication was already being discussed as a serious possibility. Both Baldwin and Queen Mary, attuned to public sentiment, understood that Edward's obsession with Wallis was a dangerous threat to the monarchy's stability and the unity of the country.

The romantic narrative frames Edward's abdication purely as a sacrifice of duty for love, but others like the eminent historians A.J.P. Taylor and Philip Ziegler argue that it was a calculated bloodless coup, to oust an unsuitable monarch. Edward's fixation on marrying Wallis Simpson was the pretext; but the British establishment had long viewed the King, a moderniser with Nazi sympathies, as a destabilising force. Determined to protect the monarchy, Baldwin played his hand with cold precision. Edward, stubborn and blind to the consequence, trapped himself in a constitutional crisis of his own making. His demand to make Wallis his queen doomed him. Baldwin and the establishment saw that Bertie, steady and obedient, was the safer bet.

When Edward visited depression-hit South Wales in November, including the derelict Dowlais Ironworks near Merthyr Tydfil, he strained Baldwin's patience to the limit. Walking through bleak towns where he famously expressed concern over the severe unemployment and poverty, he was shocked by the conditions he saw. It was here that he made his infamous remark, saying, 'Something must be done.' It was a bold statement, too bold in Baldwin's eyes, who saw it as a direct challenge to the government.[23]

Declassified Cabinet papers from 25 November 1936 confirmed the tension between Edward and Baldwin. The file CAB 23/85 revealed that the Prime Minister had informed the Cabinet of the King's determination to marry Mrs Simpson, even though he knew a constitutional crisis would ensue. He also stressed that the government and public opinion opposed the marriage due to her divorces. The Prime Minister laid it out bluntly: marry Wallis, and abdication is the only option. Edward refused to bend, testing Baldwin's patience to the limit.[24]

Years later, Edward claimed he only wanted to modernise the monarchy, not endanger it. He saw the institution as outdated, drifting from the people. Reform, not rebellion, was his aim. 'I had lots of political conceptions,' he admitted, 'but I kept them to myself.' Edward believed Baldwin, haunted by his failures on unemployment, deflected blame. 'Baldwin realised they'd done little to help,' Edward claimed, suggesting his social activism fuelled their tensions. He saw himself as a modern king; Baldwin saw him as a dangerous threat to the status quo.[25]

Desperate, Edward offered a last-ditch compromise: a morganatic marriage – Wallis as his wife, but not queen. He pressed Baldwin to consult the Cabinet and Dominions, clinging to hope. Baldwin, knowing it was futile, relayed the plan on 2 December 1936. The Cabinet shut it down. Declassified papers reveal Baldwin's frustration mounting as the walls closed in.[26]

The turning point came on 1 December 1936, when the Bishop of Bradford, Alfred Blunt, delivered a scathing speech. He urged Edward to seek 'God's grace' and condemned his lifestyle, declaring Britain needed 'a leader of youth, not a playboy'. The press ran with it. The attack, echoing wider fears about Edward's morals and lack of suitability for the role as Supreme Governor of the Church, was a fatal blow. He was out of time – and out of allies.

The crisis hit the front pages, and for many people, the full scale of the abdication scandal finally sank in. Edward's reign was teetering, and Wallis Simpson quickly became the villain. Cast as a manipulative seductress who had 'stolen' the King, she became the target of public fury. Hate mail, threats of acid attacks and even assassination poured in. Sir Dudley Forward, the King's loyal aide, was stunned by the venom in the letters. Britain was seething. Sir Dudley said later, 'England loathed her, Britain loathed her. I am always surprised that she was never murdered. They loathed her, and there are still people who loathe her too.'[27]

Once loyal allies like Winston Churchill and legal adviser Walter Monckton, who had defended Edward's right to choose his wife, now saw abdication as inevitable too. Only Oswald Mosley, leader of the British Union of Fascists, remained a vocal supporter. The nation was divided, as Baldwin feared. Rumours of a 'King's Party' to back Edward's marriage and reign fizzled. The crisis had spiralled into a constitutional standoff.

On 5 December 1936, another now-declassified memo from Baldwin outlined his final attempt to make Edward see reason. The Prime Minister said the government's position was unequivocal. The King had two choices: end his relationship with Wallis Simpson and remain on the throne, or abdicate. There was no middle ground.[28]

Back in London, Dominion governments made their position clear: they would not accept Wallis as queen, or even as Edward's wife, under any circumstances. The King's fate now rested with his younger brother, the Duke of York, who reluctantly prepared to accede to the throne. In a letter to Queen Mary, her mother-in-law, Elizabeth expressed confidence in her husband (Bertie) saying: 'If this terrible responsibility comes to him, he will face it bravely.' Some feared Edward might resist abdicating, but he knew defiance would dishonour the Crown and threaten the monarchy's existence. With no fight left, he stepped down quietly. On 10 December 1936, after just 326 days, he signed the Instrument of Abdication. The next evening, he made a historic BBC radio address, when he said, 'I have found it impossible to carry the heavy burden of responsibility and discharge my duties as King as I would wish to do without the help and support of the woman I love.' His emotional words, described as 'women's magazine language', shocked many, raising doubts about whether love alone justified such a monumental decision.[29]

Edward was out. Bertie was in. He took the regnal name George VI, honouring their father and grasping for stability. Three days from forty-one, unready and unwilling, he had hoped Edward would come to his senses. He did not. The choice broke him. The nation was split. Edward had the people, the government and the Church standing against him. Bertie's stammer and frail health cast doubt, but Queen Mary steadied the ship. The Crown would endure.

Baldwin's handling of the abdication crisis was the final significant act of a thirty-year political career. He had steadied Britain through several crises, defusing the 1926 General Strike while modernising the Conservative Party and maintaining political stability. He had experienced failures, too. His reluctance to rearm against Hitler left Britain exposed and his cautious foreign policy and failure to confront fascism, misreading the storm ahead, would haunt his legacy. He retired a few days before George VI's coronation on 12 May 1937, to be succeeded by Neville Chamberlain.

He later reflected, rather disingenuously, that Edward's abdication marked 'the end of a career of great promise'.[30] Privately, he felt relief. Baldwin died on 14 December 1947, aged eighty, at his Worcestershire home after a protracted illness.

For Princess Elizabeth, the abdication was life-changing, but it left her with a guiding truth summed up in one word: duty. It became the mantra of her reign.

CHAPTER 3

THIS GHASTLY VOID

I never wanted this. I had no training for it. [31]

GEORGE VI, 1936

As the coronation neared, whispers of doubt swirled around – was Bertie up to the task? Even he was not sure. Always in Edward's shadow, he now bore the weight that his brother had cast off. When destiny knocked, Bertie buckled, seeking comfort where he always had, in his mother's embrace. The night before the ceremony, he poured his anguish into his diary: 'I went to see Queen Mary, and when I told her what had happened, I broke down and sobbed like a child.'[32]

After all, Edward had always been the family's golden boy: glamorous, adored, the darling of the British empire. Bertie, by contrast, was the shy, stammering second son, lacking his brother's film-star good looks and easy charm. The two had been close as boys, born just eighteen months apart. But Edward's confidence sometimes masked his crueller side. His teasing of Bertie's speech impediment, though often playful, struck at his brother's deepest insecurities, leaving lasting scars on his fragile self-esteem.

At formal dinners, Bertie's devoted wife Elizabeth would sit beside him and when he began to stammer, she would squeeze his hand, or gently pat his arm, always there to steady him. A breakthrough came when she was given the name of a speech therapist, Lionel Logue, based in Harley Street, and persuaded her husband to meet him ahead of their joint 1927 tour of Australia.[33]

He agreed to meet Logue, and soon developed an intense reliance on the Australian amateur actor with no formal medical qualifications, eighty times over a fourteen-month period. They made great progress together. In one letter, Bertie proudly shared that he had spoken to his father without stammering; a rare victory over a lifelong struggle complicated by his father's harsh, domineering character. After Edward VIII's abdication in December 1936, Bertie's work with Logue intensified. Their letters show a close, supportive friendship.

As monarch, Bertie had to step up and command the stage. He had the heart, but he admitted it left him feeling what he described as 'this ghastly void'.[34] He could not have done it without the love of his wife, Queen Elizabeth. Tough, elegant, and charming, she became the face of the monarchy, tirelessly supporting the King in his hour of need. Cecil Beaton's iconic photos of her presented a glamorous image, easing the sting of Edward's sudden exit.

Rumours continued about the new king's frail health and unfitness for the throne. Some even placed cruel bets on whether he would last until his coronation. On the morning of the historic day, George VI admitted to a 'sinking feeling' and was so overwhelmed he could not eat. Yet, he silenced the doubters, embracing the burden with quiet strength and dignity. The coronation highlighted Lionel Logue's vital role in the King's life and the depth of their bond. To the shock of many, the Australian and his wife, Myrtle, were seated in the royal box; a testament to a friendship born from trust and loyalty. For the

King, having Logue nearby was more than symbolic, it was a source of reassurance and calm.[35]

Queen Elizabeth masked her turmoil, but her husband's sudden accession to the throne had shaken her to the core. Days after the abdication, she confided in the Duke of Windsor that she and Bertie were 'overcome with misery' at their new burden. Life for them had changed overnight. She told their eldest daughter that she would one day become queen regnant – unless a brother arrived. A weighty truth for one so young. Sensing the moment, Princess Margaret asked her sister, 'Does that mean you'll be the next queen?' Elizabeth hesitated. 'Yes, someday.' Margaret, ever blunt, simply replied, 'Poor you.'[36]

Sensing the tension, ten-year-old Elizabeth told her curious sister, Margaret, 'I think Uncle David wants to marry Mrs Baldwin, and Mr Baldwin doesn't like it.'[37] Elizabeth under-stood they would move, her father would be king, and her mother queen – but the true gravity of abdication was beyond her tender years.

Bertie's loyalty to Edward was shattered when he uncovered his brother's financial deceit – and soured further when he learned that Wallis called Elizabeth a 'fat Scottish cook', or on gentler days, just 'Cookie'.[38] The King had granted Edward a lavish stipend – enough to buy Le Moulin de la Tuilerie in 1938. The secluded Normandy retreat became a lasting wedge between them.[39] The rift deepened, and never healed, when George VI discovered that Edward had gifted Wallis jewels taken from the Royal Collection. Among them: Queen Alexandra's pearl and diamond necklace, a treasured heirloom from their grandmother.[40]

Even after abdicating, Edward's deceit did not stop. He kept pleading poverty to George VI while quietly amassing a fortune. By his death in 1972, he had tucked away an estimated £15–25 million – worth £150–250 million today. He lived off royal allowances while quietly investing in property, stocks, and stashing it in secret Swiss bank accounts.[41]

The new Queen Consort, Elizabeth, dismissed Wallis with a curt 'that woman', ignoring her barbs and focusing on duty. Whitehall murmurs still questioned Bertie's reign – some even whispered that Queen Mary or Prince George might take over. Elizabeth knew the monarchy needed a strong king and her role was to make Bertie believe that he was one.

On 12 May 1937, Wallis listened to the coronation alone at the Château de Candé, near Tours, in France, haunted by what might have been. Edward, in Austria, did the same. Back in Westminster Abbey, Reverend Frederic Iremonger, the BBC's Director of Religion, quietly read the service instructions from a perch above Saint Edward's Chapel – there was no running commentary. As George VI was crowned, Edward's brief reign faded away. The transition was seamless; the new king's presence eclipsed the past.

George VI granted Edward the title HRH The Duke of Windsor – his alone, never to be passed on. Edward now had one aim: to marry Wallis and secure 'Her Royal Highness' for her. But George stood firm. It fell to the Duke's friend, Sir Dudley Forward, to deliver the blow: Wallis would never be HRH. Edward crumbled, tears spilling. 'He never forgave the family, and he never got over it,' Sir Dudley recalled.[42] The wound never healed. It lasted a lifetime.

On 3 June 1937, Fleet Street reporters and photographers swarmed the Château de Candé for Edward and Wallis's wedding. The lavish estate, owned by industrialist Charles Bedaux – later arrested for Nazi collaboration – set the scene. By royal command, the family boycotted the ceremony, ignoring Edward's pleas and casting a shadow over the day.

Cecil Beaton, behind the camera lens, noted Edward's 'essentially sad' eyes. Reverend J.A. Jardine, who defied Church rules to officiate, was later defrocked, reinventing himself with the gaudy 'Windsor Cathedral' in Hollywood. Best man Major 'Fruity' Metcalfe played his part, while his wife, Lady Alexandra, quietly captured private moments. 'It was hard not to cry,' Lady Metcalfe recalled. 'To see a King of England, once idolised, marry under such circumstances was pitiable and tragic. And yet, Edward carried himself with a simplicity and dignity that was hard to describe.'[43]

On their Paris honeymoon, reality bit. At Maxim's, the Duke cut a pathetic figure asking for butter, as waiters ignored him. From a nearby table, Barbara Cartland watched, struck by the fall: a king, now irrelevant. 'When you give up the crown,' she said bluntly, 'you give up the attention.'

Blinded by vanity, Edward refused to accept his diminished status. Convinced he still mattered, he became easy prey for Nazi propaganda. Like many on Britain's right, he admired Hitler, who had flouted the Treaty of Versailles by rebuilding Germany's army in 1935. By 1936, 30,000 German troops had marched into the Rhineland – unchallenged. It was a step towards Hitler's goal: securing resources for an inevitable showdown with the Soviets.

Ignoring Churchill's warnings, Edward eagerly accepted a 1937 invitation to Germany; perhaps craving a royal reception, or wanting Wallis to taste the adulation once hers to command.

On 11 October, the Duke and Duchess landed in Berlin, touring Munich and visiting the arms giant Krupp – sparking outrage. By 22 October, at the Berghof, Edward was sitting with Hitler, humiliated yet defiant.

He mimicked Nazi salutes, spoke fluent German, and later quipped to his aide, 'Didn't I wave nicely?' What he saw as politeness sent Britain reeling. The King and Queen were alarmed, the public furious. The press pounced. *The Times* called it a diplomatic disaster; the *Daily Herald* dismissed him as a 'pawn' of the Reich.

The Duke's ties to Oswald Mosley and admiration for the Third Reich and National Socialism had already set off alarms in Britain. MI5 ramped up surveillance on both him and Wallis, whom they had watched since 1935. One declassified memo noted: 'Contact with the Simpsons is maintained . . . Mrs Simpson's secret lover [Joachim von Ribbentrop] remains unidentified. She is wary of losing the prince's affection, fearing a fate like Lady Furness, so she keeps her affair hidden.' There is no question that Wallis was seduced by the charismatic von Ribbentrop, but there is no hard evidence that their relationship was physical.[44]

After a shift towards greater government transparency and confronting historical truths, files unsealed in 1996 revealed Edward's undeniable Nazi sympathies. Originally meant to remain classified for a century, the documents had been kept by Foreign Secretary Ernest Bevin (1945–51) as part of his duty to handle sensitive diplomatic records and also exposed Edward's 'ambivalent attitude' towards the war. Churchill allegedly tried to 'destroy all traces' of telegrams detailing a Nazi plot to reinstall Edward as king. Alongside US officials, he worked to suppress evidence of the Duke of Windsor's Nazi ties, shielding the royal image from scandal.[45]

A crucial set of documents, German diplomatic papers found at Schloss Marburg in 1945 by American forces, was the most damning. They revealed that the Duke of Windsor made peace overtures to Nazi Germany and shared his belief that a Labour government would negotiate with them. Other intelligence files revealed that Father Odo, a Benedictine monk and nobleman in a Franciscan monastery, who had ties to Britain's Queen Mary (formerly Princess May of Teck) confirmed to the FBI that Wallis Simpson had a passionate affair with Joachim von Ribbentrop in 1936. During their intimacy he claimed that she passed on British secrets to her lover, who sent her seventeen carnations daily, each flower symbolising their trysts.[46]

Soviet intelligence viewed the Duke as treacherous, suspecting he negotiated with Hitler for a pro-German UK government and an alliance against the USSR. Spanish diplomat Don Javier Bermejillo reported in June 1940 that Windsor blamed 'the Jews, the Reds, and the Foreign Office' for the war and suggested bombing Britain might force peace – news that reached Franco, then Germany. The Blitz began on 10 July.[47]

Hitler pushed Europe towards war. On 12 March 1938, German forces rolled into Austria, met with cheers. The Western Allies stood by, unwilling to act. Next, Hitler set his sights on the Sudetenland, a resource-rich German-speaking region of Czechoslovakia. Alarmed but desperate to avoid conflict, Britain and France clung to diplomacy.

Knowing Britain was unprepared for war, Prime Minister Neville Chamberlain made three trips to Germany, bargaining for peace. At the Munich Conference, Chamberlain, the French leader Édouard Daladier, and Mussolini handed Hitler the Sudetenland – on the promise of no further aggression. Chamberlain returned on 30 September 1938, triumphantly declaring, 'I believe it is peace for our time.'

George VI, haunted by the Great War and desperate to prevent another, backed appeasement. He loathed Hitler but, like Foreign Secretary Lord Halifax, saw no alternative. When Chamberlain arrived home, the King, caught up in the euphoria, made a rare misstep and invited him onto the Buckingham Palace balcony, binding the Crown to one of history's most infamous policies.

It unravelled fast. On 15 March 1939, Hitler shattered the Munich Agreement, seizing the rest of Czechoslovakia. His ambitions stretched far beyond German-speaking lands – he wanted a vast empire, its resources fuelling his vision of continental domination. Britain and France, finally drawing a line, warned that an invasion of Poland would mean war. The countdown had begun.

With war on the horizon, the King and Queen set sail for Canada aboard RMS *Empress of Australia*, arriving in Quebec on 17 May 1939. Cheering crowds lined their route through Montreal, Ottawa, Toronto, Winnipeg, Calgary, Banff, and Vancouver. The tour, spanning thousands of miles, deepened Canada's bond with the Crown.

In Montreal, two Boer War veterans, both Scots, pressed the Queen with a debate: 'Are you Scots, or are you English?' With a smile, she replied, 'Since I have landed in Quebec, I think we can say that I am Canadian.'

On 8 June, the royals landed in Washington, D.C., for a historic White House visit with President Roosevelt; George VI becoming the first British monarch to set foot in the US. His mission was clear: strengthen ties and rally America against Hitler. The American public, once obsessed with Edward and Wallis, now embraced the warm and engaging new King and Queen. At the 'Hot Dog Summit' on 11 June, they picnicked with the Roosevelts at their family home in Hyde Park, New York. Served hot dogs for the first time, George looked perplexed. Grinning, Roosevelt quipped, 'Push it in your mouth.'

The visit was a triumph. George and FDR bonded, laying the foundation for the wartime Anglo-American alliance. The Queen's charm won over the press and talk of Wallis's chic style faded. Edward, stewing in exile, tried to sabotage the moment, timing a peace broadcast on NBC from France to undermine his brother's success. It failed. The king that Edward once deemed to be unfit now eclipsed him.

Throughout the 1930s, sidelined in his 'wilderness years', Churchill warned Britain to rearm. Through speeches and articles in the *Daily Mail, Evening Standard,* and *Sunday Chronicle,* he urged military overhaul. As early as July 1934, he cautioned in the *Daily Mail,* 'A terrible process is astir. Germany is arming.' Critics sneered, branding him a warmonger.

But Churchill was right. As war loomed, he slammed appeasement, comparing it to feeding a crocodile, hoping it eats you last. After Munich in 1938, he called it 'an unmitigated disaster', warning it emboldened Hitler and crippled Britain. His verdict was scathing: 'You were given the choice between war and dishonour. You chose dishonour, and you will have war.'[48]

By August 1939, Hitler and Stalin had struck a secret deal – Poland would be theirs. On 1 September, Germany invaded from the west; sixteen days later, the Soviets stormed in from the east. On 3 September, Britain and France declared war. Stunned, Hitler had believed they lacked the resolve to fight. The Second World War had begun. Appeasement lay in ruins, and so did Chamberlain's career.

As war loomed, the King spoke to the nation. Years of training with Lionel Logue paid off. His voice was steady and his message clear: Britain would stand firm. A reluctant leader, he called for unity and sacrifice. 'For it is to this high purpose that I now call my people at home and my peoples across the seas,' he declared. In that moment, George VI embodied the monarchy's true strength – unwavering in crisis.

Chamberlain, secretly battling cancer, resigned on 10 May 1940 after Norway's disastrous defeat – it was a humiliating blow for Britain. Aimed at blocking Hitler's access to Swedish iron ore, the campaign was slow, confused, and badly led. Naval losses mounted, objectives slipped away, and the operation collapsed. The failure shattered Chamberlain's credibility and hastened his fall. It came to a head during a Commons debate on 7–8 May, where senior parliamentarians, including Leo Amery and David Lloyd George, openly condemned him. Amery's cutting rebuke – 'In the name of God, go' – summed up the mood. Though Chamberlain won the vote, over 39 government MPs opposed, with between 30 and 40 abstaining slashing his majority and exposing a fatal loss of confidence in his leadership. With Hitler storming through Europe, Britain needed a fighter. The King summoned Churchill to form a National Government. Hours later, the new prime minister took charge, rallying the nation with words that would define the fight ahead.[49]

Edward and Wallis, once fixtures in the spotlight, faded into irrelevance as the nation rallied behind George VI. Meanwhile, in government circles, the King's past support for appeasement raised eyebrows. Churchill, Attlee, Eden, and Duff Cooper – along with many in the security services – feared his stance could tarnish Britain's future. MI5's Sir Vernon Kell and MI6's Stewart Menzies stayed neutral, focused on security, not politics.

The King and Churchill's early relationship was uneasy – two starkly different men. George VI, who had fought to overcome his stammer, admired Churchill's command of language, especially as Churchill had openly acknowledged his own struggles with speech. But their first meetings were tense. Caroline Erskine, daughter of the King's assistant private secretary, Sir Alan Lascelles, recalled that the King found Churchill imposing, while Churchill struggled to navigate royal protocol.[50]

With George VI lacking his brother's charisma, Queen Elizabeth (his wife, later the Queen Mother) became the monarchy's public face: tough, charming and tireless. Cecil Beaton's photos cast her as regal and glamorous, but it was her resilience that cemented her place in history.

On 13 September 1940, a German Heinkel He 111 bombed Buckingham Palace while the King and Queen were inside. Two blasts rocked the palace and the royal mews, narrowly missing them. Unharmed, they emerged as symbols of shared sacrifice – suddenly, the royals were 'one of us'.

That night, with sirens wailing and gunfire echoing, the Queen ordered champagne for dinner. Later, she famously declared, 'I'm glad we have been bombed. It makes me feel I can now look the East End in the face.' Early visits to bombed-out east London had been rough; some jeered, others hurled rubbish, seeing her finery as out of touch. But she dressed up, she said, to honour those who did the same for her.

The press hid much of the resentment, but time changed hearts. Scorn turned to solidarity, jeers to cheers. The bombing proved that even the royals were not untouchable. By staying in London through the Blitz – never fleeing abroad – the King and Queen won a nation's devotion.[51]

In autumn 1940, British intelligence warned Churchill of a possible Nazi invasion, led by Luftwaffe General Kurt Student, mastermind of Germany's airborne forces. Ever cautious, Churchill ordered a secret evacuation plan, Operation Rocking Horse, to move the King and Royal Family to a secure location, or, if necessary, to Canada.

Two hundred elite Coldstream Guards stood ready, with bodyguards and escape drivers on high alert. But the King, a Royal Navy veteran who had manned a gun turret aboard HMS

Collingwood in the Great War, refused to run. He was staying – standing his ground with his people.[52]

The King's defiance left Churchill in a bind. Warwick University's Richard Aldrich recalled George VI's resolve: 'He says everybody is going to stay and fight. I want to get my German. I want to at least kill one of the invaders, and we will all fight to the last.'

The King, as a member of the Home Guard, was issued with a Sten Mk II machine-carbine gun. Delighted, George VI fortified Buckingham Palace into a makeshift stronghold. The Queen and staff trained with handguns and rifles, with the Queen Consort, Elizabeth honing her aim by shooting rats in the gardens with Churchill's deadly gift.

Throughout the war, the King dressed the part – often in military uniform, armed with his Lee Enfield rifle and an Enfield revolver, which he wore holstered at his hip. As Commander-in-Chief, he wanted Britain to see him as a fighter, not just a figurehead. It bolstered the shy King's confidence too, the uniform giving him strength. On a 1943 visit to RAF Tempsford, the Queen was amused by a particularly British innovation: exploding horse manure, designed for sabotage behind enemy lines.[53]

Hitler's Blitzkrieg tore through Europe on 10 May 1940. France collapsed in six weeks; Paris fell on 14 June. Meanwhile, the Duke of Windsor, a major-general in title only, was stationed near Biarritz as a liaison officer. Defying orders, he fled to neutral Spain with Wallis, deepening Churchill's mistrust.

Edward's openness to German overtures fuelled suspicions, his wartime legacy forever tainted. Churchill, aware of Operation Willi – a Nazi plot to install Edward as a puppet king – moved fast. He pressured Edward into accepting the post of Governor of the Bahamas, keeping him far from Nazi reach.

When the Duke hesitated, Churchill sent a blunt telegram: take the post or face court-martial. This was not about royal duty – it was national security. After stalling again, Edward was reminded it was an order, not a request. On 9 August, the Windsors left Lisbon, switched ships in Bermuda, and reached Nassau on 17 August. There, they spent the war in isolation, far from the action and nursing grudges in exile.[54]

During the Blitz (September 1940–May 1941), Goering's Luftwaffe pounded British cities, aiming to shatter morale and industry. Heinkel He 111s, Junkers Ju 88s and Dornier Do 17s rained destruction mainly at night. In the earlier daylight raids they were escorted by Messerschmitt Bf 109s and Bf 110s.

Over 43,000 civilians perished, and cities like London and Coventry lay in ruins. But Britain did not break. The Blitz hardened its resolve. Churchill's 'Few' – the fighter pilots lauded during the Battle of Britain (July–October 1940) – soared in Spitfires and Hurricanes, while radar gave the RAF the edge. Germany's plans unravelled, and the tide began to turn.[55]

The King and Queen stayed in London, visiting bombed areas in the East End and standing with their people in 'their finest hour'. Their courage and commitment to share the nation's hardships inspired respect, solidifying the King as a symbol of strength.[56]

At fourteen, Princess Elizabeth joined the war effort, standing alongside her ten-year-old sister Margaret. She made her first public speech on BBC radio's *Children's Hour*, offering courage and hope to the Commonwealth's children. 'We are trying to do all we can to help our gallant sailors, soldiers and airmen, and we are trying, too, to bear our own share of the danger and sadness of war.'

In December 1941, the war shifted. President Roosevelt committed US troops to the European conflict after the Japanese attacked their Fleet at Pearl Harbor on 7 December, a day that the president said, 'will live in infamy'. Germany and Italy declared war on the US four days later. Britain had already endured the Blitz; the Soviets would bleed at Stalingrad in 1942–43. But once the US unleashed its industrial might, out producing Hitler and Japan in tanks, planes and ships, Hitler and the Nazis were doomed.

On 25 August 1942, war hit home. Prince George, Duke of Kent – air commodore, brother, and confidant – was killed in a plane crash at just thirty-nine. The King, devastated, said, 'I have lost my best friend and the best of brothers.' At his funeral in St George's Chapel, Windsor, royals and dignitaries paid their respects, including King Haakon VII of Norway and King George II of Greece. He was laid to rest in the Royal Burial Grounds at Frogmore, another life lost to war.

US forces surged into North Africa, Italy, and, on 6 June 1944, Normandy – as Operation Overlord was launched under General Eisenhower. Churchill, eager to witness the invasion first-hand, was stopped cold by King George VI. As Commander-in-Chief, the King declared that if Churchill went, so would he. The thought of both leaders in the line of fire forced Churchill to back down. Eisenhower sided with the King, and together they convinced him to stay put.[57]

Churchill feared not just the loss of 'the flower of British and American youth', but the collapse of democracy if the invasion failed. Deception tactics threw the Germans off, allowing the Allies to storm Utah, Omaha, Gold, Juno, and Sword beaches. The landings surpassed expectations, turning the tide of the war. Failure would have shaken both Churchill and Roosevelt's leadership.

Throughout the war, the King was a pillar of morale. He visited victorious troops in North Africa and, just ten days after D-Day, met Field Marshal Montgomery in Normandy, standing with the men of the 21st Army Group. Touring the front lines, he embodied Britain's unwavering support for the Allied cause.

Two years earlier, in the Pacific, Admiral Chester W. Nimitz had crushed Japan's ambitions at Midway in June 1942, gutting its carrier fleet and beginning the island by island advance toward Japan. By the time the Allies closed in on Berlin, only Hitler Youth and diehard old men were left fighting. Hitler, knowing it was over, put a pistol to his head in his bunker on 30 April. The Nazi Third Reich was finished.

America entering the war did not just tip the scales, it shattered them. It came at a cost – 291,557 American combat deaths – but the end was in sight. Victory was inevitable – grinding, brutal, bloody but inevitable.

On 8 May 1945, Victory in Europe (VE) Day, George VI and Churchill stood together on the palace balcony – symbols of Britain's endurance. 'God bless you all. This is your victory,' Churchill declared, shifting the spotlight to the people and the armed forces. The King addressed the nation with quiet strength: 'Today we give thanks to Almighty God for a great deliverance.' The war was over. Peace had come at last. By the time of Churchill's speech, Trafalgar Square, Whitehall, and The Mall were filled with an estimated one million people. The jubilant crowd then surged towards Buckingham Palace. The King and Queen appeared on the balcony eight times, greeting the roaring masses. Churchill joined them three times, met with thunderous applause. These moments, etched in history, embodied unity, resilience, and triumph after years of bloody sacrifice. That evening, Princesses Elizabeth, nineteen, and Margaret, fifteen, slipped out of Buckingham Palace by a back door and joined the crowds in The Mall, sharing in the public's joy first-hand. They ended up doing a conga through the Ritz Hotel at about 11.30 p.m.[58]

That night, George VI reflected in his diary: 'The day we have been longing for has arrived at last, & we can look back with thankfulness to God that our tribulation is over. But there is still Japan to be defeated & the restoration of our country to be dealt with, which will give us many headaches & hard work in the coming years . . .'[59]

Just two and a half months after VE Day, Churchill was out. The electorate, hungry for change, chose Labour's vision of a fairer society over his wartime heroics. The 1945 general election was a landslide: Labour won 393 seats to the Conservatives 197. Churchill's leadership had won the war in Europe, but the people wanted bold reforms.

Labour's slogan 'Let Us Face the Future' struck a chord with a weary nation. Clement Attlee, Churchill's wartime deputy, promised transformation – welfare, nationalised industries, economic recovery, and 'Homes Fit for Heroes'. Churchill had misjudged Attlee dismissing him as 'a modest man, with much to be modest about'. He had misjudged the mood of the nation too.

Despite being personally fond of Churchill, King George swiftly adapted, inviting the victorious Attlee to form a government. The two built a strong relationship and the King appreciated Attlee's no-nonsense professionalism. He also grew to admire Aneurin Bevan, the coal miner's son with a stammer, who as Minister of Health would deliver Britain's greatest post-war achievement: the National Health Service.

The election result signalled more than just political change – it marked the British empire's decline. The sight of Indian regiments in the victory parade underscored its fragility.

'Everything's going,' the King lamented, 'and soon I shall have to go too.'[60]

CHAPTER 4

FOR VALOUR

Never in our long history has a Sovereign, throughout his reign, been faced with greater or more continuous difficulties ... His Majesty never failed us.

LORD TEVIOT SPEAKING FOR THE HOUSE OF LORDS, 1952

The last King-Emperor remained behind in England as the sun set on the Raj. British India, as it was called, was in turmoil, and a royal visit was too dangerous. From afar, George VI watched as his cousin, Lord Mountbatten, the last Viceroy, oversaw the Empire's most significant handover.

On 15 August 1947, the King's pre-recorded address aired simultaneously in India and Pakistan via the BBC. In a short BBC broadcast in his own voice to listeners in Britain, India, and Pakistan, King George VI expressed confidence in India's future and hoped the transfer of power would bring peace, prosperity, and justice. At separate independence ceremonies in Delhi and Karachi, His Majesty's message – delivered on his behalf by Lord Mountbatten – stated: 'I am confident that the statesmanship and the spirit of cooperation ... will be the best guarantee of your future happiness and prosperity.'

The question of India's future split the nation. The newly elected left demanded an end to imperial rule, while Churchill and his loyalists clung desperately to the idea of Empire. Churchill, now Leader of the Opposition, was furious, reportedly calling Mountbatten a pawn of the Labour government and insisting on Dominion status for India as a compromise. The mission was a political minefield. He knew that whatever path he chose, he was destined to make enemies on all sides.

Attlee's government chose a no-deal exit. Mountbatten's hope for peace shattered as bloody violence erupted among Muslims, Hindus and Sikhs. In August, British India was partitioned into the new republics of India and Pakistan. Chaos followed, with massacres, rapes and displacements. Over fifteen million people were uprooted from their homes, up to two million died.

Violent uprisings occurred across the Empire. In Palestine, Jewish militias like Irgun and Haganah attacked British forces, while Arabs resisted too, forcing a withdrawal and in some cases partition. In Malaya, communist guerrillas waged war for independence. It had begun to unravel. As the Empire waned, so did the King. War, illness and duty had worn him down.

A six-week tour of South Africa drained him further. On 17 February 1947, he arrived in Cape Town aboard HMS *Vanguard* with the Queen and his daughters, Elizabeth and Margaret. The trip's defining moment was Elizabeth's 21st birthday speech, a promise of lifelong service. In an historic broadcast, she pledged: 'My whole life, whether it be long or short, shall be devoted to your service and the service of our great imperial family.' This vow not only foreshadowed her future as queen, but also solidified her leadership, reaffirming the monarchy's relevance and unwavering commitment to the Crown during a time of political change.

What the public did not know at the time was that Princess Elizabeth was secretly engaged to her third cousin, Prince Philip of Greece, now Lieutenant Philip Mountbatten, RN. Dashingly good looking and with the right royal bloodline, he proposed in the summer of 1946. The King, cautious, asked for a delay until his beloved daughter had turned twenty-one.

Elizabeth's first significant meeting with Philip had been during a royal visit to Dartmouth Naval College on 22 July 1939.[61] The impressionable princess was then thirteen; Philip was eighteen, a tall and confident naval cadet. Philip's uncle, Lord Louis Mountbatten, ensured Philip was assigned to look after the princesses.

After Philip's father's death, Louis – or 'Dickie', as he was known by his family and friends – had become his mentor, driven by fierce ambition. Married to the wealthy and scandalous Lady Edwina, Mountbatten had the means and the plan: to groom Philip as a suitor for the young princess. Edwina had inherited millions, a London townhouse, and the Broadlands country estate in Hampshire from her grandfather, financier Sir Ernest Cassel. Louis relied on her wealth to fund their lavish lifestyle.

Philip, bold and charming, became like a surrogate son to Louis and from 1938 he stayed at Broadlands. Louis, impressed by his wit and confidence, formed a bond that would shape both their destinies.

After the Dartmouth meeting, Elizabeth was smitten. Philip – handsome, confident, unfazed by royalty – played croquet, leapt over tennis nets, and charmed her instantly. When the royal yacht left, he bravely followed in a small boat while others turned back. The King called him a fool; to Elizabeth, he was fearless.

Machiavellian Mountbatten's plan was working. Elizabeth fell fast for Philip: for her, he was the one. But the King, Queen, and royal circles would resist their match for years.

When war broke out. Philip, eager to serve, joined HMS *Ramillies* as a midshipman, escorting convoys in the Indian Ocean. But even in war, Mountbatten continued to play royal matchmaker. He saw Philip as perfect for Elizabeth with his royal blood, his charm, and his grit. A good match was power, and Mountbatten never wavered in his ambition to see Philip wed to the world's most eligible heiress.

Philip proved himself in the Second World War. Serving on HMS *Valiant*, he was Mentioned in Dispatches for bravery at the Battle of Cape Matapan in 1941. In 1943, during the Allied invasion of Sicily, he saved his crew by outsmarting a German bomber, using a clever ruse to conceal the ship at night.

While Philip fought at sea, Elizabeth matured into a poised young woman at Windsor Castle under the watchful eye of her governess, Marion Crawford. Her devotion to Philip was clear, though she also had a fleeting crush on Hugh, Earl of Euston.

Philip, wary of royal constraints, considered retreating to Greece. But Mountbatten, ever the strategist, urged him on. His daughter, Patricia, recalled, 'The characters of Prince Philip and Princess Elizabeth matched extremely well. My father genuinely believed this was a very good idea.'

In 1944, Mountbatten pressed George VI to open marriage talks with the Greek king. The King, exasperated, shut him down, writing, 'We are going too fast.'

By 1945, Philip was a first lieutenant – one of the Royal Navy's youngest – aboard HMS *Whelp* in Tokyo Bay for Japan's surrender. He had served his adopted country with distinction, witnessing first-hand the devastation of Hiroshima and Nagasaki. On 2 September, as the Instrument of Surrender was signed aboard the USS *Missouri*, Philip recalled, 'Being in Tokyo Bay with the surrender ceremony taking place was a great relief.'

Throughout the war, Elizabeth kept a photo of Philip in her room, and they exchanged letters. During shore leave, he visited Windsor, but their bond remained a friendship. Philip admitted he only considered marriage seriously after the war. By 1946, he was invited to Balmoral and had applied for British citizenship.

Post-war life felt dull, and Philip grew restless. London trips lifted his spirits – and brought him closer to Elizabeth. His MG sports car and lively presence shook up palace life. Australian navy commander Mike Parker believed Philip was deeply in love, but suspected Dickie's meddling sometimes got in the way.[62]

Despite having few material possessions, Philip's charm and down-to-earth personality won the affection of many. His royal lineage opened doors to high society, but the traditional establishment and old-school courtiers were cautious of him. While Princess Elizabeth was in love and determined to marry Philip, her mother, the Queen, still opposed the match. Protective of her daughter, she found the virtually penniless Philip's bold, confident, and 'brash' demeanour off-putting. She also feared public backlash over his German heritage and the fact that his three surviving sisters had married German aristocrats linked to the Nazi regime.

When a photograph emerged showing Prince Philip's sister, Princess Sophie, at Hermann Göring's 1935 wedding to Emmy Sonnemann, it caused a stir. The lavish Nazi affair, held on 10 April 1935, saw Sophie and her husband, Prince Christoph of Hesse, seated at the top table, across from Adolf Hitler. The couple had joined the Nazi Party in 1933, with Christoph serving as an SS colonel and Hitler's intelligence chief. In her son Prince Georg of Hesse's memoir, Sophie recalled the lunch with Hitler, describing him as 'charming and seemingly modest'.[63] In a 2006 interview, Philip acknowledged his family had admired Hitler's early restoration of Germany, but stressed, 'None of them were antisemitic.'[64]

It was not only Philip's German roots that unsettled royal courtiers; his reputation as a ladies' man did too. He had enjoyed a brief summer romance with American Cobina Wright at seventeen, and she later claimed almost proposed, before they drifted apart. He also briefly went out with Canadian debutante Osla Benning and accounts suggest he fell for nightclub singer Sandra Jacques while in Australia. Five years older than Princess Elizabeth, Philip had naturally dated other women, and gossip always trailed him. His friend Mike Parker saw a different side, however: reserved and serious, a far cry from the man of scandalous rumours.

Lord Mountbatten worked tirelessly to secure dynastic success for his nephew, promoting his Britishness to counter any anti-German sentiment, even writing to influential journalist Tom Driberg to secure his support. Under Mountbatten's influence, Philip adopted the Mountbatten name, further anglicising his identity. Nothing was left to chance. On 28 February 1947, Philip became a naturalised British citizen.

When the Palace finally announced their engagement on 9 July, Philip gave Elizabeth a three-carat diamond ring made from his mother's tiara, designed by the society jewellers Philip Antrobus and by Philip himself. The princess was thrilled; she had won her man.

Philip's background may have unsettled Queen Elizabeth, but King George VI had bigger worries – the Marburg Files. These sensitive documents, uncovered by American forces in May

1945 at Schloss Marburg, detailed 'Operation Willi', a Nazi plot to manipulate the Duke of Windsor. The Nazi plan aimed to convince the Duke that Churchill and George VI had conspired to have him killed while he was Governor of the Bahamas. The files revealed that the Nazis saw him as either a puppet monarch or governor if they won the war. Churchill, fearing the scandal could shatter the monarchy, fought to keep the files buried.

After the war, historians from Britain, France and the US accessed key German records, but some were deemed too explosive to release publicly. At the time, the British government moved swiftly. Intelligence officials sent Anthony Blunt, a former MI5 officer and art historian (later unmasked as a Soviet spy), on a covert mission to Germany. Officially, he was recovering Empress Frederick's letters to Queen Victoria. Unofficially, according to later accounts, Blunt was also tasked with recovering documents that could have been politically embarrassing to the Royal Family.

Historians who have examined the Windsor File describe its contents as highly compromising, detailing contact between the Duke of Windsor and senior Nazi officials that, in their view, raised questions about his judgment and the monarchy's standing.

Years later a 2020 declassified Cabinet file revealed the British government's relentless efforts to suppress the truth. It emerged that in 1954, Churchill's government even appealed to France and President Dwight Eisenhower to restrict access. One chilling entry from a German diplomatic report dated 11 July 1940 claimed that Edward suggested bombing Britain might hasten surrender and potentially create conditions for his return as a Nazi-backed ruler. If true, it was treason. But its authenticity remains disputed among historians.

Even after he was sidelined in the Bahamas, Edward had remained a liability. FBI files later revealed US surveillance on the couple, and declassified intelligence from the FBI's 'Vault' suggested both the Duke and Duchess of Windsor harboured Nazi sympathies. The full truth remains buried, but what has surfaced is damning.

Edward vehemently denied any wrongdoing, dismissing the German Marburg Files as forgeries. On 8 December 1954, Prime Minister Winston Churchill explicitly ordered Cabinet officials to control the release of the files, to minimise Edward's role, and safeguard the monarchy's reputation. An official note claimed that Edward faced intense German pressure to remain in Europe and influence British policy, asserting he 'never wavered' in loyalty. Records indicate otherwise. Despite personal misgivings about Edward, Churchill orchestrated a high-level cover-up, historians and Cabinet papers show. When the Marburg Files emerged in 1957, censorship removed the clearest proof of Edward's Nazi sympathies – protecting royal prestige above historical accuracy.

A revealing clue comes from MP Harold Nicolson's unpublished diary, where he quotes Sir Alan Lascelles, Edward's former assistant private secretary, describing his boss: 'The man is like the child in the fairy story who was given everything in the world, but they forgot the soul.' It sums up the Duke perfectly: a man utterly lacking self-awareness, oblivious to the gravity of his own actions.[65]

As Governor-General of the Bahamas, Edward cut a pathetic figure, dogged by scandal, most notably the botched investigation into philanthropist Sir Harry Oakes's murder. In July 1943, Sir Harry Oakes was found murdered in his Nassau mansion – bludgeoned, burned, and covered in insecticide. The Duke of Windsor, then Governor of the Bahamas, ignored British authorities and flew in Miami detectives with no jurisdiction and even less competence. Their case against Oakes's son-in-law, Count Alfred de Marigny, centred on a lone fingerprint – one the court suspected was planted. De Marigny was acquitted, but deported. Whispers of cover-up followed. Edward had sidelined officials, silenced press, and stayed close to key players, including Harold Christie. Critics said he was more focused on polo and Wallis than justice. The murder was never solved. But the stench of favouritism, failure, and self-interest clung to the former King.

Was Edward a traitor or opportunist? The debate endures. Though he denied being in exile, Edward never returned home, his legacy defined by controversy and the Nazi associations revealed despite government attempts to suppress them. History remembers George VI more kindly – as the reluctant king who stepped up when Edward stood aside.

Anthony Blunt, praised by the King for his wartime secrecy, later disgraced the Royal Family when he was revealed to have been a Soviet spy in the 'Cambridge Five'. Born into Britain's elite, Blunt embraced communism at Cambridge, inspired by his fellow spy, Guy Burgess. He infiltrated British intelligence and passed state secrets, including intelligence related to the Allied invasion plans, to Moscow.

After the war, his royal ties (his mother was Queen Mary's distant cousin) secured him the post of Surveyor of the King's Pictures, enabling his double life. Blunt claimed betrayal of Britain, not the monarchy. When exposed in the 1960s, his royal connections shielded him, and the Queen Mother urged Elizabeth II to protect him. Only in 1979 did Margaret Thatcher publicly unmask him as a spy. Whether driven by communist loyalty, personal devotion to Burgess, or thrill-seeking betrayal, remains uncertain.[66]

In 1947, a bitter Edward sold his story to *Life* magazine for $100,000. Royals did not do that and George VI read it like a slap in the face. Edward followed up with his memoir, *A King's Story*. His publishers hired Charles Murphy, an American, to ghostwrite the book. It was torture. Edward could not focus, always lured away by Paris nightlife. Wallis, jealous and demanding, kept interrupting. Deadlines passed. Then she left for America, chasing Jimmy Donahue, a rich playboy. Edward chased her.

Murphy finished alone. The book was slick but hollow. He played Edward as the victim – a cruel nanny, distant mother, strict father. As the Prince of Wales, he was bored, frustrated. He was captivated by Wallis, he wrote, who was 'the most independent woman I had ever met'. Later asked why he wrote it, Edward mumbled about correcting misconceptions. The truth was simpler: he needed money.

Meanwhile post-war Britain craved hope, and they found it in Princess Elizabeth's marriage to Philip on 20 November 1947.

The previous day, Philip had raced to the wedding rehearsal in his sports car – only to be pulled over. 'Sorry, officer,' he quipped, 'but I've got an appointment with the Archbishop of Canterbury.'

On the morning of the wedding, the weight of his new life settled in. Newly off cigarettes, he shared a gin and tonic with his best man, David Mountbatten, before Countess Mountbatten found him alone. 'Am I being very brave or very foolish?' he asked. It was not doubt about Elizabeth; it was mourning the life he was leaving behind. 'Nothing was going to change for her,' she later recalled. 'Everything was going to change for him.'

Marrying the world's most eligible heiress changed Philip's status – and his bank balance. On the day of the wedding, he had literally only pennies to his name (the equivalent to about 12 pence today). His father-in-law gifted him bespoke Purdey shotguns, but Philip would remain frugal for life – once having his Savile Row tailor alter a 52-year-old pair of trousers.

Under grey skies, cheering crowds filled London's streets. Inside Westminster Abbey, Elizabeth, radiant in ivory silk, walked beside her father before royalty, dignitaries, and 200 million listeners worldwide. A rare moment of joy amid post-war hardship.

The bride signed simply as 'Elizabeth', listing her profession as 'Princess of the United Kingdom of Great Britain and Ireland'. Philip, newly titled by the King, signed as 'HRH The Duke of Edinburgh'.

One sting remained: his sisters were banned. King George VI, wary of their Nazi-linked marriages, refused to let Margarita, Theodora and Sophie attend. 'It would feel perhaps rather tactless,' said his cousin, Countess Patricia Mountbatten. 'So soon after the war, you couldn't have "the Hun".' Lady Pamela Hicks added, 'I think Philip understood, but the sisters certainly didn't. For years afterward, they would say, "Why weren't we allowed to come to your wedding?" They weren't exactly Stormtroopers.'

That night, the King wrote emotionally to Elizabeth: 'I was so proud of you . . . but when I handed your hand to the Archbishop, I felt I had lost something precious.' Yet the wedding transcended private sorrow – it symbolised hope and continuity. The young couple, deeply in love, rode through cheering crowds, were showered with rose petals at Buckingham Palace, then boarded a train to honeymoon at Lord Mountbatten's Broadlands estate in Romsey.

*

When the media hype over the royal wedding died down, Philip felt anxious about his future. Court life frustrated him. Lord Brabourne's wife, Lady Patricia, Philip's cousin, said, 'It was very stuffy. Sir Alan Lascelles, the King's private secretary, was impossible. They were awful to him, patronising him as an outsider. He laughed it off, but it must have hurt. I doubt Elizabeth noticed; her life hardly changed. His did completely. He gave up everything.'

At Birkhall, the royal estate in Scotland, Philip wrote to the Queen, his mother-in-law, pledging to build a strong, united life with Elizabeth. Yet, he was baffled by the constant presence of Elizabeth's personal maid, Bobo MacDonald, on their honeymoon. Bobo grated on him, but Elizabeth, long accustomed to having servants around, could not see his problem. To Elizabeth, her maid was a cherished connection to her past. To Philip, she was an unwelcome intrusion. It lingered unresolved. Living at Buckingham Palace for a year while Clarence House was renovated only added to Philip's frustrations with the stifling protocol.

The mounting costs of the renovation sparked public outcry, forcing the King to step in and cover the expense himself. Elizabeth recognised the strain this placed on her husband's self-esteem. George VI, sensing the challenges ahead, grew to respect Philip's struggles and warmed to him over time. The King confided to a wedding guest, 'I wonder if Philip knows what he's taking on. One day, Lilibet will be queen, and he will be consort. That's much harder than being king, but I think he's the man for the job.'[67]

Philip, fiercely independent and brimming with ideas, amused Elizabeth with his irreverence. Loyal to the Crown, he valued duty, but his free spirit unsettled palace courtiers. Countess Patricia Mountbatten observed, 'Philip had a capacity for love, and Elizabeth unlocked it.' Politicians were wary too. Harold Macmillan even noted, 'I fear this young man is going to be as big a bore as Prince Albert.'[68]

Despite his distinguished Royal Navy service, Philip was dismissed by the palace old guard as a foreign outsider, his role limited to producing heirs. Just weeks after their wedding, Elizabeth told her parents she was pregnant, but the Palace kept it quiet. She hid her bump in loose clothes, avoiding the public eye.

When Elizabeth gave birth on 14 November 1948, Philip was playing squash. Still in his gear, he joked that baby Charles looked like a 'plum pudding'. Elizabeth, groggy from anaesthesia, received flowers and champagne. The new father left the nappies to the nannies, focusing on his career, while baby Charles barely saw his mother. Yet, through it all, Philip and Elizabeth were deeply in love, enjoying a rare moment of happiness in their marriage.

In October 1949, Philip was posted to Malta, and Elizabeth joined him at Villa Guardamangia, living as a naval officer's wife, free from royal obligations. She drove around unnoticed, while Philip thrived, commanding HMS *Magpie*. Lady Pamela Hicks later recalled Philip calling it his happiest time. For a while, they lived simply, as husband and wife. But royal duty soon called them back.[69]

Elizabeth returned to Britain pregnant with their second child, Anne, born in August 1950. Philip, poised for a successful naval career, felt his future was at sea, and their time in Malta remained a cherished memory, even celebrated on their diamond wedding anniversary. But fate had other plans.

King George began experiencing serious health issues, including arteriosclerosis, complicated by his heavy smoking. In March 1949, he underwent major surgery to treat arterial blockage in his legs. This condition affected his mobility and caused considerable pain. Despite initial optimism, the operation's success was short-lived. His health steadily worsened.

In 1951, Britain celebrated the Festival of Britain with the King and Queen in attendance. In September, the King was diagnosed with lung cancer and underwent a pneumonectomy at Buckingham Palace, performed by Sir Clement Price Thomas. The nation rejoiced at his return to duty, but the surgery had left him significantly weakened.

By December, as George marked fifteen years on the throne, he was masking his rapidly declining health. He asked Elizabeth and Philip to take his place on a Commonwealth tour. On 31 January 1952, along with the Queen and Princess Margaret, he saw them off at London airport, a pack of Chesterfield cigarettes in hand. After Elizabeth had boarded the plane, he quietly asked Bobo MacDonald, Elizabeth's long-term personal maid, to look after her for him. The sadness in his eyes, she recalled, suggested he knew it was their final farewell.

A week later in Kenya, they stayed at Treetops, a magical retreat perched in a fig tree, overlooking a salt lake where elephants gathered by moonlight. Elizabeth filmed everything, enchanted by the wildlife and the jungle bathed in iridescent light at dawn – a moment she would never forget. But as they rested after a long day, devastating news broke elsewhere: her father was dead. She was oblivious to it.

The King had been in good spirits the night before, returning from a shooting party at Sandringham with Maurice Roche, the 4th Baron Fermoy, spending the evening with his grandchildren, Charles and Anne, and dining with Margaret. Princess Margaret later said, 'He died just as he was getting well.' But he was not well, they only thought he was.

On the morning of 6 February 1952, he never woke up. A blood clot, worsened by a lifetime of smoking, claimed him overnight. At 7.30 a.m., his valet, James McDonald, found George VI unresponsive. Dr James Ansell, the Surgeon Apothecary to the Royal Household at Sandringham, confirmed the death. By 8.45 a.m., Sir Alan Lascelles made the call: 'Hyde Park Corner.' Churchill, now prime minister again, called it 'the worst news' and informed the Cabinet, while Queen Mary mourned. Churchill was disconsolate.

His brother, Henry, Duke of Gloucester, rushed to Sandringham. His sister, Princess Mary, cancelled her ski trip. At 10.45 a.m., the BBC's John Snagge announced with 'great sorrow' that the King was dead. He had reigned for 15 years, 26 days, and died peacefully in his sleep. He was only fifty-six. His widow, Queen Elizabeth, heartbroken, wore black for three months.

At just fifty-one, Queen Elizabeth felt crushed by grief. 'He was my whole life,' she wrote to Queen Mary. She had never wanted Bertie to bear the crown, knowing its burden. Now widowed, she carried the pain for another half a century.

Britain mourned deeply, anxious over young Elizabeth's readiness to lead. Her mother blamed Edward's abdication for hastening Bertie's death, and never forgave him.

On the day of the King's death, Queen Elizabeth II was in Kenya, unaware her father had died. Her private secretary, Martin Charteris, urgently relayed the news to Philip, who gently broke it to Elizabeth during a quiet garden walk at Sagana Lodge. Calmly, she absorbed her loss, cancelled the tour, and began her journey home.

'What will you be called?' Charteris asked. 'Elizabeth, of course,' she replied. Overnight, her private life ended – now she belonged to Britain.

Flying back, Elizabeth changed into black. At London Airport, photographers lowered cameras in respect. Spotting the waiting black limousines, Elizabeth murmured, 'Oh God, they've sent the hearses.' Her carefree days were gone. She was now Queen Elizabeth II, bound forever by duty.

George VI had never sought the throne but rose bravely to meet it, quietly guiding Britain through its darkest hours. Yet many doubted his young daughter Elizabeth, only twenty-five, could carry that same burden. Churchill himself wept, calling her a child, but he believed in the resilience of Crown and country.

In Parliament, Churchill honoured the late King's quiet heroism: 'He shared all our fortunes and misfortunes.' He ended emotionally, invoking the Victoria Cross motto, 'For Valour', words he wrote personally on the King's wreath – a tribute to quiet courage.

For three freezing days, 300,000 mourners paid their respects in Westminster Hall. On 15 February, London paused for the funeral at Westminster Abbey, televised for the first time. As Big Ben tolled, the Royal Family followed the coffin draped with the Royal Standard, bearing the Imperial State Crown. Dowager Queen Mary watched from Marlborough House, as an era ended.

To the mournful strains of Chopin's Funeral March, after the service the royal cortège made its way to Paddington, where the royal train departed for Windsor. After a service at St George's Chapel, the King was laid to rest in the Royal Vault. London fell silent for two minutes in tribute. *The Times* observed that, despite changing times, the monarchy still commanded deep respect. Newsreels echoed the sombre sentiment: 'The King is laid to rest, preserved in death. As one life ends, a young Queen begins her reign, bearing the nation's hopes into a new Elizabethan Age.'[70]

The Duke of Windsor returned for the funeral alone; Wallis was unwelcome. If he hoped his niece would invite him back into the royal fold, he miscalculated. There was no room for a king who had walked away. The Queen, her mother, and Queen Mary pointedly excluded him from the family lunch, blaming Edward for hastening George VI's death.

George was gone; the crown now belonged to Elizabeth.

The young Queen set the tone of this New Elizabethan Age with her coronation broadcast on 2 June 1953: 'I have in sincerity pledged myself to your service, as so many of you are pledged to mine.'

Edward and Wallis, forgotten royals, watched Elizabeth's coronation from Paris – unwanted and uninvited. For Edward, it was bitter proof of a throne traded for love. They drifted into luxurious exile at Villa Windsor in Paris, hollow and alone, and would remain that way for the ensuing decades. Charles, then the Prince of Wales, visited his great uncle at his Parisian home on 4 October 1970, when Charles was twenty-one and Edward was seventy-six. It was a brief and disappointing experience. He left after forty-five minutes. Charles shared with his circle just one odd memory of Wallis: 'She had extraordinarily large hands.'[71]

In November 1971, the Duke was diagnosed with advanced throat cancer. Charles's visit paved the way for a final meeting with the Queen when she was in Paris on 18 May 1972; Edward died ten days later. The Duchess lingered, isolated and suffering from Alzheimer's disease, until 1986. Both rest at Frogmore, their gravestones quietly marking an infamous legacy.

Their Paris villa passed to Mohamed Al-Fayed, who controversially auctioned its contents for charity. The Egyptian tycoon personally promised to return heirlooms to Prince Charles but reneged, leaving Charles with little more than hairbrushes engraved with Edward VIII's insignia. Even the modest hope of reclaiming kilt pins and a Sgian Dubh knife belonging to his great-grandfather, George V, and great-great-grandfather, Edward VII, proved futile.

CHAPTER 5

TROUBLE IN PARADISE

It is quite untrue that there is any rift between the Queen and the Duke of Edinburgh.

RICHARD COLVILLE, BUCKINGHAM PALACE PRESS SECRETARY, 1957

Queen Elizabeth II's coronation on 2 June 1953 marked Britain's renewal. Wartime austerity faded, and pride surged with news of Hillary and Tenzing's British-led Everest victory. It had dawned cold and wet, one of London's chilliest June days. Shivering soldiers warmed themselves with brandy-soaked sugar lumps. Yet the day turned magical: a radiant 27-year-old queen crowned beside her dashing consort. After austerity, crowds roared 'Rule, Britannia' and 'Land of Hope and Glory'. Her fleeting vision of grace in the Gold State Coach stayed etched in memory. The *New York Times* hailed her as a safeguard against darkness; *Time* called her a beacon of hope.

To ease tensions, Elizabeth named Philip as chair of the Coronation Committee, giving him purpose. He pushed for television coverage, outraging traditionalists. Churchill thought it undignified; Archbishop Fisher and the Queen Mother feared losing sacredness. But Elizabeth, backed by Philip, insisted; she saw television as a powerful bridge to her people. The broadcast became a fairy-tale triumph. An estimated worldwide television audience of 20 to 27 million watched in the UK and many millions more worldwide the deeply religious ceremony, a defining milestone in television history.

Elizabeth valued tradition, often saying, 'My father did it this way.' Philip, restless and frustrated by royal routines, quipped, 'If porridge was customary at every meal, Lilibet would have it.'

In an ITV interview with Alan Titchmarsh in May 2011 as part of a special marking Prince Philip's 90th birthday, he admitted he was 'naturally disappointed' about giving up the Navy. 'Being married to the Queen, my first duty was to serve her,' he explained. 'You make compromises – that's life.'

Philip, a natural leader, struggled without an official role, constantly clashing with palace traditionalists suspicious of his foreign background. When they moved into Buckingham Palace, he battled outdated customs, clashing openly with stubborn courtiers he called 'the blockers'. Yet he carved out a purpose. Determined to modernise, Philip refused to be sidelined, pushing causes the Queen could not openly champion. Brigadier Miles Hunt-Davis observed, 'He built a role where none existed.'

Philip also fought hard to give his surname to Elizabeth and their children, but the Queen Mother resisted. Quiet battles played out behind palace walls, with Elizabeth caught between family loyalty and Philip's anger. The Queen Mother distrusted Philip and his ambitious uncle, Lord Mountbatten. Determined to protect the Windsor legacy after the abdication crisis, she and Queen Mary – backed by Churchill – forced Philip to accept that Elizabeth's children would bear the Windsor name.

Philip was furious. 'I am just a bloody amoeba,' he raged, feeling emasculated. Elizabeth stood firm. On 9 April, Clarence House confirmed: the royal children were Windsors. Devastated, Philip turned to flying as an escape, quickly mastering solo flight.

On 7 March 1954 at Yarra Ranges, Victoria, Australia, Philip burst from a cottage, the Queen on his heels, hurling a tennis racket and shoes. Then she spotted the camera crew, grabbed him, dragged him inside, and slammed the door.

The Commonwealth Film Unit had come for a staged royal moment with koalas. Instead, they stood frozen. Soundman Loch Townsend coolly exposed the film and handed the reel to the Queen's panicking press secretary, who took it with relief.

Later, Elizabeth emerged from the cottage, this time smiling. 'Sorry for the little interlude,' she said. 'It happens in every marriage. Now, what would you like me to do?'

The footage vanished, but the film that the crew were making, *The Queen in Australia*, packed cinemas. Decades later, researcher Jane Holley Connors unearthed the tale in her university thesis. Just another moment in a brutal six-month tour – about 44,000 miles, 13 countries, 500 engagements. The Crown pressed on.[72]

At the end of their long tour, the Queen and Philip were eventually reunited with their children, Charles and Anne. They stood on the Buckingham Palace balcony, waving to the crowd. Four appearances, nearly 11 p.m., and yet they lingered. Only when the palace lights dimmed did they drift away.

Sir Winston Churchill welcomed her home. 'I assign no limits to the reinforcement this journey has given to the health, wisdom, sanity, and hopefulness of mankind,' he said. She was at her peak. Philip kept her steady. He was her anchor. Churchill later reflected, 'In the first years of the Queen's reign, the adulation –

you wouldn't believe it. Safer not to be too popular. You can't fall too far.'

Elizabeth and Churchill had grown close. He left their weekly meetings wiping away tears, still chortling. Her private secretary, Sir Alan Lascelles, recalled their talks were 'punctuated by peals of laughter'. On 9 April 1955, secretly weakened by strokes, Churchill resigned at the age of eighty. In his final toast, he called Elizabeth 'a young, gleaming champion'. She replied with a handwritten letter. 'My first Prime Minister,' she wrote. 'To whom both my husband and I owe so much.'

As Elizabeth grew into her role, Philip drifted. On the long Commonwealth tour, he had felt free; more importantly he felt needed. Back in Britain, the old court closed in around the monarch. He was locked out. Once more restless and isolated.

Churchill's exit changed everything. The Queen, once his pupil, stood alone. She admired him, but only in his absence did she step fully into the role for which she was born.

Then came the Suez Crisis. The new prime minister, Sir Anthony Eden – a man in a hurry, with sharp suits and slick hair – kept the Queen in the dark. He had waited too long in Churchill's shadow. When he finally got the top job, it crushed him.

Suez was his downfall. He saw the Egyptian president Gamal Abdel Nasser as another Hitler. He plotted in secret. On 29 October 1956, Israeli forces invaded Egypt to seize the Suez Canal after Nasser had nationalised it. Britain and France had a secret pact: Israel would strike, and they would pose as 'peacekeepers'. Eden ordered the records destroyed. It did not matter. The truth got out. President Eisenhower shut him down without firing a shot. The pound crashed. Britain buckled. Eden had no way out. Furious, Eisenhower used the International Monetary Fund (IMF) to squeeze British loans, forcing a retreat.

Humiliated, Eden resigned in January 1957. Harold Macmillan took his place.

Eden always denied collusion, but the records said otherwise. His legacy? A lesson in ambition and failure. The Suez Crisis left scars. It exposed Britain's decline. *The Times* put it plainly: 'He was the last prime minister to believe Britain was a great power and the first to face a crisis proving she was not.'

The reckoning was national. The Queen was not spared. In 1957, Lord Altrincham, John Grigg, editor of the *National and English Review*,[73] sparked controversy by criticising her public image, urging her to evolve from a diligent, beautiful figure into someone more relatable. His remarks were so provocative he was even attacked in the street, slapped by Philip Kinghorn Burbidge of the League of Empire Loyalists, who declared, 'Take that!' Burbidge was fined 20 shillings for the assault.

The Queen and her advisers were shaken. Philip was right, change was needed and fast. Her first televised Christmas message that year marked a step towards modernisation. Yet her cousin, the Earl of Harewood, noted she still struggled to connect with a changing world. John Grigg criticised the courtiers as 'tweedy' and out of touch, blaming them for the Palace's disconnect. Though Martin Charteris dismissed the critique, balancing tradition and progress remained a delicate challenge.

While the Queen faced these difficult problems alone as monarch, Philip, thirty-two and restless, longed for his naval roots. Rumours of strain in their marriage swirled as he escaped palace life with his navy friend Lieutenant Commander Mike Parker, slipping off to Soho for lunches with actors and artists in their 'Thursday Club'. The Queen tolerated his outings, though she wrinkled her nose at the port-soaked returns. When she suggested he represent her aboard HMY *Britannia* for the 1956 Melbourne

Olympics, he eagerly accepted, hoping for renewed purpose. Restless, he and Parker embarked on a six-month world tour.

Then in 1957, scandal exploded when the *Baltimore Sun* ran the headline: 'Queen, Duke in Rift Over Party Girl', hinting at an affair involving Philip. Many pointed to the stage actress Pat Kirkwood, linked to Philip's circle since 1948, when rumours first surfaced while Elizabeth was pregnant. With ties to society photographer Baron Nahum and the Thursday Club, Kirkwood became tabloid fodder. Philip was furious. 'He was very angry and deeply hurt,' said his friend Mike Parker.

Dismayed by the swirling rumours, the Queen broke protocol by authorising her press secretary, Commander Colville, to issue a rare denial about her personal life. The Palace said: 'It is quite untrue that there is any rift between the Queen and the Duke.' Meant to quash speculation, the statement backfired, fuelling Fleet Street's belief that there was no smoke without fire.

As Colville prepared the statement, news of Parker's own marital troubles broke. His wife, Eileen, had filed for divorce during the world tour, sparking a media storm around Philip's private life. Parker resigned as the Duke's private secretary and returned to London, met by a swarm of reporters. Expecting support when he spotted a palace aide in the crowd, he was met instead with blunt dismissal: 'From now on, you're on your own.' To Parker, it was a stark reminder of the Palace's ruthless detachment. Once out, you were truly out.

Mike and Eileen Parker's divorce became tabloid gold, with his closeness to Philip fuelling more rumours of royal marital strain. The press hinted the split could expose damaging secrets about the monarchy. Eileen later revealed that both the Queen and Philip had urged Mike Parker to stay, but he chose to resign. Granted a divorce on 28 February 1958 over his adultery with

Mary Alexandra Thompson, Eileen claimed her lawyer, Meryn Lewis, had leaked the story to the press without her consent.

Speculation over Philip's affairs surged. The *People* editor Harry Ainsworth even impertinently urged Elizabeth to name him 'Prince Consort' to keep him 'busy at home', warning his undefined role risked more lengthy separations.

In a public show of unity in February 1957, the Queen travelled to join Philip aboard HMY *Britannia* in Lisbon, where they spent two days together before a state visit hosted by President Craveiro Lopes. Exuding marital solidarity at events such as a public welcome at Black Horse Square, they toured key sites, including the Jerónimos Monastery.

Later that month, at a lunch hosted by the Lord Mayor in London, Philip – joined by his outgoing secretary Mike Parker – batted off media rumours, instead reflecting on his tour: 'I find it rather difficult to realise that I've been around the world . . . nearly 40,000 miles . . . all because I was asked to start off the Olympic Games.' He emphasised the value of Commonwealth unity, noting, 'If we don't make sacrifices for it, we shall have nothing to hand onto those who come after us.' He could not resist a dig at the fickle press, adding that the press is a 'professional intruder' and you can't complain about it.

Years later, Pat Kirkwood recounted her one night out in 1948 with Prince Philip, after he saw her starring in the revue *Starlight Roof* at the London Hippodrome theatre. He and his friend, the court photographer Baron, dined and danced with her until dawn, ending with scrambled eggs at Baron's flat. She categorically denied any affair, with her fourth husband, Peter Knight, later offering up their correspondence to prove 'there was no illicit relationship'.

Reflecting, Kirkwood recalled, 'A lady is not normally

expected to defend her honour . . . I would have had a happier life if Philip had gone home to his pregnant wife that night.'[74] She had asked Philip to publicly refute the rumours, but in a letter, he replied that 'invasion of privacy, invention, and false quotations are the bane of our existence.'

He did nothing.

CHAPTER 6

FORBIDDEN BONDS

She [Princess Margaret] could have married me only if she had been prepared to give up everything.[75]

GROUP CAPTAIN PETER TOWNSEND, CVO, DSO, DFC, 1978

Group Captain Peter Townsend was a war hero. A Battle of Britain ace and trusted in King George VI's court. To young Princess Margaret, however, he was more than a dashing aide. He was her knight; the man of her dreams. But fairy tales do not last. Townsend was sixteen years older, married, and caught in a love story that would grip the nation. His wartime marriage to Cecil Rosemary Pawle had given him two sons, Giles and Hugo. But war strains a marriage and by 1952, it had unravelled. Rosemary's affair with John de László sealed its fate.[76]

At seventeen, Margaret stepped into the light. Poised and radiant, she moved with confidence and the camera loved her. The world watched. But whispers followed. Peter Townsend was older, married, and bound by class and duty. Still, he was drawn to her. She to him. Margaret became a royal icon of the 1950s – elegant, magnetic and untouchable. A girl no longer. From her late teens, she broke rules: she smoked in public, a cigarette holder balanced between her fingers. It suited her.

She mixed with stars and scoundrels. Days began at noon and nights blurred into parties. Yet she was flawless. Friends bowed, murmuring 'Ma'am'. Criticism slid off her, like rain on glass. Rumours tied her to tycoons and nobles. But her heart was already spoken for.

In 1947, Princess Elizabeth and Princess Margaret had accompanied King George VI and Queen Elizabeth aboard HMS *Vanguard* on a royal visit to South Africa. At seventeen, Margaret had blossomed. Aboard HMS *Vanguard*, far from court formality, she was free. The King insisted on life at sea without rigid protocol. Royals and sailors mingled as near equals. Margaret, restless and radiant, thrived. Among them was Peter Townsend, the King's equerry. His presence stirred something deeper. This was no ordinary voyage: it was the spark of something lasting.

At the equator, the crew held their wild Crossing the Line ritual. Townsend reportedly took his ducking with a smile. His gaze strayed to Margaret – and she noticed. Everyone did. By now his broken marriage was an open secret. Her girlish crush, no longer innocent. The King, who genuinely liked Townsend, said nothing. If he saw more in the blossoming friendship, he did not let on.

Others were less kind. Senior courtiers saw Townsend as an opportunist, a social climber. 'Cradle-snatcher,' they whispered. He was too old and too low-born. No match for a princess. By the time the tour ended, the rumours had begun to spiral out of control, outside royal circles. Margaret and Townsend did their best to guard their love, hidden in plain sight.

When Margaret lost her father, she lost her anchor. He had called Elizabeth his *pride*, but Margaret was his *joy*. He had spoiled her, given her everything. Now, she was adrift. Shattered, she turned to Townsend. He was her refuge, her escape. A link to her father. Even at the racecourse, where he rode as an amateur jockey, she followed and cheered him on. Now divorced, he was within reach. Marrying him would shake the nation. Defy the Church and upend royal tradition. But the world was changing, she thought. She had hope.

At first, they remained in the shadows, waiting. Townsend, now on the Queen Mother's staff, carried the stain of divorce. In the 1950s, that was enough. The monarchy was still haunted by abdication. He knew the odds: slim at best. Still, he held on. He trusted in the Queen's love for her sister. For him. Elizabeth, contented in her own marriage, was kind, but cautious. She urged patience. Time, she hoped, might offer a way out.

In June 1953, the monarchy took centre stage with Elizabeth's coronation, a dazzling spectacle beamed around the world on television. The new queen was the star. The stage was set. A grand act of royal theatre. Margaret played the captivating supporting role. The event sealed the monarchy's popularity like never before.

But one moment changed everything. Leaving the abbey, Margaret broke protocol. She had promised to avoid Townsend in public. She did not. She saw him in the crowd and went over to him. Without hesitation, without thought. She spoke to him openly with the world watching. She even brushed a piece of fluff off his uniform. The press caught it all. The chemistry. The reckless abandon. The story was theirs. Now, the Queen had a dilemma.

The Sunday tabloid the *People* was the first to confirm the romance: Margaret and Townsend's love affair was now more than rumour. Marriage to a divorced man? Unthinkable, the paper's judgemental editorial thundered. The Palace, on the back foot, panicked. Townsend had to go. On advice, the Queen agreed to send him abroad to Brussels for a two-year posting as air attaché at the British Embassy. He was exiled, but only after Margaret had left the country.

Margaret was sent on an official overseas tour – fifty-four events in sixteen days through Rhodesia with the Queen Mother. At Leopard Rock Hotel, the Queen Mother broke the news: Townsend would be gone when she returned. The next morning, Margaret locked herself in her room. Four days of silence. Four days of heartbreak. A princess in a gilded cage, with less freedom than any commoner, she thought. The official excuse was influenza. The press called it 'diplomatic flu'.

Back in Britain, her pain was clear. The public took her side. Polls showed overwhelming support for her right to marry whomever she chose. The establishment looked cold and out of touch. The echoes of 1936 rang through the palace. It was love versus duty – again. Margaret told Elizabeth that she and Townsend had a plan. They would marry. The Queen hesitated over public opinion, the Church, and the risk of division. She proposed a deal. Wait two years, no contact. At twenty-five, Margaret could choose freely for herself. The princess agreed. Maybe as a test of love. The family hoped time would cool her passion. It did not. She wrote to Townsend daily and thought of him constantly.

In 1955, decision day loomed. Margaret set off on a royal tour of the West Indies, radiant and carefree. She saw the finish line ahead. The Queen Mother urged caution. From Birkhall, on 9 September 1955, she wrote:

> My Darling Margaret,
> I wonder if you know how hard this is for me. I want only your happiness, and I know how torn you are. I think of

> you constantly. Speaking of hard things does not lessen my love for you.
> Your very loving Mummy.

Despite later romanticised portrayals, Margaret was not as powerless in her choice as the press claimed. A 1955 letter revealed her determination to make the decision herself. Six days before her twenty-fifth birthday, Margaret wrote to Prime Minister Eden:

> I expect the press will speculate about my marrying Group Captain Townsend, especially on my birthday. I won't see him then, but in October I'll return to London and hope to meet him on his leave. Only by seeing him can I decide if marriage is right. By late October or early November, I hope to share my decision.

The letter, cold and to the point, suggests her love for Townsend was waning, her certainty fading. She appears confident, in control, casting doubt on the notion that she sacrificed her great love purely for duty. Had she not just moved on?

As she celebrated her twenty-fifth birthday at Balmoral, the nation – or at least Fleet Street, whose editors loved the circulation-boosting story – held its breath, waiting for her decision. Margaret had two options: firstly, to renounce all her royal rights and privileges and become plain Mrs Peter Townsend; secondly, give up any idea of marrying him altogether. She wisely took time to decide, moving through her duties with a bowed, weary air. After weeks of anguish, Margaret made her choice.

At Clarence House, under siege by the press, she met Peter Townsend. She told him first. Marriage was impossible. It had to end. The public got a carefully worded statement. The princess and Townsend framed it as duty, not pressure. Not sacrifice. Not the cost of keeping her crown.

Margaret's words were deliberate:

> I have been aware that, subject to my renouncing my rights of succession, it might have been possible for me to contract a civil marriage. However, mindful of the Church's teaching that Christian marriage is indissoluble, and conscious of my duty to the Commonwealth, I have resolved to put these considerations before any others.

Then, the final line:

> I have reached this decision entirely alone, and in doing so I have been strengthened by the unfailing support and devotion of Group Captain Townsend.

It was over.

Dr Geoffrey Fisher, the Archbishop of Canterbury, welcomed the news. 'What a wonderful person the Holy Spirit is,' he said. Fleet Street went on the attack, slamming the establishment for pressurising the princess to put duty before love. Others lauded her decision as 'courageous'.

Margaret was available again. Young men of class and wealth lined up. Among them was Billy Wallace – a playboy, socialite and old friend. He proposed three times. On the third, she said yes. It did not last. He cheated on her. When she found out, the engagement ended abruptly. No grudge, no drama. Years later, on 9 October 1965, she attended Billy's wedding to Elizabeth Hoyer Millar. She smiled throughout, as if nothing had ever happened between her and the groom.

In public, she dazzled. In private, she drifted. Clarence House was grand, but empty. She lived with her mother, filling her days with high society, but the emptiness remained. The warmth faded and generosity turned to impatience. The charm, once effortless, gave way to hauteur. She demanded the impossible. When denied, few escaped her wrath.

As Margaret neared thirty, her smile returned. She was happy again. The reason? Anthony Armstrong-Jones. A photographer and a charmer. A man who moved between high society and the bohemian world she craved. From the start, he fascinated her. Their romance, built in secrecy, pulled her into a life of theatre, fashion, and freedom.

On 26 February 1960, they announced their engagement. The world was stunned. For months, she had slipped away to his tiny dockside flat in London's East End. No one had seen it coming.

A few months earlier, in July 1959, Peter Townsend married a much younger, beautiful twenty-year-old Belgian heiress and actress, Marie-Luce Jamagne. They had three children, including Isabelle, who worked as a Ralph Lauren model in the late 1980s and 1990s. The family later lived in Le Moulin de la Tuilerie, once home to the Duke and Duchess of Windsor. In his 1978 memoir, *Time and Chance*, Townsend reflected on Margaret, understanding the sacrifice she faced. 'She could have married me only if she had been prepared to give up everything – her position, her prestige, her privy purse. I simply hadn't the weight, I knew it, to counterbalance all she would have lost.' He was spot on. Unlike her uncle, the Duke of Windsor, she was not prepared to abandon the trappings of royalty for love.[77] Denied happiness once, Margaret now seized her moment.

She chose a handsome, sexually exotic commoner, Armstrong-Jones, over foreign princes and titled suitors. A bold choice and a modern one. Not everyone approved. Queen Ingrid of Denmark reportedly snubbed the wedding, offended by a social slight.

On 6 May 1960, Margaret married at Westminster Abbey. The first royal wedding televised in colour, it was a spectacle of tradition and modernity. Armstrong-Jones stood at the altar, composed as Prince Philip escorted Margaret down the aisle. She looked radiant. The future gleamed with promise.

Beneath the glitter, cracks had already formed. It was a union of opposites. The groom had stepped into a world he would soon resent. On their honeymoon aboard *Britannia*, Margaret discovered Mustique. She fell in love with the island, its freedom, its quiet. Colin Tennant, 3rd Baron Glenconner, gifted her a villa – Les Jolies Eaux. It became her retreat, the only place she ever truly owned. Her husband hated it and never returned. The differences had begun.

Margaret's shine began to dim too, as critics slammed her lavish spending and neglecting her public royal duties. She pushed the Queen for bigger and better accommodation at Kensington Palace and was eventually handed a whole wing of the palace to call home.

Tony, stripped of his career, struggled as a royal consort. At events, he trailed behind Margaret, looking miserable. Salvation came when he was appointed as artistic adviser to the *Sunday Times* magazine. A job. A purpose. His talent as an outstanding portrait photographer silenced the critics.

When Margaret became pregnant, the Palace gave him an earldom. They became the Earl and Countess of Snowdon. Their son, David, was born. The spotlight returned and the Sixties roared. They embraced the scene – rockers, film stars and late nights. In 1964, they introduced their daughter, Sarah. They smiled for the cameras, but behind closed doors, the cracks widened.

Margaret, used to smooth royal paths, frequently clashed with Tony, who was restless and defiant. She expected devotion, but he refused to be tamed. In London, he played his part. Abroad, he disappeared; with no calls or letters. Margaret, once adored, the centre of everything, found herself alone. And she grew bitter.

Margaret craved excitement. In 1966, she found it with the jazz pianist and writer Robin Douglas-Home, nephew of the former Conservative prime minister, Sir Alec Douglas-Home. It did not last. Tony found out and Margaret, unwilling to risk divorce, ended it with a letter. She wrote that she would reconcile with her husband. Eighteen months later, Douglas-Home, battling depression, took his own life with a barbiturate overdose. Margaret said nothing publicly, but she was shaken.

Lonely and trapped in a failing marriage, Margaret sought comfort elsewhere. A string of unsuitable men followed. Peter Sellers claimed an affair, but changed his story with every telling casting doubt. She grew irritated and banished him. Mick Jagger. Warren Beatty. David Niven. The gossip pages had a field day. Some names were true, others were fantasy. But Margaret did not care.

Tony had his own affairs and everyone knew it. Returning from Japan in 1970, he faced the press. Reporters fired questions about his marriage and his private life. He stayed cool, the royal composure learned from his in-laws. He denied everything, but by then, the truth was clear. The Snowdons were barely speaking.

Margaret knew about the mistresses: Lady Jacqueline Rufus-Isaacs, journalist Ann Hills, and photographer Lucy Lindsay-Hogg, who would become his second wife. Others were rumoured, like Marjorie Wallace and Cleo Goldsmith. Unlike Margaret, Tony was discreet, which made all the difference. He played the role of the wronged husband. The press, where he had many friends in high places, chose to believe it – and he did not mind one bit.

At forty-three, Margaret fell in love with Roddy Llewellyn, eighteen years her junior, after they were introduced by her friend Lady Anne Glenconner in 1973 at the Café Royal in Edinburgh. His boyish good looks, youth and charm revived the middle-aged princess, bringing her three years of happiness. Still married to Snowdon, she took Roddy to Mustique for a romantic holiday. A leaked photo ended the secrecy and effectively ended the marriage.

Snowdon, with feigned wounded pride, and more than a touch of hypocrisy to those who knew the truth, declared: 'I'm naturally desperately sad in every way that this had to happen. I would just like to say three things to you. Firstly, to pray for the understanding of our two children. Secondly, to wish Princess Margaret every happiness for her future. And thirdly, to express with the utmost humility, my love, admiration and respect I will always have for her sister and her mother.'

There was no going back. The Queen had always liked Tony and appreciated his diplomacy, which kept him in royal favour for years. Meanwhile Margaret dismissed his broadcast as an act and defied him even more brazenly. Within weeks, she reunited with Roddy. She did not care who knew or what they thought. On 19 March 1976, Snowdon announced their formal separation after sixteen years of marriage.

Middle-aged and out of favour, Margaret's public standing had never been lower. Their marriage ended on 11 July 1978, following two years of separation. Princess Margaret was the first senior royal to divorce since 1901, when Princess Victoria Melita ended her marriage to Grand Duke Ernest Louis of Hesse.[78]

At fifty, Margaret faced heartbreak when Roddy Llewellyn ended their strained eight-year relationship in 1981, falling in love with and later marrying Tatiana Soskin, the daughter of Russian-born British screenwriter and film producer, Paul Soskin. Despite being labelled a 'floozy' by the press, the princess kept a friendship with Roddy, even blessing his marriage. He defended their relationship and expressed regret for any embarrassment he may have caused, later becoming a father to three daughters: Alexandra, Natasha and Rosie.

As new royal scandals appeared from the next generation of royals, Margaret retreated from the spotlight, finding solace in her relative obscurity. In her later years she grew closer to the Queen, their shared experiences of privilege and duty deepening their bond. Her declining health – worsened by smoking – would lead to lung surgery and multiple strokes, dimming her vibrant spirit. Despite her struggles, Margaret took pride in her children, David and Sarah, who lived quietly and without scandal, embodying her legacy. Her final years were overshadowed by sadness, lingering regrets, and the poignant memories of lost love.

Even in her twilight years the princess still loved to party. On 25 October 1990, she joined Princess Diana at a banquet at the Victoria and Albert Museum in honour of the Italian president's state visit. Diana, draped in a stunning fuchsia pink silk gown by Victor Edelstein and crowned with a tiara, was the centre of attention, as ever, radiating elegance. Princess Margaret, in blue silk, was happy to be no longer the star attraction. But ever the social butterfly, she stayed to the bitter end, revelling in the evening's festivities.

Diana's Scotland Yard bodyguard Ken Wharfe, who had agreed to stay on after dropping off his charge back home earlier, returned to watch over Margaret. He recalled their short journey in a Rolls-Royce back to Kensington Palace as anything but dull. When the car jolted, Margaret, who was a little tipsy, tumbled into the footwell, laughing off the mishap. Upon arrival, the princess discovered she did not have a key. Wharfe offered to wake the butler, but Margaret quipped, 'You won't wake him, he'll be drunk.' Thankfully, the butler defied her expectations.[79]

In 1992, Margaret and Peter Townsend met one last time at Kensington Palace. It was closure. She was sixty-one. He was seventy-seven. 'He looked the same,' she said later. 'Just grey-haired.'

Townsend died in 1995, aged eighty, in France. Leaving him had been her great personal tragedy. What was once scandal would barely matter now, but it shaped her. Her love story became something larger – a symbol of life stifled by duty. Of sacrifice. Of what might have been.

The princess moved into Clarence House with her mother, where they supported each other until the end, as Margaret faced her battles with lung cancer. The Queen Mother's devoted servant William Tallon, dubbed 'Backstairs Billy', who served her for fifty years, recalled the princess would always ask for lunch to include an egg dish. It would serve as 'Margot's' breakfast, as she rarely rose before noon.

Lord Charteris, before his death aged eighty-six in 1999, dismissed the idea that courtiers sacrificed Margaret. 'Maybe she sacrificed herself, but that's different,' he said.[80] Margaret lived a life of privilege, but was isolated from ordinary experiences, never shopping, cleaning, or dealing with everyday struggles. She famously likened her lack of privacy to being 'a goldfish in a bowl'.

Princess Margaret died on 9 February 2002, aged seventy-one, after a stroke at King Edward VII's Hospital in London. Prince Charles honoured his vibrant and talented 'darling aunt' as a 'a wonderfully free spirit, who loved life and lived it to the full.'

The real tragedy of Margaret's life was losing the man she truly loved. A choice that broke her. A wound that never healed.

At her funeral in 2002, the Queen spoke to Lady Anne Glenconner, perhaps reflecting on the Townsend affair, or maybe wanting to rewrite it. 'It was rather difficult at moments,' she said. 'But I thank you for introducing Roddy. He made her really happy.'[81]

Margaret's life was a battle: duty versus love. The same dilemma that haunted the monarchy for decades. Elizabeth, torn between the Crown and her sister's heart, tried to balance compassion with duty. Duty won.

CHAPTER 7

A BURIED FILE

In the raucous period when authority figures were denied respect even when they deserved it, Prince Philip became the subject of unfounded rumours, simply for his association with figures like Stephen Ward.[82]

RICHARD DAVENPORT-HINES, 2013

In February 1960, Prime Minister Harold Macmillan noted his 'dismay' at Prince Philip's 'almost brutal attitude' towards the Queen. The fight was over a name. Elizabeth, the first reigning monarch to give birth in over a century, announced her third pregnancy in 1959. But when Prince Andrew was born on 19 February 1960, joy was overshadowed by Philip's old frustration. His children did not bear his name. This time, Philip would not back down. He had an ally – Lord Mountbatten.

A strategist, he was a war hero who never forgot a slight. To Mountbatten, the exclusion of their name was not just tradition. It was an insult. A deliberate erasure. And after being denied the right before, Philip had had enough.

To Palace old-school courtiers like Sir Michael Adeane, the Queen's private secretary, Mountbatten was a dangerous influence, a man whose loyalty concealed ruthless ambition. They saw him as the force behind Philip's growing push to reshape the monarchy, a threat the Queen could not afford to let too close.[83]

Philip found an unlikely supporter – Edward Iwi, a relentless lawyer and self-styled constitutional expert. A man who lived for legal battles, Iwi took up the cause with zeal. On 10 August 1959, Mountbatten met him in secret. A compromise was suggested: Mountbatten-Windsor. A name Dickie had long whispered into the right ears.

By September, Iwi pressed harder. He warned Prime Minister Macmillan that without action, the royal child would bear 'the badge of bastardy': a prince bearing only his mother's name. Philip would not stand for it and neither would Mountbatten.

The issue escalated fast.

Lord Chancellor Kilmuir got involved. An internal inquiry dug into royal surnames, uncovering that the British throne had once belonged to the Guelph family before Windsor was adopted during the First World War.

Iwi's persistence alarmed Kilmuir. He urged Macmillan to handle him 'in friendly terms'; the man had a knack for exposing legal loopholes. Macmillan pushed back. Royal surnames were symbolic, he argued. Iwi was not deterred.

On 17 November 1959, he fired back: 'No one is infallible. If the Royal Family never had a surname, then the 1917 Proclamation changing the name to Windsor would never have been necessary.' Still, he would not be silenced.

Soon, he had found another ally – the Bishop of Carlisle, Thomas Bloomer. The bishop questioned the fairness of denying a child his father's name. He chose his words carefully. But the message was clear.

Iwi did not let up. He had 'strong conscientious feelings' against a legitimate child taking only its mother's maiden name.

He believed 'many right-thinking people' agreed. Some dismissed him. One official joked, 'Not to be confused with the Browne-Windsors.' Others, like Sir George Coldstream, were less amused. 'One is sorely tempted to cane him for being so cheeky.'

But Iwi was relentless. And the Crown took notice. The debate weighed on the Queen; pregnant and exhausted, she was brought to tears. Elizabeth was torn – loyal to Philip but devoted to Windsor. She confided in Deputy Prime Minister R.A. Butler that she 'absolutely set her heart' on a change.

Just days before Prince Andrew's birth, she made her move. A declaration: Mountbatten-Windsor would be the surname for descendants without royal titles. A quiet compromise. A hidden name, waiting to be used. Whitehall was satisfied. Butler told Macmillan it had 'taken a great load from [the Queen's] mind'. The fight was over. Philip had won, at least in part.

The Queen's announcement in the *London Gazette* showed 'Mountbatten-Windsor' as the family name for certain descendants without altering the Windsor dynasty, a change that would require an Act of Parliament. To Philip, this was an ideal compromise, and the *Daily Herald* trumpeted his triumph with the headline: 'Philip wins fight for the Royal Mountbattens'.

Vindicated, Iwi secretly joined Lord Mountbatten at his home the next day, slipping in discreetly. There, alongside a jubilant Prince Philip, the three toasted their hard-won victory. Fleet Street, under Palace pressure, buried the Queen–Philip rift story; but three years later, when Philip's name was loosely tied to the explosive Profumo Affair, with its heady mix of sex, politics, scandal, betrayal, and Cold War intrigue, circulation-hungry editors could not get enough.

The scandal that shook Britain's establishment centred on Stephen Ward, an artist and society osteopath with intelligence ties, who invited nineteen-year-old model Christine Keeler to stay at his Wimpole Mews flat. Ward introduced Keeler to elite circles, where she had brief affairs with the Secretary of State for War, John Profumo, and Soviet naval attaché Yevgeny Ivanov, sparking Cold War security fears. The drama erupted in 1962 when jazz promoter Johnny Edgecombe, competing for Keeler's attention with Jamaican-born singer and chef Aloysius 'Lucky' Gordon, fired shots outside Ward's flat. As Keeler revealed her affairs with Ivanov and Profumo, who was married to the actress Valerie Hobson, the story spiralled into a full-blown national scandal.

Stephen Ward had ties to Prince Philip through the 'Thursday Club' – the exclusive, all-male dining and drinking society in London where aristocrats, celebrities and royalty gathered for boozy, carefree evenings. These fascinated the press and unnerved the government. A skilled portraitist, Ward had sketched Philip, his associates, and even Princess Margaret. Philip's connection to Ward was limited, but it did not stop the satirical magazine *Private Eye* fanning the flames with a baseless 'Man in the Mask' claim about him, infuriating Philip and his circle.[84]

In the 2020 BBC documentary *Keeler, Profumo, Ward, and Me*, journalist Tom Mangold revealed a twist: Soviet spy Yevgeny Ivanov was not just Ward's friend, but an MI5 target. Stephen Ward, ever the patriot and encouraged by the intelligence community, aimed to flip him into a double agent. The government, however, saw Ward as a liability, someone who could expose Profumo and ignite a national crisis.

A meeting on 27 March 1963 between Home Secretary Henry Brooke, Metropolitan Police Commissioner Sir Joseph Simpson, and MI5 head Sir Roger Hollis led to Ward's phone being tapped and police stationed outside his osteopathy practice. This in turn led Ward's high-society friends to distance themselves from the therapist. By May, a desperate Ward called Macmillan's office, begging for a meeting. A declassified National Archives memo revealed that Sir Timothy Bligh, Macmillan's private secretary, was so rattled by the call that he rushed to brief the Prime Minister at the House of Commons and consulted Sir Joseph Simpson,[85] who confirmed Ward's imminent arrest.

In his 22 March 1963 Commons statement, Profumo insisted there was 'no impropriety whatsoever' in his ties to Keeler, but the memo marked Ward as the 'smoking gun' the government was desperate to silence. Under mounting pressure, on 5 June 1963, Profumo admitted lying to Parliament, the public and his colleagues – ending his career, damaging Macmillan's government, exposing Britain's elite, and contributing to the Conservatives' 1964 election defeat.

At his Old Bailey trial, Ward was charged with living off the earnings of prostitution, mainly linked to Christine Keeler and her friend Mandy Rice-Davies. Judge Sir Archie Marshall steered the jury towards conviction, stressing that none of Ward's influential friends had come to his defence. MI5 could have verified Ward's role in attempting to turn Soviet spy Ivanov, but stayed silent. The intelligence agency's chief, Sir Roger Hollis, withheld key evidence confirming Ward's cooperation with the security services, allowing him to be painted as a delusional fantasist, despite his loyal service to the state.

The trial ended on 31 July 1963. Despairing, Ward took a fatal overdose of sleeping pills at a friend's Chelsea flat. Rushed to St Stephen's Hospital, he remained in a coma until his death on 3 August. He was found guilty in absentia and died without regaining consciousness.

Later evidence showed that Stephen Ward had been a scapegoat in a conspiracy by powerful figures intent on silencing him before he exposed Profumo. British intelligence, aware of Profumo's affair with Keeler and her ties to the Soviet spy Ivanov, had assigned Ward a handler, 'Woods', to set a honey trap for Ivanov, convincing Ward he was acting in national security interests.

Prime Minister Harold Macmillan tasked Lord Denning with leading a judicial inquiry into the Profumo Affair, which resulted in the Denning Report published on 26 September. It inevitably condemned the dead Ward, portraying him as self-serving and morally ambiguous, casting him in a negative light, while absolving Profumo. Ward was the scapegoat. Despite queues to buy the report, its revelations were few, with sensitive details locked up for years and held in secret files.

However, Denning did criticise the government for its slow response to the scandal. 'The conflict of loyalties, the sense of betrayal, the feeling of shame, and above all, the indignation at being misled have gone deeper than could have been imagined,' the report said. It summed up the public outrage at Profumo's lies and the moral failures among individuals in high places. But Denning found no national security breach, leaving some disappointed.

When BBC journalist Jack Hardiman Scott questioned Macmillan, he denied the Denning report's impact on his own position, but the public backlash left him in an untenable situation. The public no longer trusted him or his government. After weeks of uncertainty, he finally resigned on 10 October 1963, citing ill health as the reason. The Queen, acknowledging his service, sent him a handwritten note, wishing him well and a 'speedy recovery'.

Prince Philip's acquaintance with figures central to the scandal, however loose, intrigued investigative journalists for many years. They included Clive Irving, the distinguished reporter who set up the *Sunday Times* groundbreaking investigative unit, Insight, which later probed the royal link to the Profumo Affair. Irving and his team untangled the complex web of influences at play from society circles to the upper ranks of the British security services. They investigated the 'Thursday Club', whose members – including Ward – often gathered at artist Felix Topolski's studio on the South Bank. When interviewed, he boasted about knowing Ward and his circle, but refused to discuss Philip.[86]

The newspaper investigation attracted the interest of the British security services. Irving later revealed that an MI5 officer calling himself 'Mr Shaw' contacted him and requested a personal meeting; assuring him it was nothing to be alarmed about – 'just a matter of courtesy'. When they met, the intelligence officer and his two colleagues knew about every step the journalist and his team had taken during their probe. They had been shadowing their every move.

Among the most sensitive records of the Profumo Affair are the *Stephen Ward prosecution papers* at the National Archives (CRIM 1/4140), which remain largely closed on personal-data grounds. They have no officially confirmed release date. Separately, the Cabinet Office's confidential evidence gathered by Lord Denning in 1963 – material ministers have described as containing 'sensational personal items … which would be embarrassing if released' – is to be withheld until 2063, a full century after the scandal. Those files were *preserved despite moments when destruction was considered*, including a false 1977 claim by Denning that they had been destroyed. Supporters of the late Ward, among them Mandy Rice-Davies, who died aged 70 in December 2014 after a cancer battle, long argued that opening these records could help clear his name and expose the powerful figures they believe were shielded by an official cover-up.

Composer and theatrical titan Andrew Lloyd Webber, who produced the West End musical *Stephen Ward*, called the sealed documents 'explosive', citing a 'totally reliable' high-level source. Meanwhile, royal allies, frustrated by the lingering rumours linking Prince Philip to the scandal, suggest he would have preferred the files unsealed during his lifetime, to clear his name and stop the incessant rumours.

In June 2013, Lord Lloyd Webber stood in the House of Lords. He wanted answers. The key Profumo Affair file remained sealed. Why? 'This gives rise to an awful lot of unhealthy speculation,' he said. 'Goodness knows where it could lead.' He then warned that secrecy only fed the rumours. 'I can't believe that if I'd been involved, someone like me would receive protection like this.' Then came the question of Prince Philip. 'All we know is that Ward and Philip knew each other,' he said. 'Ward sketched him several times.'

Philip's link to the Profumo Affair remains speculation. Rumours, not proof. A 1963 FBI file recorded gossip from Thomas Corbally, an adventurer and occasional spy. He claimed that Philip was involved. No evidence; again, just whispers. Corbally had tipped off US authorities about Profumo and the Soviet spy Ivanov. He knew Ward. But there was no proof that Philip ever met Christine Keeler, or Mandy Rice-Davies. Only that Ward had met him multiple times.

In July 1963, as the Profumo scandal raged, a well-dressed stranger entered a London gallery and swiftly bought every Stephen Ward portrait of the Royal Family – paying £5,040 in five-pound notes, a huge sum in today's money, and vanishing without giving a name. The sudden disappearance of the artwork, amid Ward's explosive trial, sparked fevered speculation. Many believed the buyer was none other than Sir Anthony Blunt: the Queen's Surveyor of Pictures, a Soviet spy, and keeper of royal secrets buried in the Marburg Files.

In his posthumously discovered memoirs, Ward claimed that Philip had attended at least one of his parties in Cavendish Square with a woman named Mitzi Taylor. Others said her name was Maxie Taylor. In her own memoirs, Christine Keeler even alleged that Ward treated Philip as a patient.

With Ward's name tarnished and his ties to the elite under scrutiny, the theory took hold: Blunt was said to have been sent quietly to erase any trace of royal association. The Palace denied involvement. But the sketches – and the questions – vanished.

CHAPTER 8

FAIR GAME

I have in my heart a sense of hope for the future and confidence in the great possibilities which lie ahead.

QUEEN ELIZABETH II, 1969

Prince Philip perched high on an Indian elephant, cradling a .458 Winchester rifle. A trembling, tethered buffalo drew the tiger out, and with one shot, the beast fell. The Queen stood by as her husband posed triumphantly with the kill, flanked by the Maharaja and Maharani of Jaipur. Broad smiles lit the family's faces in the photo. By day's end, Philip had added a crocodile and six mountain sheep to his tally, while his wife observed in silence.

Historically, tiger hunts were justified by the threat they posed to villagers, but by 1961, an era of change and rebellion, they were relics of a bygone age. The timing was disastrous. On a royal visit, the couple looked like figures from the British Raj, even as India's prime minister Pandit Jawaharlal Nehru condemned such hunts as elite cruelty. The British and Indian press erupted, lambasting the royal couple for accepting the Maharaja's invitation, with *Time* magazine reporting that Fleet Street editors had questioned Philip's ethics.

A week later in Nepal, hosted by King Mahendra, Philip dodged the bullet. Mahendra, hoping to bolster his prestige with a tiger shoot in Chitwan National Park, assembled 327 elephants and set up white canvas to hold the tiger, so it would not escape. Philip needed to find a good excuse not to shoot another trophy without offending his host. He appeared with a bandaged trigger finger, claiming a painful infection. Mahendra, aware of the press scrutiny, accepted the story with no offence taken. Two royal courtiers shot and killed the tiger instead. Afterwards, when the royal party went rhino hunting, Philip again did not fire a shot.

The Duke was branded Britain's biggest hypocrite. The controversy peaked when it was revealed that, behind the scenes, Philip had been quietly working to set up the World Wildlife Fund, a guardian of nature, which he would officially launch just four months later. How could he preach conservation while hunting endangered species for sport?

His reputation barely intact, on 29 April, Philip joined Prince Bernhard of the Netherlands to announce their retirement from big game hunting and to highlight the importance of protecting endangered species. Together with intellectuals like Sir Peter Scott and Julian Huxley, they founded the World Wildlife Fund and issued the 'Morges Manifesto', saying, 'We must save the world's wildlife.'

The tiger hunt revealed a harsh reality: the royals had to evolve or risk fading into obscurity. Time had moved on, and clinging to outdated traditions in order to please royal hosts with declining influence threatened their relevance. For the Queen and Philip, it was a sharp wake-up call.

By the Sixties, the once steadfast monarchy seemed rigid and out of step with a changing world. To the younger generation, the royals symbolised colonial relics and outdated traditions.

Amid the Vietnam War and rising street protests, calls to abolish the monarchy grew louder.

The Empire cast a long shadow. Across Africa, flags were being changed and independence was the buzzword. Once loyal to the British Crown, old allegiances were ending abruptly. The Queen watched on steadily as nations reclaimed their names and their voices; ditching her as their head of state, and becoming republics. Immediately, critics spoke of financial reparations for the blood spilled and fortunes taken. Elizabeth, bound by duty and conscience, walked a narrow path, neither absolving nor denying, simply enduring. The world moved forward, but the weight of history lingered, with demands that Britain pay for the brutality of its empire.

Sir Winston Churchill's funeral on 30 January 1965, six days after his death at ninety, marked the end of an era: a passing from the old order to the new. The Queen, in her condolences to the great statesman's widow Lady Clementine, honoured his 'many-sided genius', courage, and leadership. The farewell coincided with Britain's transformative 'Swinging Sixties', a decade of change defined by the Beatles, the Rolling Stones, women's liberation, the hippy movement, sexual and social revolution. Class barriers and sexual prejudices crumbled as fashion and music reshaped the nation's identity.

It was a decade in which television surpassed radio as the dominant mass communication medium, with three-quarters of the population owning or renting bulky, cathode-ray tube models, often encased in polished wooden cabinets to double as pieces of furniture. By the end of the decade, this figure rose to about 95 per cent. Recognising this shift, Philip urged Queen Elizabeth to embrace the medium, and she made her first televised Christmas message from Sandringham in 1957; the start of a royal tradition that has since become a part of many families' Christmas Day celebrations.

Philip play-acted to ease the Queen's understandable nerves before making her TV debut. Courtiers recalled that the hallways echoed with her laughter as he ran up and down, brandishing a pair of false teeth to keep her and their children entertained. He even sent a playful message to the director: 'Tell her to remember the wailing and gnashing of teeth.'

Ronald Allison, the Queen's press secretary from 1968–78, remembered that 'Prince Philip was very much holding her hand through all of this.' Christina Aldridge, daughter of Peter Dimmock, the producer for the BBC broadcast, recalled, 'The Queen was rather nervous, and Prince Philip, aware of this, stood behind the camera making encouraging, even ridiculous faces, helping her to relax and smile.' The monarch's Christmas televised broadcast was a significant step in modernising the monarchy, as it allowed for a personal connection with the public by bringing the Royal Family into people's living rooms.

In January 1963, Labour leader Hugh Gaitskell's sudden death aged fifty-six from lupus erythematosus, a rare autoimmune disease, cut short the career of a man widely seen as a future prime minister. It paved the way for Harold Wilson's rapid rise to power. Labour, out of government since 1951, rallied behind the slogan '13 Wasted Years', capturing middle-class frustration with the Tories and an electorate hungry for a change of direction.

Grammar-school educated and from a lower-middle class background, Wilson was markedly different from earlier prime ministers. An academic, he was a shrewd moderniser, yet cultivated a favourable rapport with the Queen. With a relatable persona and an intellect honed through rigorous academia – graduating with first-class honours in Philosophy, Politics, and Economics (PPE) from Oxford and becoming one of the century's youngest college dons at the age of twenty-one – he was widely respected.

Wilson relished a 'relaxed intimacy' with the Queen, in whom he found a trusted ally. After their first meeting, she notably invited him for a drink and allowed him to smoke his iconic straight billiard pipe during their audiences. He took immense pride in their association, even displaying a photograph of them together on the wall of the study at his holiday home called Lowenva on St Mary's, in the Isles of Scilly.

As Elizabeth grew more confident in her constitutional role and developed a warm working relationship with Wilson, Philip felt increasingly isolated. He sensed that he was no longer her primary adviser and was becoming a spare part at court. Refusing to be sidelined, he aimed to modernise the monarchy. In his mid-forties, Philip recognised how out of touch the institution had become, especially with younger generations, and how dangerous that was.

His involvement with his own initiatives such as the Duke of Edinburgh's Award Scheme and London Youth equipped him with valuable insights. He scrutinised outdated palace practices, growing frustrated with the inefficiencies he found, like separate kitchens for royalty and staff, which wasted money and resources. He was shocked when told that the tradition of keeping a bottle of whisky by the Queen's bed stemmed from Queen Victoria's cold remedy request; an order that had inexplicably persisted.

Concerned about the monarchy's vulnerability, he warned the Queen bluntly that proactive modernisation was essential. While some courtiers resisted change, Philip believed that increasing accessibility to the public would enhance the Royal Family's popularity. Determined to rejuvenate the institution, he embraced the spirit of the era, considering even unconventional ideas.

With the public's growing fascination about outer space, especially after Soviet cosmonaut Yuri Gagarin's historic first orbit of the Earth in 1961, Philip, a keen pilot, became obsessed by the subject. His curiosity about the cosmos and thirst for knowledge was unquenchable. In 1969, the Queen hosted the Apollo 11 astronauts Armstrong, Aldrin, and Collins at Buckingham Palace and the royal couple also met Apollo 8's Frank Borman, celebrating their groundbreaking achievements. Avidly collecting books on extraterrestrial life and UFOs, Philip had a lifelong interest in space exploration. He even subscribed to the *Flying Saucer Review*, saying, 'There are many reasons to believe that they [UFOs] exist.'

Philip recognised the power of television and its potential to bypass what he viewed as a sneering press. 'You have mosquitoes. I have the press,' he said disdainfully during a visit to a Caribbean hospital in 1966. It led to his landmark television interview on BBC's *Panorama* on 29 May 1961. Interviewed by Richard Dimbleby about the Commonwealth Technical Training Week, Philip stressed the need for skilled worker training, marking the first time a royal faced questions on camera.

In October 1966, tragedy struck the coal-mining village of Aberfan in South Wales, when a colliery spoil tip collapsed, resulting in the deaths of 144 people, including 116 children. After the final victim was found, the Queen and Philip visited the site to pay their respects. Delayed by eight days, the Queen was visibly moved. She later admitted her regret at not going sooner, believing it would have diverted attention and hindered recovery efforts. William Heseltine, who joined the Royal Household in 1966 as the Queen's press secretary before later becoming her private secretary, noted that she fully understood the importance of showing sympathy and being present, remarking that the tears she shed endeared her to the grieving locals.

In a 1968 television interview on *Face the Press*, Philip said that instead of avoiding scrutiny, the Royal Family should foster a two-way relationship with the public.[87] He warned the Queen privately that the royals could no longer remain in their 'gilded tower' and needed to engage openly with people. Meanwhile, a new breed of forward-thinking courtiers at Buckingham Palace, led by Heseltine, grew increasingly concerned about waning interest in the monarchy, particularly in Australia and New Zealand.

Despite the remarkable success of the Queen's first Commonwealth tour, her 1963 return to Australia was a low-key affair, with local critics bemoaning Britain's shift towards Europe at the expense of Commonwealth ties. This prompted calls among former colonies for independence and for the monarchy to be ditched in favour of self-governing republics, with their own elected head of state. The Queen and her advisers had to act, and fast.

The Queen was open to suggestions, and when Philip saw an opportunity to test his theories, he seized it. In 1968, Lord Brabourne, a television producer and the son-in-law of Lord Mountbatten, proposed a 'fly on the wall' documentary about the Royal Family. Inspired by the idea, Philip championed the project to film the royals in their everyday lives and chaired the committee to explore this initiative.

Some courtiers warned the Queen against it, saying it could diminish public respect for the monarchy. It sparked a clash of visions at the palace: one path focused on tradition and the past, while Philip urged adaptation to avoid sinking into irrelevance. By 1968, as the Queen Mother neared seventy and traditional figures like Churchill were gone, Philip's influence grew, particularly since Lord Brabourne suggested that the documentary would be an excellent way to introduce twenty-year-old Prince Charles ahead of his investiture as the Prince of Wales.

Eventually the Queen backed it, accepting it aligned with the spirit of a changing Britain. Her influential press secretary, William Heseltine, an Australian, backed it too, believing it stood for a necessary shift in public relations. Victorian essayist Walter Bagehot had warned against letting daylight in on royal magic a century earlier, but now the cameras were in, and everywhere.[88]

Filming began in 1968 under the direction of Richard Cawston, head of the BBC Documentary unit. For months, he captured forty-three hours of unscripted footage at Buckingham Palace, Windsor Castle and Balmoral. The Queen and the Royal Family found it challenging to adapt to the crew's presence in what was usually their private and personal space. Notably, Philip snapped at the crew during a shoot at Balmoral, saying, 'Get away from the Queen with your bloody cameras!'

Although the documentary aimed to highlight the human side of the monarchy, its narration by Michael Flanders kept an official tone, emphasising the monarchy's significance. After eighteen months of production, the finished film depicted a year in the royal life, highlighting the Queen's work alongside world leaders, and featuring charming moments such as her visit to a sweet shop with her youngest son, Prince Edward.

Philip was pleased with the documentary's portrayal of his family as sporty, displaying Charles waterskiing, himself flying a plane, and the Queen driving her car at surprising speeds. The Queen less so. She thought the two-hour film was too long. When *Royal Family* aired on 21 June 1969, it was seen as a public relations masterstroke, captivating the two-thirds of Britain's population who tuned in. Criticism, however, soon followed, including accusations of casual racism over the Queen joking about an official visitor resembling a gorilla.[89]

The film blurred the boundaries between the royals' public duties and private lives, encouraging Fleet Street editors and the public to see the family as 'fair game'. Some commentators such as journalist John Grigg (later Lord Altrincham) said the project was folly, believing it opened the door to intrusive journalism and the rise of paparazzi.[90] Princess Anne's assessment was characteristically blunt. 'I thought it was a rotten idea,' she said.[91] The Queen considered it a strategic error and ruled against future broadcasts, except for a single repeat transmission in 1977. In 2011, a brief breakfast scene from the film was shared with the National Portrait Gallery and later appeared on YouTube, gaining over 500,000 views.

The monarchy teetered on the edge of obsolescence. Without doubt the film opened doors, but some of those doors were meant to stay shut. Mystery was traded for modernity; it was necessary but costly. Relevance came, but so did exposure and control of the narrative soon slipped from their grasp. While initially effective, the documentary laid the groundwork for the relentless press scrutiny and paparazzi culture that would shadow the monarchy for years to come.

In 1969, Philip faced more criticism. His remarks on NBC's *Meet the Press*, where he claimed the monarchy was 'broke' and might have to downsize, led to a backlash. While his statement was correct, it sparked outrage; critics derided him for lamenting the need to give up polo, a hugely costly, elitist hobby, Negative headlines followed, and dockworkers in Bermondsey mockingly offered to chip in for a polo pony, highlighting the public's disdain for his predicament.[92]

His comment, rather than garnering public sympathy,

triggered criticism and led to debates in a parliamentary Select Committee about a proposed royal pay raise. One member, Willie Hamilton MP, mocked the idea that the Royal Family might endure the 'supreme hardship' of cutting back on such extravagances, as he put it. Barbara Castle, a fiery left-winger in Wilson's Cabinet, pointed out the widespread lack of sympathy for Philip's financial woes, emphasising the disconnect between the royals and the public.

Charles's investiture as the Prince of Wales at Caernarfon Castle on 1 July 1969 was carefully staged to highlight Welsh heritage and royal tradition while countering rising nationalism. Sent to the University College of Wales in Aberystwyth to learn Welsh, Charles viewed the move as political rather than cultural. Despite genuine threats against him, the Queen, Philip, and Prime Minister Wilson agreed that cancelling the prince's term there would be a PR disaster for both the monarchy and the government.

Before his departure, on 1 March 1969 Charles recorded his first radio interview on BBC's Radio 4 *Today* programme, where he admitted to feeling 'apprehensive'. When the broadcaster Jack de Manio asked about his attitude towards the hostility against him, he replied, 'I don't blame people demonstrating like that. They've never seen me before. They don't know what I'm like. I've hardly been to Wales, and you can't really expect people to be overzealous about the fact of having a so-called English prince to come amongst them.'

On the eve of his investiture, Charles boarded the Royal Train to Wales with his parents, aware of the stakes. Bombs had exploded, and two men had died preparing one meant for the ceremony. To Welsh nationalists, the event symbolised oppression. Security was at its tightest and nerves frayed, but the Crown pressed on. Thankfully, the investiture went smoothly.

Charles rode through Cardiff, knelt before the Queen at Caernarfon, and took his oath wearing a purple velvet cloak. After fanfares and cheers, he dined aboard the Royal Yacht, relieved and happy. The next day, Charles began a week of solo visits in Wales, warmed by unexpected cheers. Back at Windsor, he hoped for praise, but his parents offered none; it was not their way.

Charles was three when fate made his mother the queen. A shy boy, he shrank from his destiny, clashing with his brash, alpha father. Unlike his fearless sister Anne, who charged ahead, Charles hesitated, cautious and always second-guessing. He would ask his Scottish nanny, Helen Lightbody, 'Should I go?' only feeling safe once she assured him and replied, 'Yes, go.' Where Anne felt strength, Charles felt the weight of a man born to be king.

Philip's strict, cold parenting strained their bond. Instead of pride, he brought pressure, trying to toughen Charles. The distance grew, leaving a lasting emotional chasm. The Duke feared Charles was spoiled by others, especially the Queen Mother. Believing in 'tough love', he countered with sarcasm and cutting remarks, adding to the strain. Teatime was not a warm family gathering; Sir Martin (later Lord) Charteris, the Queen's senior adviser, noted that even their interactions lacked affection. He recalled, 'The Queen is not good at showing affection either.' Although there were lighter moments, such as when the Queen tried to teach Charles horseback riding aged four, which backfired because Charles found the idea so terrifying.

Philip took charge of shaping the future king. Out went comfort; in came Gordonstoun – a cold, relentless boarding school where Philip had thrived. He wanted Charles to follow, to be tough and unbreakable. But Charles, introspective and gentle, was not the rugged son Philip envisioned and grew up feeling he would never be enough for his father.

Many people, including the Queen and the Queen Mother, considered Philip's choice of Gordonstoun a mistake.[93] Concerned for Charles's well-being, she pleaded with the Queen to reconsider and wrote that Eton would be a better fit, allowing Charles to grow up with his peers and stay connected to his family. She wrote to the Queen on 23 May 1961, 'All your friends' sons are at Eton, and it is so important to be able to grow up with people you will be with later in life . . . I do hope you don't mind my writing my thoughts on this subject, but I have been thinking and worrying about it all.'

Her plea fell flat. Philip justified his decision by emphasising the importance of discipline and resilience in his son's childhood, saying, 'Children may be indulged at home, but school is expected to be a spartan and disciplined experience.' Charles described his time at Gordonstoun, where he faced bullying, as 'hell on earth'. With his parents aloof, he found solace in the Queen Mother, whose nurturing presence filled the emotional void and became vital to his life.

Charles's childhood letters to her reveal a mix of doting affection and deep misery. He masked his struggles at school with humour, recalling his trumpet lessons: 'I can hear the music teacher shouting, "Ach! Zoze trumpets! Stawp zoze trumpets!" So, I gave up my trumpet.' Mostly his memories of the place filled him with dread. In a private letter on 9 February 1963, he noted about boarding at Gordonstoun: 'I hate coming back here and leaving everyone at home . . . I hardly get any sleep at the House because I snore and get hit on the head the whole time. It is absolute hell.'

The so-called 'Cherry Brandy' incident only worsened his plight. It occurred when the prince, then aged fourteen, went on a sailing trip to the Isle of Lewis. He innocently ordered a cherry brandy at a pub, the Crown Inn, only for a journalist in the bar to file a report to a newspaper about his underage drinking. When his housemaster warned other boys against picking on the prince, it backfired, leading to relentless torment. 'He was bullied,' recalled Ross Benson, the respected *Daily Mail* foreign correspondent and *Daily Express* diarist, who was a contemporary of the prince at Gordonstoun.

When Charles complained, Philip admonished his son in letters, urging him to be more resourceful. 'This did not help,' Jonathan Dimbleby wrote in his 1994 authorised biography.[94] According to his youngest son, Prince Harry: 'He was crushingly lonely for most of his time there. The wonder is that he survived with his sanity intact.'[95] It led him to cling to his teddy bear for comfort, which he took with him everywhere for years.

At seventeen, the prince underwent a significant transformation during his two terms in 1966 at Timbertop, an outdoor education school in Australia run by Geelong Grammar. 'I took him out there a boy,' said his acting equerry, Squadron Leader David Checketts, 'and brought back a man.'

Returning to Gordonstoun, Charles excelled. He was appointed Guardian (head boy), proving himself to be honest, honourable and hardworking. By now he had developed a self-absorbed exterior to shield any vulnerability. Robert Chew, the principal during Charles's tenure, said the prince's time at the school has often been misrepresented. Chew noted Charles's leadership and active school involvement, and said that his experience at Gordonstoun was not as harsh as commonly portrayed.

Charles once claimed that the people who raised him were not his parents, but 'inevitably the nursery staff'. When he aired his grievances about feeling emotionally neglected and misunderstood by his parents – spelled out in his authorised biography by Jonathan Dimbleby – it upset both Philip and the Queen. Rather than supporting Charles, his sister Anne chastised him for his self-indulgence, saying she found it 'extraordinary' for anyone to claim their mother did not care or lacked warmth. She insisted that the Royal Family was a 'happy unit' where they enjoyed each other's company and kept effective communication. 'I simply don't believe there is any evidence whatsoever to suggest that she wasn't caring. It just beggars belief,' she said.[96]

Despite Anne's defence, negative stories about the Queen and Philip's parenting methods persisted. In March 2002, writer Graham Turner in the *Daily Telegraph* portrayed the Queen as a distant mother who did not provide her children with firm guidance. In the article, an unnamed 'private secretary' was quoted as saying that the Royal Family would have been in a far better state had the Queen 'taken half as much trouble about the rearing of her children as she has about the breeding of her horses.'

Turner also quoted the former Dean of Windsor, Michael Mann, who recalled how Anne herself came to see him before her second wedding and complained that she had been unable to talk to her mother about it. He also revealed that former senior aides discussed the desperation the Queen and Philip felt about their relationship with their children. Elizabeth was said to have felt tremendous guilt over her frequent absences during Charles's early years.

Philip, when confronted, was defensive about his parenting skills. In a 2011 ITV interview with broadcaster Alan Titchmarsh, to mark his ninetieth birthday, he dismissed the idea of consciously fulfilling a role as the Queen's consort or as a father, answering disdainfully, 'I was a father. Are you a father? Well, do you think about it?' His brusque response reflected his no-nonsense approach to life. The way he raised his son was his business.

CHAPTER 9

THE CAMILLA DILEMMA

I suppose the feelings of emptiness will pass eventually.[97]

PRINCE CHARLES, 1973

Brian Connell, a dapper, trim-bearded broadcaster, put Prince Charles on the spot. 'Should the woman you marry be a royal or titled lady?' he asked.

Charles chuckled nervously, paused, and replied, 'When you marry in my position, you're choosing someone who could become queen. She must be special, meet public expectations, and understand the role.' A foreign princess had that advantage, he admitted. Then he added, 'The only trouble is, I would prefer to marry someone English . . . or perhaps Welsh . . . British.'

The exchange was awkward. It aired on 26 June 1969, in a joint HTV-BBC television special, just days before Charles's investiture as Prince of Wales. Facing questions from Cliff Michelmore and Connell, Charles seemed naive – but he was not wrong. He was expected to marry a virgin aristocrat. Not a Roman Catholic. Someone fit for royal duty.

But at that moment in time, marriage was not his focus.

He followed Lord Mountbatten's advice: sow wild oats first, settle down later. For Charles, marriage was duty. If it came with love that would be a bonus.

Charles met his first serious girlfriend, Lucia Santa Cruz, at Trinity College, Cambridge, in 1970. The 28-year-old daughter of the Chilean ambassador to the UK impressed him with her beauty and intellect, speaking four languages. An accomplished writer, she later published a book, *Three Essays on Chilean Women* (1978). During their carefree romance, Charles even introduced Lucia to the Queen, but it eventually faded. They parted as friends.

Charles was not preoccupied with finding a bride at Cambridge, or even a serious girlfriend. Instead, he had his studies, amateur dramatics and personal ambitions, like learning to fly. In his second year at Trinity College, he formally requested permission from the Queen to take flying lessons with the Royal Air Force. With Philip's backing, the Queen finally relented, and in 1968, Charles was filmed flying a red de Havilland Chipmunk at RAF Tangmere.

After graduating in 1970 with a 2:2 degree in Archaeology, Anthropology, and History,[98] he trained as a jet pilot at RAF Cranwell and attended Britannia Royal Naval College. He began his Royal Navy service on HMS *Norfolk* on 5 November 1971.

Earlier that year, Lucia moved to a flat in Belgravia and became friends with her neighbour, the spirited debutante Camilla Shand, who shared her flat with Virginia Carington, daughter of Lord Peter Carington, 6th Baron Carrington (1919–2018), who was a heavyweight in British politics. A Conservative peer, he served as Defence Secretary, then Foreign Secretary, and later led NATO.

From an early age Prince Charles knew his wife would have to be more than a partner – she would be an integral part of the monarchy. Then he met Camilla Shand. Witty, confident, unimpressed by titles. She had the right background: Church of England, she was born into privilege on 17 July 1947, and mixed in the right circles. Her father, Major Bruce Shand MC and Bar, was a war hero twice decorated for bravery in combat, now a wine merchant. Her mother, Rosalind, was the daughter of Roland Cubitt, 3rd Baron Ashcombe. An old bloodline and a solid name.

Her family lived between a townhouse in South Kensington and a country home, The Laines, an eighteenth-century country house in Plumpton, East Sussex. Her great-grandmother, Alice Keppel, had been King Edward VII's mistress, and Camilla liked to remind people of it at school. She loved horses, hunting and country life. Academia was not her strength. She left school with only one O-level, but excelled where it mattered for a young woman of her class – socially.

In her late teens, she was launched into London's debutante scene. She was quick-witted, vivacious, and impossible to ignore. A favourite among young aristocrat male suitors. Among her admirers was Andrew Parker Bowles, a handsome, popular Household Cavalry officer, who was seen as a good catch. But not a faithful one. Eventually, Camilla had enough of his philandering ways.

She moved into a flat in Westminster and fate intervened. Her neighbour, Lucia Santa Cruz, had an idea. She knew Charles. One evening, she introduced them. They clicked, instantly.

Camilla did not treat him like a prince. She treated him like a man. Charles later said he had never felt so at ease with anyone. Her wit, her ease, her love of the countryside – he was drawn in. She was comforting and captivating; she thrilled him like no woman before. By late autumn 1972, Charles was smitten. But Camilla's heart was still tied to Andrew Parker Bowles. Only when duty sent him to Germany did the tether break.

For a while, Charles and Camilla were inseparable, but the Royal Family was not so impressed with his choice. Mountbatten was wary, believing she was not queen material. The rules were clear: a direct heir to the throne such as Charles must marry a virgin. Camilla did not qualify. Mountbatten encouraged the affair, up to a point. He even let the young couple use his country house Broadlands as a retreat. To the ruthless royal mentor, she was 'good mistress material' – but nothing more. A shrewd judge of character, he also sensed she was still in love with Parker Bowles.

Duty intervened. The Royal Navy took Charles away. In early December 1972, Charles was assigned to HMS *Minerva* for an eight-month Caribbean tour. Before sailing, he took Camilla aboard and showed her the ship. They had lunch, and he despaired that it would be 'the last time I shall see her for eight months'.

To be fair, Camilla had made no promises to her royal suitor, who was a year and four months her junior. When Andrew Parker Bowles returned, nearly eight years her senior, they picked up where they left off.

Afterwards, Mountbatten wrote to Charles. His advice was blunt:

'In a case like yours, the man should sow his wild oats and have as many affairs as he can before settling down, but for a wife, he should choose a suitable, attractive, and sweet-charactered girl before she has met anyone else she might fall for.'[99]

While Charles was at sea, Camilla got engaged. On 4 March 1973, she said yes to Parker Bowles. They married on 4 July at the Guards Chapel, Wellington Barracks in London. It was a grand wedding and British high society turned out in full. On the surface it looked like a good match. It was not. His affairs were an open secret and marriage did not put an end to them.

Nevertheless, Charles and Camilla stayed close. She remained his confidante. When her son Tom was born, she asked Charles to be his godfather, and he agreed.

By the age of twenty-three, Charles had had several girlfriends, but his relationships were chaste compared to what he sought with more experienced women. One such love was Lady Dale Tryon, an Australian heiress nicknamed 'Kanga'. Charles first met her in 1966 while studying at Geelong Grammar, and their friendship was rekindled when she moved to Britain to work for Qantas. As Dale Harper, daughter of a printing magnate, in 1973 she had married Anthony Tryon, 3rd Baron Tryon, becoming Baroness Tryon. Charles appreciated her refreshing lack of deference and she understood him.

The prince, now free, enjoyed his time as the world's most eligible bachelor, sharing intimate dinners with the beautiful film star Susan George, famous for *Straw Dogs*. Their intimate relationship was never confirmed, but she called him her 'special individual' and always addressed him as 'Sir'. Knowing he needed a queen, Charles admitted, 'I've fallen in love with all sorts of girls . . . but marriage is basically a strong friendship.'

Charles flew to Singapore in January 1974 and joined HMS *Jupiter* as a communications officer. His presence caused a stir whenever the frigate docked, especially in San Diego, where crowds gathered to greet him. During shore leave, he developed a friendship with Barbra Streisand, whom he met on the set of her film, *Funny Lady*. He was mesmerised by her talent, wit and charm, and she fondly recalled their time together, joking, 'If I played my cards right, I could have wound up being the first Jewish princess!'

Charles dated several women in the next few years, including Lady Jane Wellesley, who dismissed the idea of marriage with her famous quip to the press, 'Do you honestly believe I want to be queen?' In 1975, still in no hurry to wed, Charles said he thought that thirty was the right age for marriage. He was romantically linked to Lady Sarah Spencer in 1977, but their relationship ended after she spoke to the press, calling Charles 'not ready for marriage' and saying she would marry only for love. Another prospect, Davina Sheffield, was ruled out when it was reported that she had lived with a boyfriend.

Once back in the UK, Charles honed his flying skills and qualified as a helicopter pilot at Royal Naval Air Station Yeovilton, later joining 845 Naval Air Squadron aboard HMS *Hermes*. In February 1976, he commanded the coastal mine-hunter HMS *Bronington*, where an incident involving a snagged anchor chain resulted in considerable damage to the Royal Navy's equipment and criticism from his superiors, leaving him eager to move on from active service. Shortly after, he used his £7,400 severance pay to set up the Prince's Trust, the start of his life as a philanthropist, while also becoming an early advocate for environmental issues, seeking harmony between society and nature.

Attitudes were changing fast. The royals seemed dull, as familiar as an old armchair. With the arrival of Australian newspaper publisher Rupert Murdoch, the Fleet Street press had become far less deferential; they now wanted salacious stories, especially juicy royal scoops, which always boosted circulation. Many years later, Murdoch declared, 'The British monarchy has become irrelevant to this generation of Australians,' underscoring his republican stance and shaping the editorial tone of his media empire.[100]

In 1974, the royals hit the front pages – and this time, for all the wrong reasons. Just four months after her wedding to Captain Mark Phillips, Princess Anne survived a kidnap attempt.

On the night of 20 March, Anne and Mark were returning from a charity film screening in a maroon Rolls-Royce. With them were her lady-in-waiting, Rowena Brassey, and her protection officer, Inspector James Beaton of Scotland Yard.

As chauffeur Alexander Callender drove down The Mall, a white Ford Escort cut them off only 200 yards from Buckingham Palace. Inspector Beaton stepped out, thinking it was road rage and he was shot in the shoulder. The attacker was Ian Ball, who was armed and unhinged. He wanted to kidnap the princess and demand £2 million in £5 notes.

The Scotland Yard officer now stood between Ball and Princess Anne. He took another bullet and tried to return fire, but his gun jammed. Next, Ball moved to the rear door, but Anne and Mark fought to hold it shut. A royal night out had turned to chaos. But Anne never left the car.

Somehow, Inspector Beaton got back on his feet, wounded and still trying to protect them. Ball fired into the car and Beaton took a bullet in the hand, deflecting it. Then a third shot hit him. This time, he went down and did not get up.

Driver Alexander Callender stepped in next, but Ball shot him in the chest. Ball then lunged for Anne, grabbing her forearm. Mark Phillips pulled her back and her dress tore. At gunpoint, Ball ordered her out of the car, but Anne did not flinch. 'Not bloody likely,' she snapped back. A struggle followed. Mark later admitted he was terrified. 'I felt like a caged animal,' he said, as police hesitated to move.

At first, Police Constable Michael Hills thought it was just a car crash. Then Ball shot him in the stomach as he approached. Journalist Brian McConnell and Ron Russell, a former heavyweight boxer, jumped in to help. McConnell was shot too. Seconds later, Russell stepped up and threw a single punch –

hard and clean. It rocked Ball back and ended it. He tried to run, but Detective Constable Peter Edmonds, who had arrived on the scene, chased Ball down and caught him. In under ten minutes the chaos was over.

The new home secretary, Roy Jenkins, ordered a report for Prime Minister Harold Wilson, but he insisted the investigation remain 'broadly confidential'. Scotland Yard said nothing. Buckingham Palace said less. Some reports claimed Ian Ball was mentally ill. Others hinted at something larger – a network, maybe. Nothing was confirmed.

In response, royal protection was stepped up. But the Palace drew a line. The Royal Family, they said, 'had no intention of living in bullet-proof cages'.

At the Old Bailey on 4 April, Ian Ball pleaded guilty to attempted murder and kidnapping. He got life in a mental health facility. He told the court, 'I did it because I wished to draw attention to the lack of facilities for treating mental illness under the National Health Service.'

The Queen later awarded the George Cross to Inspector Beaton[101] and bravery honours to PC Hills, Ron Russell, PC Edmonds, John Brian McConnell, and Alexander Callender.

In 2006, Russell recalled meeting the Queen. She told him, 'The medal is from the Queen of England, the thank you is from Anne's mother.'

Meanwhile, Prince Philip, ever dry, had his own take: 'If the man had succeeded in abducting Anne, she would have given him a hell of a time in captivity.' In August 2025, the *Daily Mail* reported that Ball has been quietly released on probation in 2019 and is now campaigning to clear his name. Princess Anne and royal security chiefs were informed of the decision.

*

On his reaching thirty, the media pressure began mounting on Charles to choose a bride. Lord Mountbatten believed Amanda Knatchbull, his granddaughter and Charles's second cousin, was a good match, but lacking the passion for a royal life, she rejected his proposal in 1979. He went on to romance Scottish heir Anna Wallace, who ended the relationship due to his lingering attention on Camilla Parker Bowles. After her daughter Laura's birth in April 1978, Charles and Camilla had rekindled their relationship. Aware of the risks, he embraced the affair; although she remained unsuitable as a royal wife, he maintained his bachelor lifestyle with Camilla as his mistress.

While her son dithered in his search for a suitable bride, the Queen and her advisers were eager to use the Silver Jubilee in 1977 to reinforce the monarchy's image and authority. But at first the public were not buying into it. Britain was emerging from a severe economic crisis marked by high inflation and public spending cuts, following an IMF bailout. With murmurs of hostility and scepticism, Palace officials were aware of the ongoing mood of industrial unrest and financial strain.

It was the punk rock era, and anti-establishment protests were commonplace. If the royals wanted a party, the consensus was they should pay for it themselves. Actress Helen Mirren, who later accepted a damehood and earned an Oscar for her role as Elizabeth in Stephen Frears' 2006 film *The Queen* to mark her eightieth birthday, recalled, 'At the time of the Silver Jubilee, I was a grumpy anti-monarchist. I didn't celebrate and was appalled by the celebrations.' She was not alone. The Socialist Workers Party's 'Stuff the Jubilee' campaign blasted the monarchy for its extravagance during economic hardship, spreading their message with badges and flyers. Punks upped the ante, calling the Jubilee fascist. The Sex Pistols' 'God Save the Queen' single was banned by the BBC, but made waves when the band brazenly performed it on 7 June while cruising the Thames, mocking the Queen's grand procession.

The Queen, however, was determined to connect with her people. After studying her grandparents' schedules during their Silver Jubilee, she set about replicating them. Encouraged by Philip, who believed visibility would generate momentum, the Queen's journey began in Glasgow on 17 May 1977. The royal couple then travelled the country, culminating in a national celebration with street parties and parades. Elizabethe was dubbed the 'People's Queen', revitalising the Royal Family's authority during a time of momentous change.

Two years later, the Royal Family's world was shattered. On 27 August 1979, Earl Mountbatten was assassinated. An IRA bomb, planted by Thomas McMahon, tore through his boat off the coast of Mullaghmore, in the Republic of Ireland. Mountbatten, aged seventy-nine, died instantly. So did his great-grandson Nicholas, fourteen, and local boat boy Paul Maxwell, fifteen. Doreen Knatchbull, Dowager Lady Brabourne, died the next day, aged eighty-three. The IRA claimed responsibility and McMahon got a life sentence. In 1998, under the Good Friday Agreement, he walked free.

Charles was devastated. Mountbatten's murder hit him like a hammer blow. His mentor, his guide, was gone in an instant. In 2015, Charles returned to Mullaghmore. He was shown the site by Mountbatten's grandson Timothy Knatchbull, who survived the blast. The pain was still there. Charles admitted he had felt like he wanted to 'die too'.

Mountbatten had shaped Charles – more than anyone. He was the grandfather the prince never had. George VI died when Charles was only three. He never knew his other grandfather,

Prince Andrew of Greece. The grief was deep and the anger real.

'At the time I could not imagine how we would come to terms with the anguish of such a deep loss,' Charles said years later in Sligo. 'Through this dreadful experience, I now understand in a profound way the agonies borne by others on these islands of whatever faith or political persuasion.'

He still carries the pain. He always will.

A few years later, the press began asking hard questions. What did the Queen, Philip, Charles, and the establishment know about the real Mountbatten?

For decades, he was hailed as a war hero and patriot. But in 2019, declassified FBI files painted a darker picture. They described him as 'a homosexual with a perversion for young boys'. The legend cracked. Among the accusers was the American socialite Elizabeth de la Poer Beresford, Baroness Decies, who called Mountbatten and his wife Edwina people of 'extremely low morals'. Her words added weight to long-held suspicions. And the questions and allegations have not gone away.

Next came the claim from Norman Nield, Mountbatten's wartime driver. He alleged that he was ordered to bring young boys – aged eight to twelve – to Mountbatten's home. He claimed they were given brandy and lemonade. No court ever proved it, but the details stuck. The debate still burns, leaving Mountbatten's legacy to stand no longer untouched.[102]

What if something had been overlooked? Could the Crown afford to acknowledge the allegations, or did the preservation of Mountbatten's heroic image serve as a necessary shield for the institution itself? As a central figure in Elizabeth's and Charles's court, these alleged scandals involving Mountbatten reflected the challenges that faced the Royal Family, underscoring the delicate balance of power, trust, and belief.

Lonely, timid, and restless, more than he would ever let on, Charles knew he needed a bride, and an heir. The pressure was not only from the royals; it was inside him. Duty called, and he knew he had no choice but to answer. His choices were bound tight. No Catholics. No divorcees. Tradition demanded purity too, a girl without a blemish, a virgin. In July 1980, Charles attended a weekend barbecue at Philip de Pass's house, in Petworth, West Sussex. Among the guests was Lady Diana Spencer, Lady Sarah's younger sister.

Diana recalled, 'I was asked to stay with some friends in Sussex and they said, "Oh, the Prince of Wales is staying," and I thought, I hadn't seen him in ages.' She added, 'He'd just broken up with his girlfriend and his friend Mountbatten had just been killed. I said it would be nice to see him. I was so unimpressed. I sat there and this man walked in, and I thought, well, I am quite impressed this time round. It was different.'

When she was alone with Charles for a moment, Diana told him, 'You must be so lonely. It's pathetic watching you walking up the aisle with Mountbatten's coffin in front, ghastly, you need someone beside you.' Whereupon to her shock the prince leapt on her and started kissing her. 'I thought, urgh, this is not what people do. And he was all over me for the rest of the evening, following me around like a puppy.'[103]

From then on, the couple dated mostly through phone calls in those early days, meeting only thirteen times before Charles proposed on 6 February 1981. To his surprise, she agreed. Neither of them was sure; was this love, or just a call of duty?

CHAPTER 10

A LAMB TO THE SLAUGHTER

Don't worry, dear, it'll only get worse.

PRINCESS GRACE TO LADY DIANA SPENCER, 1981

On 8 September 1980, the *Sun* headline shouted: 'He's in Love Again: Is Lady Di the New Girl for Charles?' That was the name now – Lady Di. It stuck. Arthur Edwards, the legendary Fleet Street photographer, had first seen her in July at a polo match, with the sun on her gold 'D' necklace. It caught the light. Hawk-like, he spotted it. He asked her name – Lady Diana Spencer – and asked if he could take her photo. She agreed.

Later, near Balmoral on assignment covering the Braemar Games, Edwards spotted Charles about to go fishing by the River Dee, and she was there again, acting as his ghillie. Edwards was in the car with reporter James Whitaker of the *Daily Star*, and his photographer, Ken Lennox. Whitaker recalled a flicker of green behind a pine. 'I caught sight of a green wellington boot poking out from behind a pine tree,' he said. 'She held a make-up mirror – not fixing her face, just watching me from across the river.'

She did not move, did not blink. Just watched. Still as a deer.

Edwards was poised to get a photo of the woman as an irritated Charles packed up the rods. Gone.

As Lennox walked down to flush her out, Diana emerged. Click. Edwards had the film in the bag. They had it. The story. The moment. 'I knew she was important because the prince was trying to hide her. I recognised her as the same girl I had photographed at the polo. At the Braemar Games I asked about her and was told she was at the castle for the weekend and Charles was following her around like a lamb,' he said.

Edwards rang Harry Arnold, the royal reporter at the *Sun*. Arnold was in Kent, but that did not matter. Edwards knew this one needed front-page firepower, and Harry was the man to spin it into orbit, giving the story maximum projection.

The next day, the *Sun* splashed it big, using Edwards's polo shot from July:. Lady Di, the necklace flashing. Inside, they ran the riverside pictures too. Whitaker had filed the same story in the *Daily Star*. Same moment, same boots, same mirror. He got an inside lead, but the *Sun* team had the front page.

It marked the start of a long, fraught relationship between Lady Diana Spencer and the press. From that moment, the shy teenaged daughter of the 8th Earl Spencer was pursued relentlessly by Fleet Street reporters and photographers.

Ten days later, the *Sun* struck again. Front page. Byline: Harry Arnold. Headline: 'Charlie's Girl!' Another shot by Arthur Edwards. Lady Diana, the shy nursery teacher from Young England School in Pimlico.

That morning, Edwards had shown up early and asked if she would pose. She said yes. He walked her to the park, with two kids in her arms. Then the trap snapped. A swarm of paparazzi burst from their cars. With the cameras firing, light hit her skirt and her legs showed through. She froze but held the children.

Later, Edwards returned with Harry Arnold. She told the reporter, 'You know I can't say anything about the prince or my feelings for him.' He accepted it, then cleverly asked, 'Does your mother know?' Diana replied, 'Oh yes, she knows.' They had their confirmation.

The machine was rolling now. Royal watching. It sold newspapers and it made money. A lot of it. Years later, at her funeral, her brother Charles said it straight. Named for a goddess of the hunt, Diana became 'the most hunted person of the modern age'.

Recalling the chaos, Diana recalled on tape to her friend Peter Settelen, 'They chased me everywhere – thirty of them.' She had no support from Charles, the police, or Buckingham Palace's press office. Charles wanted to help but could not; Scotland Yard protection only applied once they were engaged. After the Young England photo, several reporters would turn up every day, bombarding her with questions as she left her London flat, 60 Coleherne Court, on Old Brompton Road. They had singled her out as the next royal bride.

Once the story caught fire, there was no slowing it. Charles felt the walls closing in. Years later, he told a friend, 'To have withdrawn, as you can no doubt imagine, would have been cataclysmic. Hence, I was permanently between the devil and the deep blue sea.' He did not stop there. 'The power and influence of the media driving matters towards an engagement and wedding were unstoppable,' he said.[104] The tide was too strong and he went with it.

The pressure was building. Still, duty first, his father reminded him. Charles confided to a friend, 'I'm terrified of making a promise I might regret. It's an unusual plunge into unknown circumstances that disturbs me, but I hope it will be the right thing in the end.'[105]

Lady Diana initially thought Prince Charles's marriage proposal was a joke and replied, 'Yeah, okay,' before realising he was serious. He reminded her, 'You do realise that one day you will be queen,' but later she recalled an internal voice warning, 'You won't be queen, but you'll have a tough role.' Their engagement was announced on 24 February 1981. Asked to sum up their feelings, Charles said, 'Just delighted and happy. I'm amazed she's brave enough to take me on.' When pressed about love, Diana replied instantly, 'Of course.' Only for Charles to add the now infamous line, 'Whatever "in love" means.'

Gentle and shy, Diana's life experience was a world apart from that of Charles. They barely knew each other. It was effectively the last of the great arranged royal marriages. Charles later acknowledged they were incompatible. In that awkward engagement interview, Diana said, 'It wasn't a difficult decision . . . it was what was wanted,' quickly adding, 'It's what I wanted.' She began to have second thoughts at once, confiding in her sisters. It was too late to pull out. 'I felt like a lamb to the slaughter,' she said.[106]

Before they wed, Charles had already begun to doubt Diana's suitability as his wife. He confided to friends, 'I desperately wanted to get out of the wedding in 1981, having realised how awful the prospects were.'[107] He was concerned by her erratic mood swings, which he struggled to cope with. Leading up to the big day, Diana would often burst into tears for no obvious reason. Just days before the wedding, she told her sisters she feared he still loved his former mistress, Camilla Parker Bowles.

What Charles did not know was Diana had been battling undiagnosed bulimia for months. '[My husband] put his hand on my waist and said, "A bit chubby here, aren't we?"' she recalled to biographer Andrew Morton.[108] 'And the Camilla thing.

I was desperate, desperate. I remember the first time I made myself sick. I was so thrilled because I thought this was the release of tension.'

It was a troubled time in the country as recession bit deep. Riots burned in Brixton and Toxteth. There were two nations now – one watching a royal wedding in gold and lace, the other scraping by in boarded-up streets, angry and unheard. Pride did not reach everyone.

Through it all, the Queen held steady. At Trooping the Colour, six blank shots cracked the air. A teenager, Marcus Sarjeant, had pulled the trigger. The Queen calmed her horse, Burmese, and rode on; stone-faced and unflinching. Sarjeant, aged seventeen, was jailed for five years under the Treason Act 1842, but served three years.

Then came the wedding. It lit the gloom. The night before, crowds poured into London. Hope filled the pavements. London breathed again. The ceremony went ahead on 29 July 1981. The pretty English girl became HRH The Princess of Wales, third lady of the realm, behind Their Majesties the Queen and the Queen Mother. Her wedding dress, designed by the husband-and-wife team David and Elizabeth Emanuel, was silk taffeta, specially woven, with fabric piled high. Hundreds of metres of tulle shaped the petticoat. Thousands of pearls and sequins sparkled on the lace. If Diana was nervous, she never showed it.

Her bridesmaid India Hicks said, 'As a young girl, you thought she was everything a princess should be, very beautiful . . . and yet and yet, there was a certain nervousness about her.' The wily old courtier, Lord Charteris, recalled, 'I will look back on the marriage of the Prince and Princess of Wales as one of the greatest things I've ever seen. A tremendous feeling of excitement about it, and it looked perfect. I saw no clouds on the horizon, I saw nothing but sunshine and happiness.'

The world marvelled as 600,000 spectators lined the route from Buckingham Palace to St Paul's Cathedral, cheering on the royal couple, while further afield thousands more hosted street parties across the UK. An astonishing 750 million people tuned in globally, making it the most-watched television event at that time. The new Princess of Wales captivated all who saw her as she made her way down the red-carpeted aisle, with her 25-foot-long train. It was hailed as the 'stuff of fairy tales' by the Archbishop of Canterbury, Robert Runcie. Yet, it quickly became clear there would be no 'happily ever after', as both Charles and Diana soon regretted their union.

Princess Diana's first instinct, upon learning of Camilla still being on the scene, was to run. But her family held her back. Behind the newlyweds walked the Queen and the Earl Spencer, and behind them lay the shadow of Charles's mistress. The tragedy began there, impossible to reel back. Amid the national joy, the public obsession with Diana was born. She was not merely a princess; she was an event.

Everywhere Diana went, the world's press followed. She connected with the British public like no royal before her. They adored her. She was not a stiff figure from the House of Windsor; she was a fresh breeze, full of glamour and charm. She brought film-star allure, but with the gravitas of a future queen. Across the country crowds packed the streets, bearing gifts and flowers.

Diana was rare. Style, status, and warmth – all wrapped in one. She had grace and humour, and a way of making people feel important. She lit up rooms. On overseas tours, crowds cheered. She thought they had just showed up and genuinely did not know it was for her.

Almost overnight, she was a fashion icon. But not simply for the clothes. She spoke through them, sending quiet signals in fabric and cut. As her confidence grew, so did her edge – military jackets, Cossack coats, sharp lines and bold colour. Even her hair set trends. 'Fashion isn't my big thing,' she'd say. 'I like bright colours. My husband likes me smart.' For a time, they looked the part – Charles and Diana, the star couple. The public saw the sparkle, not the strain.

Diana dazzled. Through no fault of hers, she made Charles look like an afterthought. The press revelled in the contrast, stirring the pot. It gnawed at him. Charles wanted the stage like he had always had it; he wanted to be heard. He spoke his hard truths at the podium, while she stood beside him, glowing. After a keynote speech, the press did not quote him, unless it was to ridicule him. They wrote about her dress. Her smile. Her hair.

But there were problems inside the marriage, too. Issues that had been swept aside, such as Diana's youth and the brief time they had spent together before marrying, grew into insurmountable problems. Charles sought professional help, not only for Diana but also for himself, to cope with their strained, incompatible marriage; a move that deserved some credit, as a former royal aide noted.

Dr Alan McGlashan was quietly brought in after Diana distanced herself from royal medics like Sir John Batten, who was reported to have had serious concerns about her mental health and feared genetic implications for the royal line. The royal doctors dosed her on antidepressants and behavioural therapy, but Dr McGlashan's assessment differed sharply from the earlier medical advice. After eight sessions, he concluded, 'She is a normal girl with emotional troubles, not a pathological case.'

Charles has since faced criticism for his treatment of Diana, ignoring his lifetime of service, vision, and passion for humanity. His detractors focus on his neglect of his young bride and his adultery, branding him unfit for kingship, while overlooking her many affairs. Over time Charles has learned to live with this distorted image, especially after Diana's death, realising that no amount of effort can erase the stains on his reputation. He feels he let down not only the monarchy but also himself and Diana by not calling off the wedding, when he knew it was wrong.

What frustrates the King even now is that Diana's version of what happened is still believed, despite being, in his view, 'a tissue of lies' fed to a sympathetic but gullible press. It is wrong in his opinion that they have become 'historical fact'. One widely circulated falsehood was the claim that he and Diana had spent two nights together aboard the Royal Train, a notion Diana and her family denied. The Duke of Edinburgh was so furious about this, he was said to have sent Charles a strongly worded letter, seen only by the sender and recipient, warning that his reputation as a gentleman and Lady Diana's honour would be at risk if he did not propose. In fact, sources have said the letter was warm and sympathetic and in no way put pressure on his son.

The tryst-on-the-train story was also a damaging fabrication, as the incident never happened. The *Sunday Mirror* claimed an impeccable source for the story – local police assigned to watch the train – but the Queen's press secretary, Michael Shea, firmly objected. Editor Bob Edwards refused to apologise, instead planning to publish their correspondence under the headline 'Prince Charles and Lady Diana', which the Palace reluctantly accepted. Charles could not win, whatever he did.

Diana was devastated by the story, knowing it falsely implied Charles had been unfaithful while she slept miles away. In December 1980, her mother, Frances Shand Kydd, wrote a

In 1917, with German bombers over London and anti-German sentiment rising, King George V rebranded the monarchy-ditching Saxe-Coburg-Gotha name and created the House of Windsor. It was swift, symbolic, and shrewd – anchoring the Crown to Britain and helping it survive war, revolution, and doubt.

Right: Prince Edward's open affair with married Wallis Simpson embarrassed the Court and infuriated his mother Queen Mary, who famously asked at the 1935 Jubilee Ball, 'Who is this woman?' before the prince stormed off. As George V's health declined, family tensions mounted, and the prospect of Edward's reign loomed.

Left: Edward's flirtation with German overtures during the war cast a lasting shadow. To block Nazi plans to use him as a puppet king, Churchill forced the new Duke of Windsor into effective exile as Governor of the Bahamas, backed by a threat of court-martial. Reluctantly, Edward and Wallis sailed to Nassau arriving in August 1940, where they spent the rest of World War II sidelined and bitter.

Right: Princess Elizabeth adored her uncle 'David', as she called Edward VIII. His abdication in 1936, when she was just ten, changed the course of her life – and left her with a single guiding word that defined her reign: duty.

On 12 May 1937, the day of his coronation, King George VI – who fondly called his family Queen Elizabeth and his daughters, Princesses Elizabeth and Margaret Rose 'we four' – confessed to a 'sinking feeling' and couldn't eat. But he rose to the occasion with quiet strength, silencing doubters.

On VE Day, 8 May 1945, King George VI and Churchill stood on the palace balcony as a million people filled The Mall. 'This is your victory', Churchill told the cheering crowds. The King gave thanks 'for a great deliverance'. That night, Elizabeth and Margaret joined the celebrations, conga dancing through The Ritz. In his diary, the King wrote: 'Our tribulation is over' – but warned of 'many headaches' still to come.

On 13 September 1940, a German bomb struck Buckingham Palace while the King and Queen were inside. They emerged unhurt. In that moment they became symbols of shared sacrifice. 'Now we can look the East End in the face', the Queen said. Early visits to the East End during the Blitz had drawn jeers, but after the palace bombing, scorn turned to solidarity.

Above: Ahead of his wedding, Prince Philip celebrated with laughter, cigars, and two stag nights – one official (pictured) at The Dorchester, the other private at The Belfry Club. On the wedding morning, sharing a quiet gin and tonic with his best man, he asked, 'Am I being very brave or very foolish?' It wasn't doubt about Elizabeth, it was grief for a life left behind. He had just pennies to his name when he married Princess Elizabeth.

Left: In April 1947, Princess Margaret and Peter Townsend were photographed in South Africa oblivious to the media storm to come. After George VI's death, Margaret turned to Townsend, her anchor in grief. Divorced and devoted, he was within reach but marrying him would defy Church and Crown. For a time, they waited in hope. But the monarchy still bore the scars of abdication. In the end, Margaret chose duty over love.

On 2 June 1953, Queen Elizabeth II's coronation marked Britain's postwar renewal. Despite cold rain, crowds roared as a radiant 27-year-old was crowned beside her dashing consort. News of Everest's conquest lifted spirits, and after years of austerity, pride returned. *The New York Times* called her a safeguard against darkness; *Time* called her a beacon of hope.

At Treetops at Aberdare National Park in Kenya, Elizabeth became Queen. Flying home, she changed into black. Spotting the waiting limousines, she whispered, 'Oh God, they've sent the hearses.'

Balmoral was the Queen's sanctuary, where Philip proposed, where she laughed, danced, and found peace among family, her corgis, ponies and nature. It was her haven in life, and where she died.

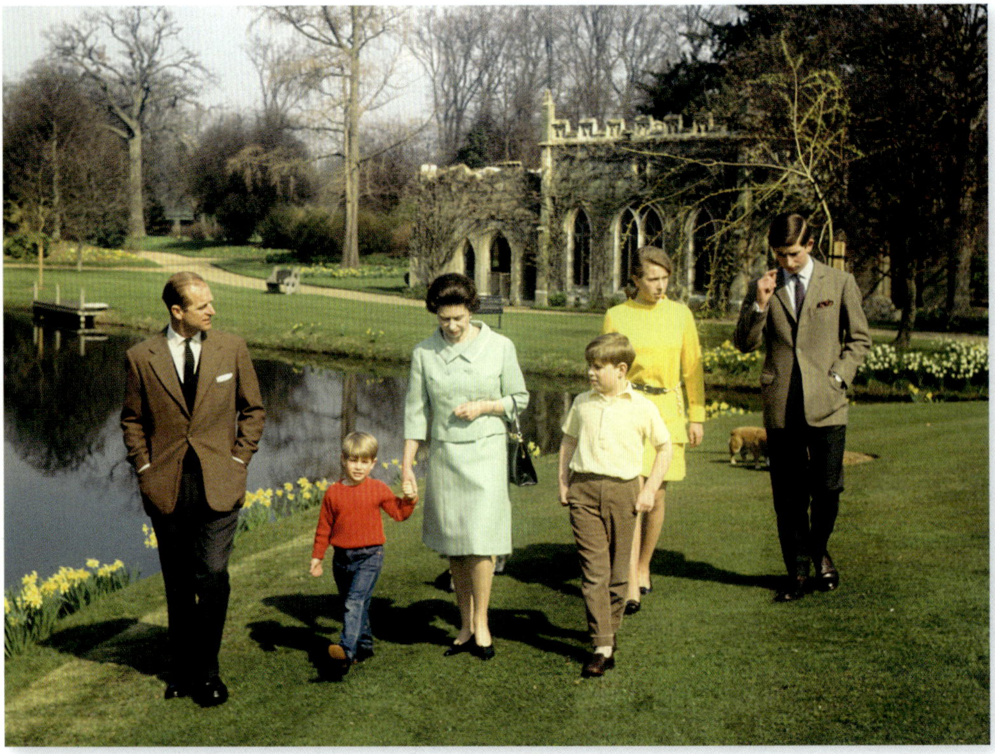

© PA Images / Alamy Stock Photo

The royal family pose in the gardens of Frogmore House, in the shadow of Windsor Castle, an image of ease and unity in 1968. That same year, behind the scenes, plans were underway for *Royal Family*, a behind-the-curtain documentary bringing the Windsors into Britain's living rooms and the modern age.

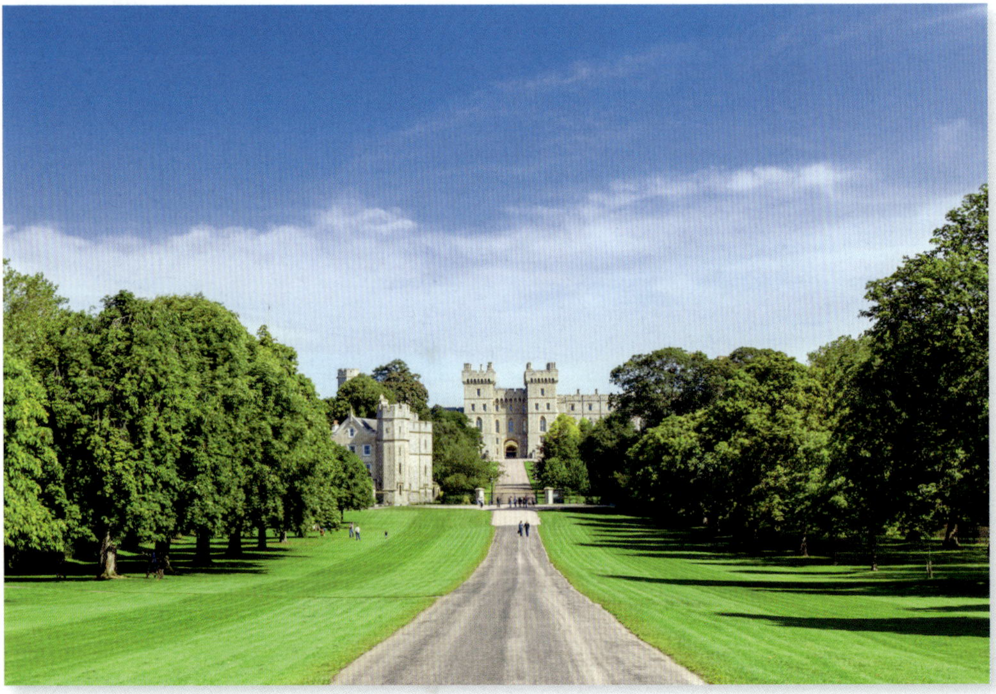

© Ian Dagnall / Alamy Stock Photo

forceful letter to *The Times*, denouncing the 'lies and harassment' Diana had faced since her romance with Charles became public.

This enduring fabrication has haunted Charles, propelling him towards marriage in a bid to protect their honour, despite its complete lack of truth. He explained to a close friend later, 'The most extraordinary and pernicious of these is that I secreted Diana on board the Royal Train on the eve of our wedding. This was endlessly denied at the time. The truth is the *Daily Mirror* [*sic*] had mistaken a private secretary's blonde secretary for Diana. The press obstinately stuck to this story. Then, years later, they pushed the invention even further, claiming it was Camilla [on board the Royal Train] after all.'[109]

In 2007, the *Daily Telegraph* wrote, 'Her [Camilla's] unpopularity was such that an irate shopper was reported to have thrown a bread roll at her in a supermarket in Wiltshire.' The report made Charles's blood boil, because it was completely unchecked and untrue. He told a friend, 'Another persistent lie is that the duchess had bread rolls thrown at her by angry shoppers in a store in Chippenham. This was in fact a fabricated media exercise stunt, which involved actors throwing bread rolls at one another. A lookalike actress was employed and placed in the store in Chippenham.'[110]

Charles, friends have revealed, 'wept' the night before his wedding to Lady Diana Spencer, feeling torn between his future wife and his former love, Camilla. Hence, he totally rejects another false claim that he smuggled Mrs Parker Bowles into Buckingham Palace for a secret tryst the night before marrying Lady Diana. He told a close friend, 'The idea that this could have happened is beyond belief, yet this monstrous nonsense has persisted.'

Charles acknowledged the existence of other fabricated

stories, including one about Camilla being with him while he was skiing in Switzerland, lamenting that there seems to be no remedy for such lies. While some may cling to the veracity of these fanciful tales, those close to the King believe in the sincerity of his denials.

Diana was still unsettled by Charles's vague comments about 'whatever "in love" means' during their engagement television interview, when she boarded the royal yacht *Britannia* for their honeymoon. Significantly, Camilla had been among the invited guests at the wedding ceremony in St Paul's, and although Charles was loving and attentive to his bride, he continued to make daily phone calls to his ex-mistress. His valet Stephen Barry noted in Tina Brown's *The Diana Chronicles* that the prince became irritable when he missed these calls.

Charles also received cufflinks from Camilla, personalised with two Cs entwined like the Chanel 'C', which, when Diana confronted him, he admitted to her without concern. His new wife was demanding and tensions rose early in the marriage. She even resented him sitting for hours at his easel painting watercolours. One day he returned to find she had destroyed his painting and all his painting materials. This marriage, he soon realised, was a mismatch and would be an uphill struggle.

On 21 June 1982, just ten days after Diana's twenty-first birthday, Charles left the private Lindo Wing of St Mary's Hospital, Paddington, beaming after the princess had given birth to Prince William at 9.03 p.m., following a labour of over thirteen hours. Charles shared the news with a delighted Queen and Queen Mother, and the press quickly spread word across the globe.

Asked how he felt, Charles replied, 'It's a bit difficult to tell,' before adding, 'relieved and delighted.' About the baby, he shared, 'He's in marvellous form' with 'fair, blondish hair', likely to change, but he could not yet say who he resembled. Then came, 'Is he the prettiest baby in the world?' Charles smiled, 'Well, he's not bad.' Finally, a cheeky question about the crowd's chant – 'Well done, Charlie, let's have another one!' – made him laugh. 'Bloody hell! Give us a chance . . . ask my wife. She might not be too pleased just yet.'

Despite her smiles, the princess was struggling both physically and mentally after the birth. She later recalled the agony she endured during the photo session, her stitches causing her pain as she strained to stand and smile for the cameras. Once the car turned the corner, out of sight from photographers, she burst into tears. She could not wait to lock herself away with her precious baby at Kensington Palace, shielded from prying eyes. Unlike earlier royal infants, this child was born into the relentless scrutiny of modern media; the first future monarch born in a hospital rather than behind palace gates. In a nod to family tradition, the baby's name was agreed: Prince William Arthur Philip Louis, blending both parents' wishes.

Charles was thrilled with his son and grateful to have been by Diana's side. The Queen quipped, 'Thank heavens he hasn't ears like his father.' Diana's Spencer bloodline meant that William would be potentially the first Stuart blood descendant to take the throne since Charles II. Privately, she admitted to friends that not everything was 'hunky-dory'.

Despite public joy over William's birth, Diana was overwhelmed by postpartum depression, and she felt excluded from decisions about the christening. Distressed by the rigid royal demands, she felt isolated and deeply unhappy. Her moods swung wildly, revealing a raw side few had seen before. She craved comfort, a hug, a shoulder to cry on, but Charles was not emotionally equipped enough to give it to her, due to his cold upbringing. He blamed himself for the mess that was unfolding. Diana may well have been on an emotional roller-coaster, but he was bound to duty, too distant. He lacked the natural warmth and emotional tools to handle her. It never got better.

Princess Diana, overnight the most famous woman on Earth, faced immense pressure. Some in Charles's circle suggested she needed professional psychiatric care. Diana was highly strung and impulsive at times, but far from insane. Painting her as a 'nutcase' was easy; the truth was much more complicated. The Queen understood that Diana might just be a woman overwhelmed with the royal world and the attentions of the press. She urged Charles to be patient.

The princess later revealed she suffered from bulimia nervosa, though friends initially attributed her dramatic weight loss to stress. When she eventually shared her struggles, it was shocking but made her more relatable, as Diana had a rare ability to turn her personal struggles into powerful advocacy.

At William's christening, the Queen noticed Diana's distress and suggested she offer her finger for the crying baby to suck. William calmed briefly, but screamed each time her finger was removed. Only six weeks after giving birth, Diana later recalled feeling desperate, saying, 'It was all decided around me. Hence the ghastly pictures.'

CHAPTER 11

SEPARATE LIVES

We were very, very close to each other the six weeks before Harry was born, the closest we've ever, ever been and ever will be. Then suddenly as Harry was born it just went bang, our marriage, the whole thing went down the drain.[111]

PRINCESS DIANA ON HER RELATIONSHIP WITH PRINCE CHARLES

By the time Prince Harry was born on 15 September 1984, the once-celebrated marriage of the Prince and Princess of Wales was already damaged beyond repair. Charles had drifted back to Camilla; a relationship Diana had long come to suspect.

Her pregnancy with their second child had sparked a fleeting moment of joy for the couple. Diana said Charles had hoped for a girl. Instead, they got a healthy boy with flame red hair. The prince's offhand remark – 'Oh God, it's a boy . . . and he's even got red hair' – cut deep. Diana never forgot or forgave it: 'Something inside me closed off.' She had kept the baby's gender secret throughout the pregnancy, anticipating his disappointment.[112]

Any sense of renewed connection between the royal couple quickly dissolved. Within weeks of Harry's birth, Charles had resumed his intimacy with Camilla. The distance between the royal couple widened further. They remained committed parents in public, and continued playing to the cameras as a couple, but behind palace doors, the emotional detachment was stark. The Queen knew it and along with Prince Philip, she encouraged them to work at their marriage.

Diana's own search for love and affection led her in 1986 to James Hewitt, a dashing cavalry officer with a mop of red hair, hired to teach her riding. Their affair unfolded over five years. But crucially, it began two years after Harry's birth – making the persistent paternity rumours not only cruel but completely unfounded.

Harry was born into a gilded cage already overshadowed by his parents' private estrangement. His birth did not mend the cracks in the royal marriage – it merely exposed them further. From the start, Harry knew his place: William was the heir, Harry the spare.

The rivalry sparked when they were young. Aged six, Harry snapped from the backseat of Diana's car: 'You'll be king, I won't – so I can do what I want!' Diana and her bodyguard Ken Wharfe, who listened in, were stunned.

Staff fawned over William, and his family did too. The Queen Mother always gave him precedence. Harry? Left out, but undeterred. He was cheekier, wilder, more fun. His nanny, Olga Powell, did not sugar-coat it: 'Harry, I love you, but I don't like you.' He was a handful; he loved playing her up and playing to the crowd.

At nursery school, he tugged at his music teacher Mr Pritchard's trousers through assembly. When challenged, he grinned: 'I can see your willy.' He was sent straight to the head. When Diana was called in, she could hardly stop laughing.[113]

Behind the laughs, there was a storm. Diana clung to motherhood to make up for her loveless marriage. While Charles loved his boys, his heart had moved on. Diana was painted as the victim at this time. But not all staff saw her as the sainted mother portrayed by the press. Some found her cunning and deeply manipulative. One bodyguard, pushed to breaking point, emptied his gun into a tree, saying, 'That should wake them up.'

Charles and Diana, trapped in a failed marriage, reached a quiet understanding. A truce of sorts. During the week, he kept to Highgrove, while she would remain at Kensington Palace. Weekends were shared on a rota; they were rarely both in residence. Charles one weekend, Diana the next.

It was neat, and cold, but it worked for them.

For Diana, it meant space, and the freedom to see James Hewitt on her terms. When he stayed at Highgrove, he had a room but rarely used it. His overnight stays were discreet, his arrivals timed to dodge the press. He blended in. He joined in poolside games with William and Harry and the Scotland Yard protection officers, laughing, splashing, and play-fighting.

William and Harry adored the fun. When Diana was once thrown into the water fully dressed, she roared with laughter. The boys had no idea he was their mother's secret lover. To them, Hewitt was simply another smiling face, another uncle figure while their busy father was away working – not the man sharing their mother's bed.

When he was in their company, Charles did not do roughhousing. The bodyguards did. William and Harry would storm into Inspector Ken Wharfe's room shouting, 'Ken, do you want to fight?' It was not a question. One went for the head, the other for the groin. There was nothing playful about these play fights, they meant business.

Charles would pop his head around the door and peek in, more bemused than amused: 'They're not being too much bother, are they, Ken?' He cared, of course he did. He loved his boys, but from a distance.

Through it all, Diana tried to shield her sons from the royal chaos. They went on holidays with both parents, trips to Spain, yacht outings with the King and Queen of Spain. The illusion of normalcy held – just.

William's schooling continued at Wetherby and then Ludgrove School. He excelled at sport, drama and leadership. But an accident in 1991 exposed the cracks between Charles and Diana. Struck on the head by a golf club at school, William was rushed to hospital by PPO Sgt Reg Spinney. Diana was alerted at lunch and rushed to William's bedside. He was operated on at Great Ormond Street Hospital in London. Charles? He left his son's bedside and went to the opera. While Diana held William's hand during surgery, Charles hosted European Union officials at *Tosca*, then boarded the Royal Train. Diana never truly forgave him. 'What kind of dad are you?' screamed the *Sun*.

Harry visited his brother the next morning. William later joked about the scar: 'I call it [my Harry Potter scar] because it glows sometimes and some people notice it – other times they don't notice it at all. I got hit by a golf club when I was playing golf with a friend of mine. We were on a putting green and the next thing you know there was a 7 iron, and it came out of nowhere and it hit me in the head.'[114]

The boy who swung the golf club was never identified.

Trapped in a loveless marriage, Diana threw her heart and soul into being a loving mum. She would take her sons on holiday without her busy father – instructing protection officer Inspector Wharfe to scout out possible holiday destinations and recce them.

Necker Island, a private retreat in the Caribbean owned by Virgin boss Sir Richard Branson, proved Diana's escape hatch. After a cold Christmas at Sandringham, blanked by the royals, she had had enough. In January 1989, she took up Branson's offer: a break in the sun, without Charles.

Just Diana, William, Harry, and a handpicked family crew. Charles told the boys he was working. Diana did not explain – she did not need to.

Secluded beaches, Balinese-style villas, snooker under beamed ceilings, jet-skis at the ready. The moment the island came into view, the tension lifted. Their host Richard Branson met them at the dock. While Diana sunbathed, the boys ran wild. There were pool games, beach swims, lobster barbecues under the stars. Heaven, at last, for a while.

It did not take long before Fleet Street showed up. Boats bobbed offshore, with long lenses aimed at the sand. Cameras were seized and flights banned. Still, the press kept coming.

Undeterred, Diana returned to Necker Island in April 1990 with William and Harry. Once more, photographers swarmed – this time, a flotilla of over sixty boats. For the press, Diana had become an industry unto herself; her images, especially in swimwear, were a goldmine, selling newspapers worldwide.

When she raged at her security detail that the press intrusion was frightening the boys, her bodyguard Wharfe tried damage control – a quiet deal to keep the worst at bay. It helped, but the spell was broken. For Diana, Necker was more than a holiday. It was freedom. A place to breathe, laugh, and love her sons, who would cherish these memories. But even at Necker, there was no real peace; the world found her.

In August 1992, Charles and Diana took their boys on a holiday for the second year running aboard the yacht *Alexander* –

a floating palace loaned to them by the Greek shipping magnate John Latsis. They joined the ship at Levkas Harbour in Greece for what would be their last holiday together. The end was coming, but for now, under the sun, they shared one last moment of joy as a family.

Below the surface of the marriage, the cracks were deep. It had run its course. Both Charles and Diana knew it. The affairs – Camilla, James Hewitt, and others – were no longer secrets. What was not clear, however, was how it would all end. What would be the catalyst?

They were already dealing with the fallout of Andrew Morton's *Diana: Her True Story*, serialised in the *Sunday Times* and published in June 1992. It detonated like a bomb within the walls of Buckingham Palace. The book laid bare the chasm in the Waleses' marriage, detailing Diana's profound unhappiness, suicide attempts, battles with bulimia, and Charles's affair with Camilla Parker Bowles.

At the time, both Morton and the Palace denied Diana's involvement. However, it later emerged that the princess had been the mastermind and primary source of the entire project, secretly recording her candid revelations and passing the tapes to the author via an intermediary.

The fallout was seismic: public sympathy surged for Diana and the monarchy's façade crumbled. Charles, crestfallen, was exposed as a failure as a husband and a cheat.

Then on 23 August, after they returned from their tense family holiday cruising the Greek islands, came that catalyst. It was the publication of a transcript of the so-called 'Dianagate tapes' recording the princess on the phone to her male friend James Gilbey, heir to the Gilbey's gin fortune, who had known Diana since childhood. The *Sun* splashed the story across its front page and several pages inside. The transcript of an intimate phone call made on New Year's Eve 1989 showed Gilbey calling Diana 'Squidgy' and 'Squidge', hence the scandal also being dubbed 'Squidgygate'.

During the conversation, Diana expressed her deep unhappiness in her marriage, stating, 'I just felt so sad and empty and thought, bloody hell, after all I've done for this fucking family . . .' She also voiced her concern that she might become pregnant with her lover's child. At one point, Gilbey tells her, 'Oh, Squidgy, I love you. Love you. Love you.'

The scandal sparked numerous conspiracy theories regarding the origins of the recordings. It emerged that in January 1990, retired bank manager and radio enthusiast Cyril Reenan claimed he had inadvertently intercepted a call between Diana and Gilbey using his home scanning equipment. He later sold the tape to the *Sun*. Adding to the intrigue, 25-year-old typist Jane Norgrove from Oxfordshire also asserted that she had recorded the same conversation.

These coincidental interceptions raised significant questions about the security of royal communications and fuelled speculation about possible eavesdropping by intelligence agencies. Analysis by surveillance experts uncovered anomalies in the recordings, such as unexpected data bursts and background hums, indicating potential tampering or rebroadcasting of the original tapes. Were these really chance interceptions? Many doubted it.

Home Secretary Kenneth Clarke faced criticism for allegedly blocking a thorough investigation into the leaks over fears that probing too deeply might expose sensitive operations or further damage the reputation of the security services.

There was no way back.

Before the formal separation was announced, Diana made a

quiet visit to Prince William at Ludgrove School. She sat William down and told him the truth – or as much of it as she could. She explained that she and Charles could no longer live under the same roof, but they still loved him and Harry. William pressed for answers, she did her best to respond.

At least when John Major announced the separation in Parliament in December 1992, William was not shocked. He was ready. He had long been Diana's anchor. Her emotional crutch. The boy who became her companion. He once told her he wanted to be a policeman — 'so that I can protect you'.

And when the divorce came – and with it, the loss of her royal HRH rank – it was William who wrapped his arms around her and said, 'Don't worry, Mummy. I'll give it back to you one day, when I'm king.' A promise he could not keep.

Perhaps Diana leaned too hard on him. She knew it and so did her private secretary, Commander Patrick Jephson RN, who warned her against doing it, as he feared William was too young, too sensitive for the burdens she placed on him.

But she did not stop. William, just a boy, had become 'the man in my life'. And he carried the burden – all of it.

CHAPTER 12

SPECIAL FRIENDS

Philip is a man who enjoys the company of attractive, intelligent younger women. Nothing wrong in that . . . He has special friends, like Penny [Romsey]. But I am quite sure, quite sure, certain, he has never been unfaithful to the Queen.

PATRICIA, 2ND COUNTESS MOUNTBATTEN, AND PENNY ROMSEY'S LATE MOTHER-IN-LAW

Prince Philip's close friendships with beautiful women have long been the subject of intense speculation. When asked outright about his possible infidelity by journalist Fiammetta Rocco, during an interview in December 1992, he sharply replied, 'Good God, woman! Have you ever stopped to think that for years I've not moved anywhere without a police officer accompanying me? How the hell could I have got away with anything like that?'

Yet, even under the watchful eye of Scotland Yard's elite SO14 squad, scandal touched his family. Charles carried on a long affair with Camilla, while Diana had relationships with her bodyguard Barry Mannakee, Major James Hewitt, and others like Oliver Hoare. Philip's daughter, Anne, had her own entanglements, including an affair with Tim Laurence, later her husband, and another with her bodyguard Peter Cross. In 1984, when Cross was moved from duty, Anne continued to see him privately, using the codename 'Mrs Wallis' in their secret meetings. The relationship ended after Cross sold his story to the *News of the World* for £60,000.

Throughout his long marriage to the Queen, Philip was often linked in the tabloids to glamorous women such as Katie Boyle, Merle Oberon and Anna Massey. But reliable evidence of any such liaisons has never emerged, and his friends, notably Gyles Brandreth, stressed that Philip always denied such affairs outright. His close friend Hélène Cordet, whom he had known since youth, also faced speculation about her child's paternity after Philip became his godfather, although her son Max always denied any connection.

Philip's friendships extended beyond socialites. Daphne du Maurier, author of the bestselling novel *Rebecca* and the wife of Lieutenant-General Sir Frederick 'Boy' Browning, shared what many called an 'emotionally intimate' bond with him.

Alexandra 'Sacha' Hamilton, Duchess of Abercorn, twenty-five years his junior, also admitted to enjoying a 'passionate friendship' with Philip. The beautiful Sacha, tied by blood to Russia's Romanovs as well as the British royals, and wife of James, the 5th Duke of Abercorn, spoke of the 'highly charged chemistry' they shared. She admitted to Gyles Brandreth, 'The heart came into it in a big way.' Though it was not a 'full relationship', she said, the passion lived in their ideas, in the trust and connection that bound them close.[115]

Royal biographer Sarah Bradford went further and spoke plainly. In her 2011 book, *Elizabeth II: Her Life in Our Times*, she flatly called Philip an adulterer, though evidence produced was scant. 'The Duke of Edinburgh has had affairs, full-blown affairs and more than one,' she wrote. 'He has affairs, and the Queen accepts it. I think she believes that's how men are.'[116] She added that Philip 'never chased actresses'. His tastes were different, according to Bradford, always younger, often beautiful, invariably an aristocrat, and usually married.

Yet, despite these lurid stories, the Queen and Philip's marriage remained strong. His friend and biographer, writer Gyles Brandreth, noted that Elizabeth's faith in Philip was unwavering.[117] Brandreth also touched on another taboo, wild speculation about the Queen's own fidelity. Persistent gossip claimed that Prince Andrew's father was not Philip but the Queen's racing manager, Henry 'Porchey' Porchester, later 7th Earl of Carnarvon. But after raising it in *Philip: The Final Portrait*, Brandreth writes. 'I think we can take it as read that the Queen has been faithful throughout her married life.' The dates made nonsense of the rumour: Philip returned from *Britannia* in April 1959, Andrew was born on 19 February 1960. As Brandreth observed in his book Andrew was 'a happy by-product of the Queen and Philip's post-Britannia reunion.'[118]

Indeed, friends and staff described Philip's marriage to the Queen as filled with love and private affection. Mountbatten's butler, Chief Petty Officer William Evans, recalled the physical spark between them too, seeing Philip pinch the Queen's bottom at Broadlands and chasing her up the stairs to the bedroom, playfully calling them 'a pair of teenagers'. Throughout their marriage, which produced four children, the couple's love, mutual respect and trust remained, standing as a quiet yet powerful response to years of speculation.

In July 1982, Michael Fagan, a jobless father of four, broke into Buckingham Palace and entered the Queen's bedroom. It was his second intrusion: weeks earlier he had slipped in unnoticed, drunk Charles's wine and urinated in a dog's bowl.

When interviewed, Fagan said that after he drew back the curtain on her bed, the Queen was shocked. 'She jumped up and said, "What are you doing here? What are you doing here? Get out. Get out."' She fled, her bare feet skittering across the floor. The only help arrived in the form of footman Paul Whybrew – 'Tall Paul' at six-foot-four – who kept Fagan calm by offering him a drink while they waited for police officer Robert Roberts to arrive. Home Secretary Willie Whitelaw submitted his resignation to Mrs Thatcher. However, she declined his offer, and Whitelaw remained in his position.

Tried at the Old Bailey that September, he was acquitted after just 22 minutes of jury deliberation, as trespass was not a criminal offence. The *Sun* summed up the verdict in a single word: 'Bonkers!'

Once the uproar had died down, the press switched tack and jumped on the details exposed in the trial. After all, Fagan's break-in had revealed that the Queen and Prince Philip slept in separate rooms – a surprise to most everyday people used to sharing a bed with their spouse. Royal commentators put it down to upper-class tradition, but the tabloids still asked the question: where was Philip? Why had he not been there to protect her? In the end, their sleeping arrangements stirred more talk than the fact that a stranger could wander right into the Queen's bedroom unchallenged.

Friends insisted the Queen and Philip did usually share the same bed, but claimed the Duke had simply slept in his own quarters that night due to an early engagement the next morning.[119] Lady Pamela Hicks, Philip's ever-loyal first cousin, had a more credible explanation. 'In England, the upper class always have had separate bedrooms,' she said. 'You don't want to be bothered with snoring or someone flinging a leg around. Then when you are feeling cosy you share your room sometimes. It is lovely to be able to choose.'

What is not in question, however, is Philip's penchant for the company of beautiful women, especially as he grew older. He enjoyed the company of lively, full-spirited women, and usually ones who were safely married. One such lady was Penny Romsey, thirty-one years his junior, and wife of his godson and second cousin, Norton Knatchbull, Lord Romsey, later the 3rd Earl Mountbatten. Penny enjoyed a 'highly personal' relationship with the Duke spanning many years. Tall, slender and blonde, she looked every bit the part of a fashion model. Yet it was her sharp mind and quick wit that had earned her a principal place in royal circles.

Despite her humble roots – her father Reginald Eastwood had left school at fifteen to work as a butcher – Penny had married into aristocracy and found herself managing a vast, historic estate. Her father had become wealthy by founding the Angus Steakhouse restaurant chain, which he eventually sold for millions, allowing Penny an upbringing in the best of both worlds: grounded yet with a taste for the finer things in life.

Since 1975, when Norton first introduced his girlfriend Penelope Eastwood to Charles and then Philip, she had become a beloved presence within close royal circles. Penny was refreshingly natural – warm, humorous and intelligent, but neither brash nor flirtatious. Philip was attracted by her easy charm, wit, and femininity. Penny later shared his interest in carriage driving, a passion that became their bond. Philip once explained how he came to it: 'I gave up polo at fifty, looked around for what was next. We had horses and carriages, so I borrowed four and went to Norfolk to practise.' In his second race, he admitted, he had finished near last, though the challenge only deepened his passion for the sport.

In Penny (now Countess Mountbatten), Philip found a kindred spirit, a woman as resilient as she was beautiful. Their friendship, natural and unpretentious, grew into one of Philip's most cherished connections, a source of laughter and companionship long into his later years. Senior palace courtiers called it the 'Penny Romsey situation'. She was so much a part of royal life that household staff nicknamed her 'And Also', because Philip always added her to royal guest lists, sometimes after they had been drawn up.[120]

In March 1996, a private telephone call between Philip and Penny was leaked and published by the *News of the World.* They spoke of family matters – Charles and Diana's divorce, Camilla, even the Queen Mother's hip. The press dubbed it 'Dukegate.' Though the call was more friendly than intimate – Penny even passed the receiver to her husband, Norton – the very fact of its leak enraged Philip and raised unwelcome questions. The tabloids smelled blood, and questions followed. The royal walls, so often silent, now faced the unrelenting scrutiny of the world.

Meanwhile, Penny carried on with her life as usual, even when her husband, Norton, left her for Lady Nuttall, a fashion designer, and took up with her in the Bahamas. When that fell through, he returned to Broadlands but kept his distance, moving into a cottage on the estate.

Penny became an integral part of royal life, spending weekends at Windsor Castle, often updating Philip and even the Queen on events beyond palace walls. The Queen, it seemed, was relaxed about their friendship; the three of them would sometimes settle in for a quiet evening, watching television together.

Even in his later years, when carriage driving became difficult, Philip and Penny shared a love of painting watercolours, another opportunity to spend time together. He was a masterful dancer, a regular on the floor at the Royal Yacht Squadron Ball in Cowes, where he would often be seen gliding her effortlessly alongside.

By now, the Queen had made peace with Philip's flaws – his bluntness, his charm, his eye for a beautiful woman – knowing his loyalty ran deep. Even when he nearly caused a diplomatic stir in 1986 with a careless remark about a British student in Xi'an getting 'slitty-eyed' if he stayed much longer in China, she trusted his counsel. In his later years, his flirtations – along with his so-called 'gaffes' – did not faze her; what counted was his steady love and unshaken respect.

Publicly, Prince Philip once reflected on his 73-year marriage, saying at their 1997 Golden Wedding Anniversary that 'tolerance' is the key to a happy marriage. 'I think the main lesson we have learnt is that tolerance is the one essential ingredient in any happy marriage,' he said. 'You can take it from me, the Queen has the quality of tolerance in abundance.' Privately, he once remarked to the wife of a senior courtier, who was introduced to the Duke by her husband at a palace garden party, 'You're far too good for him,' before pithily adding his pearl of wisdom, 'The secret to a successful marriage is to have separate interests and spend a lot of time apart, take it from me.'[121]

CHAPTER 13

THE PEOPLE'S PRINCESS

I feel like everyone else in this country today, utterly devastated . . . She was the people's princess, and that's how she will stay, how she will remain in our hearts and in our memories, forever.

BRITISH PRIME MINISTER TONY BLAIR, 1997

Following the tumult of 'Squidgygate', the royals faced another devastating phone scandal in January 1993 – this time involving Charles himself. In a leaked recording of an intimate six-minute conversation with his married lover Camilla in December 1989, the prince expressed a desire to 'live inside [Camilla's] trousers' and joked about being reincarnated as a tampon. Dubbed 'Camillagate', it shattered Charles's image and confirmed Camilla as his mistress, bolstering public sympathy for Diana.

The backlash was brutal. Charles took it from all sides – hecklers in the street, headlines that cut deep, and fire from clergymen in the pulpit. The Bishop of Durham, David Jenkins, did not hold back. He called the prince unfit to reign, claiming he had lost moral ground. He even compared him to Edward VIII. The public had spoken, loud and clear.

Charles needed to fight back and fast. He turned to Commander Richard Aylard, his private secretary, and broadcaster Jonathan Dimbleby. They had a plan: a frank TV documentary, *The Private Man, the Public Role*, and a sanctioned biography. Charles agreed. He wanted a reset, but truth had its price. Aylard urged him to talk plainly about Camilla. Charles hesitated, then gave in. He wanted to move forward. A clean break.

The documentary laid out his work, his ideals and his pressures. But none of it stuck. What people remembered from it was the moment he said it – yes, he had been unfaithful. Briefed about the question in advance, Charles was ready. Dimbleby asked if he had been 'faithful and honourable' to Diana.

'Yes, absolutely,' he replied. Then came the killer follow-up. He paused. 'Yes . . . until it became irretrievably broken down, us both having tried.'

It landed like a thunderclap. His confession aired on 29 June 1994, as the country watched.

Diana did not flinch. That same night, she stepped out in a black silk dress by Christina Stambolian. Short, off-the-shoulder and bold, it was dubbed the 'Revenge Dress'. The *Sun* headline called her: 'The Thrilla He Left to Woo Camilla'. In that moment, Diana took back the stage. And never gave it up.[122]

And just like that, the rest of the documentary detailing Charles's good works over a quarter of a century was drowned out. A telephone poll by the *Sun* said two-thirds of respondents said he was 'unfit to be king' after his adultery confession.

The backlash was worse than any criticism he had ever faced. His own family were stunned. Pundits and churchmen renewed their cries: they said Charles was a liability, unfit to ever reign. Some urged he should step down as heir and be replaced by his son William. Historian Dr David Starkey tried to cut through the noise. British kings, he said, had divorced, separated – even taken male lovers – without shaking the throne. This was no constitutional crisis. Just scandal.

The Queen and Prince Philip were appalled. Charles's public confession of adultery had blindsided them. In the private offices and press office at the palace, it landed like a slap. It also marked the end of the charade – Camilla filed for divorce the following year.

But Charles did not back down. If anything, it steeled him. He stood by Camilla, and promised her emotional and financial support. He faced down his family.

The 'War of the Waleses' continued to play out in the press. Camilla was now labelled 'the most hated woman in Britain', and vanished from public view. Hounded, hidden and hated. Charles moved to protect her. He hired loyal ex-royal protection officer Sgt Andy Creighton to drive her and watch over her. He shielded her movements; kept her safe and kept her close.

Amid the media storm, Charles knew one thing: he had to step up as a father. The separation from Diana made that clear. But duty called, and his schedule rarely let up. He needed help.

Enter Alexandra 'Tiggy' Legge-Bourke. Tiggy was not a nanny, she was more like a big sister. She joined William and Harry on ski trips in Klosters, sailed with them on summer cruises, and gave them a sense of freedom. She gave the princes what they needed. 'Fresh air, a rifle, and a horse.'

The boys adored her. Diana did not. Sadly, she was caught in the crossfire, and became collateral damage. An innocent figure pulled into the bitter wreckage of a royal marriage unravelling in full view.

Diana was busy plotting her revenge. She hatched a secret plan; a tell-all interview on BBC's *Panorama*. In a bid to secure the interview, BBC reporter Martin Bashir spread lies about Tiggy to Diana. At one meeting, Bashir presented a fake dossier filled with shocking smears about the Prince of Wales, feeding Diana's fears. One of the wild claims was that Charles was 'in love' with Tiggy and planning a holiday with her. Absurd as it seemed, Diana believed it, and it soon consumed her. While Charles was charming and flirtatious, any risqué postcards he exchanged with her were merely playful banter.[123]

Without any evidence, Princess Diana became obsessed with the idea that Tiggy and Charles were involved in an intimate relationship and that she had lost their baby. Diana confronted her about the affair at the palace staff Christmas party in December 1995, humiliating the young woman. Her family considered legal action if the claims continued, but an internal inquiry by Sir Robert Fellowes, the Queen's private secretary and Diana's brother-in-law, found the accusations to be completely baseless.[124]

The strain between Charles and Diana affected their sons. At fourteen, William's sensitivity showed when he asked his parents not to attend Eton's 'Fourth of June' celebration, marking King George III's birthday with a day of festivities for students and their families. He feared that the media circus around them would ruin it for his classmates. Instead, he invited Tiggy to go in their place, a decision that upset Diana and took Charles by surprise.

By now, Diana was certain *Panorama* was her way out. No tabloids, no spin. Just her, speaking straight to the public she knew still loved her. It would be a clean, defiant strike against a Palace she felt had cast her off. And she meant it to hit Charles where it hurt.

On 20 November 1995, 22.8 million people tuned in. Diana did not hold back. 'There were three of us in this marriage,' she said. The line cut like a knife. She made it clear – she was not going quietly. 'I'll fight till the end,' she said. 'I have a role to fulfil, and two children to bring up.'

She knew exactly what she was doing; poised and measured, aware of her effect. Like a stage veteran hitting every mark. When Bashir asked if Charles was fit for the 'top job', she struck without raising her voice: 'I would think that the top job would bring enormous limitations to him . . . and I don't know if he could adapt to that.' And when pressed, should William skip ahead? She smiled with a dagger behind it: 'My wish is that my husband finds peace of mind, and from that, other things follow.'

It was not just an interview. It was a challenge to the Crown itself, a rapier thrust to the heart of the monarchy. The fallout was immediate. Headlines questioned the line of succession. People called for William to step up and for Charles to be sidelined.

Diana was elated, at first. She rang friends, asking, 'What did you think of my performance?' But the next morning, regret hit like cold water. 'Did you see it?' she asked her friend, the healer Simone Simmons. 'You made a fool of yourself,' Simmons replied. Others close to her agreed. Diana was shaken. Later, she confessed to her friend, *Daily Mail* journalist Richard Kay, that she wished she had not questioned Charles's right to be king.

Critics pounced. 'Who advised this?' they demanded. Diana later admitted that Sarah, the Duchess of York, and Ruby Wax had encouraged it. Desperate times had led to a desperate choice of advisers. Even her close friends and supporters questioned her judgement, some even her sanity.

Diana had kept the *Panorama* interview secret. Not even her trusted private secretary, Patrick Jephson, knew about it. Nor did she tell her press adviser Geoff Crawford, who refused to work with her afterwards and returned to his duties as deputy press secretary to the Queen. But she did give a warning to William and his housemaster, Dr Andrew Gailey, who urged her to come in person to Eton College to explain to her son what was happening. She did and told William not to worry, saying he might even like it. He did not, at all.

When the broadcast aired, William felt betrayed. At school, he faced taunts from his fellow pupils. Classmates mocked his mother's wide-eyed delivery, her confessions, her pain on full display. Her admission to 'loving and adoring' James Hewitt was excruciating for the teenage prince.

Harry, still at Ludgrove School, was shielded. The joint principals, Gerald Barber and Nichol Marston, kept newspapers away from the other boys. They also made sure the boys did not see the programme. But William had watched it. And he called her afterwards, angry and hurt. 'I'll never forgive you,' he told her. It was the one time he turned on her.[125] Years later, in May 2021, William expressed his deep sorrow over the BBC's failures, saying that reporter Martin Bashir's deceit had amplified his mother's 'fear, paranoia, and isolation' and worsened his parents' relationship.[126]

Diana had forced the Queen's hand. Four weeks after *Panorama* aired, Her Majesty acted. She wrote to Charles and Diana, urging them to divorce and end the chaos. On 21 December, Buckingham Palace made it official: Her Majesty had requested they part ways and they had agreed. Diana, who once vowed never to go quietly, was cast out. She lost her HRH title, which felt petty to many people. She was still the mother of a future king; stripping her of that honorific made her look like a martyr. She was not, but it played that way.

The early divorce negotiations were fraught. Diana's access to her boys was threatened, but a settlement was reached with shared custody. She secured visitation rights – one weekend in five – but with the boys away at boarding school, the time felt scarce. She left as Diana, Princess of Wales, with a strong settlement: £17 million up front (about £34 million today), plus £400,000 a year (around £800,000 today). A confidentiality agreement sealed her departure. The fairy tale was long dead. But now, at least, the ordeal had an ending.

Rattling around Kensington Palace alone was tough, but by August 1996, when the divorce was completed, Diana had found a newfound sense of freedom. She had transformed into a global icon of fashion and elegance. At last, she was free.

In January 1997, ITV aired a televised debate, *Monarchy: The Nation Decides*, hosted by Sir Trevor McDonald, which included a telephone poll on the future of the royals. Diana urged friends to call in and support its abolition, driven by her desire to prevent Charles from becoming king. In the end, the result was decisive – 66 per cent for keeping it, 34 per cent for abolition. When the discussion on the programme then turned to Camilla's potential as queen, Harry asked, 'Who's Camilla?' William responded, 'Don't you know?' Diana swiftly intervened, saying, 'Hold on a minute, Harry, it's time for bed. Come on.'[127]

After the divorce, Diana and Charles found moments of harmony. Once, Charles's helicopter landed near Kensington Palace, and he called ahead to ask if he could use the loo. Diana agreed and, on the phone, she joked with Simone Simmons, 'Oh, I've got to go. My ex needs the toilet.' When Charles finished and headed back to his car, Diana ran out, teasing, 'Same time next week?' hinting that they had had a sexual encounter. Caught off guard, Charles turned bright red but laughed. The police officers were left baffled. It was a glimpse of their old rapport – a reminder of their better days.[128]

Diana sought a new purpose, a new public role. She aimed to become the 'Queen of People's Hearts',[129] as she called herself, and to many, that is exactly what she became. She understood power and knew that proximity was key, so she sought ties with New Labour, even working to win over Prime Minister Tony Blair. But by 1997, her political moves – focused on AIDS and landmine clearance – had begun to draw negative headlines. She both shunned and courted the press, mastering the delicate dance. The pace grew relentless, more frantic. Her visit to Bosnia that summer, and an earlier trip to Angola, backfired. Conservative MP Nicholas Soames, Charles's friend, called her a 'loose cannon'. She in turn told BBC's Jennie Bond, in a clear statement of purpose: 'I am a humanitarian.'

For a time, Diana found some comfort in the arms of Pakistani heart surgeon Hasnat Khan, whom she called 'Mr Wonderful'. When they began dating, Diana sent her assistant, Victoria Mendham, ahead to the pub or restaurant where they were due to meet to check out what he was wearing and ensure no paparazzi were outside. She told friends she was in love with him, he was 'the one'.

Unlike the others, he wanted nothing from her. Hasnat Khan was grounded, private, a man of purpose – everything Diana admired. A heart surgeon, with steady hands and a steady life. She dreamed of something simple with him: marriage, a modest house, and a sense of normality. They slipped into pub corners at the Anglesey Arms in Chelsea. Diana wore a dark wig to stay anonymous. No flash dinners, no royal spectacle. Just two people, quietly enjoying a love affair. Sometimes they would eat at the Berni Inn, a basic steakhouse chain. She liked that.

But Hasnat was no dreamer. He saw what life with Diana

meant. No career and no peace. A life forever swallowed by her fame. To have a future, he told her, they would need to move to Pakistan. Start afresh. Away from the press, the palace, the weight of her name.

Diana tried. She went to Pakistan and met his family. She measured the life, but it was not hers. They would not accept her, and she could not pretend to be someone she was not. Yes, there was love, but they both knew there was no future. She knew that he would not be pinned down, exposed to a media circus, and she could not follow him.

When Hasnat would not commit to her, on the rebound Diana turned to Dodi Fayed, the playboy son of billionaire Harrods owner Mohamed Al-Fayed. It was the final twist in her story. That summer, she went public with Dodi, only weeks after her split from Hasnat. It began with a family holiday aboard Mohamed's 195-foot luxury yacht, *Jonikal.*

First, Diana and her boys had stayed with Mohamed Al-Fayed and his family at his luxury villa in the South of France. It did not go well. It was tense. William clashed with his mother and Harry had a spat with one of Fayed's children. They did not care for Fayed himself either. Paparazzi hounded them, lenses everywhere. They just wanted out, back to Balmoral with their father, the Queen, and the wider Royal Family. Scotland could not come soon enough.

But while Diana was there, she was wooed by Dodi, who invited her back to the yacht to spend her free time with him. She accepted. It was the start of their whirlwind connection that lasted just fifteen days. She was bowled over by him. With access to his father's huge wealth, he offered Diana a life of luxury – jets, limos, security – all the trappings she was used to. He could take care of her, and she found that appealing.

'She was tired, for sure, but yes, she sounded happy. She said she was happy,' her friend, journalist Richard Kay, said she told him so in their last conversion. Photos from the Mediterranean showed Diana's joy, unguarded and radiant. She did not care if she was photographed. Could they have had a future? Was there really a secret engagement? It is hard to say.

In Balmoral, Charles was in his Lord of the Isles kilt, Harry was relaxed, but William felt uneasy under the public eye; all agreed to pose for a photocall close to the river. Diana called her boys that night. They were preoccupied playing with their cousins and understandably wanted her off the line quick. How were they to know this would be the last time they would speak to her? What happened next shook the monarchy to its core, sparking doubts about Charles's fitness to be king and leading top establishment figures to question his suitability. By morning, 31 August 1997, Diana was gone, her life extinguished due to a car crash in a Paris tunnel.

The intoxicated driver of the luxury W140 series, black Mercedes-Benz S280, Henri Paul, was speeding to escape pursuing paparazzi who followed them on mopeds. Diana, her companion Dodi Fayed, and Paul – all unbelted – ultimately did not survive. She was 'religious' about putting on her seatbelt, according to her sister, Lady Sarah McCorquodale. 'Why didn't she put it on that night? I'll never know,' she said. Only her bodyguard, Trevor Rees-Jones, lived, though he was seriously injured. Dr Jean-Marc Martino tended to Diana at the scene. The ambulance took one hour and 43 minutes to transport the princess to the Pitié-Salpêtrière University Hospital, because French protocol prioritised on-site stabilisation and slow travel to avoid worsening her critical injuries. Despite two hours of surgery once there, she succumbed at 4.53 a.m.

In Balmoral, Charles was awakened with the news of her crash and later, her death. Grieving, he wept and told the Queen, who recommended letting his sons sleep. At dawn, he broke the terrible news to William, then Harry. Charles sat on Harry's bed, placed a hand on his knee, and quietly said, 'Darling boy, Mummy's been in a car crash . . . they tried, darling boy. She didn't make it,' leaving Harry alone with his grief, as the weight of her loss settled deeply into both sons' lives.[130] The Queen shielded the boys from the media storm, a kindness they later valued. Years on, William admitted it gave them space to mourn, though the world cast the Royal Family as being cold and Diana as a saint.[131]

After Princess Diana's tragic death, Prince Charles, overriding royal hesitations and the Queen's initial stance, insisted on bringing her body back personally from Paris to the UK, ensuring she was treated with dignity and acknowledging the nation's profound grief. Accompanied by Diana's sisters, Lady Sarah McCorquodale and Lady Jane Fellowes, Charles flew to Paris on a BAe 146 CC2 of the Royal Squadron, specifically configured to accommodate the transportation needs on that solemn occasion.

The first dilemma was where to bring her body upon return. Most assumed she would rest in St James's Palace, but the Queen at first thought otherwise. Diana was no longer HRH, no longer a royal. Charles, to his credit, insisted her body be taken there, the only fitting choice, where it lay in the Chapel Royal for the public and family to pay their respects.

Charles was devastated. He sought solace with a familiar face, the Queen Mother's long-time servant and confidant, William 'Billy' Tallon, whom he had known since he was a boy. He went to the Gatehouse Lodge, where Billy lived, and opened his heart.

He confided in Tallon, saying, 'You know, we were very much in love in the early days.'[132]

Diana's death sparked a global wave of shock and mourning, almost pagan in intensity. For many, it felt like losing family. She had a way of connecting with people that explained the hundreds of thousands who flooded London, sobbing and leaving flowers. They did not know her, but they believed they did. People were distraught, struggling to grasp the news. Prime Minister Tony Blair struck the right chord, summing up the nation's feelings when he said, 'I feel like everyone else in this country today, utterly devastated . . . She was the people's princess, and that's how she will stay, how she will remain in our hearts and in our memories, forever.'

At Balmoral, the Queen and her family remained stoic and silent. Traditional prayers were said for the Royal Family at Crathie Kirk, but not for Diana – not a word. Tradition and protocol held them firm. Within hours of Diana's body being returned to Britain, it was clear that the public demanded a national lament. Queen Elizabeth faced stinging criticism for staying at Balmoral, making her appear detached from the nation's grief.

Prime Minister Blair felt compelled to act. He and his close advisers feared the Queen had seriously misread the public mood. It was all uncharted ground. Alastair Campbell, Blair's influential press spokesperson, experienced the tense mood on the streets first-hand when walking through the crowds on his way to Buckingham Palace for planning meetings about the funeral. He warned Blair that anger was thick, the threat of violent disorder very real. People blamed the royals, whispering that if they had treated her better, if Charles had been a good husband, Diana would still be alive. The crowds swelled, voices grew sharper, and hostility mounted.

People began to question their loyalty to the Crown. Headlines like 'Show Us You Care' in the *Daily Express* rattled the Palace, even the Queen herself. Christopher Hitchens remarked that in the week after Diana's death, Britain became a 'one-party state'; criticising the 'tear-stained hordes' for their intense reaction. The flag was not at half-mast at the palace, and that also stoked public anger. When told it was not protocol, people grew even angrier. The Union Flag was hoisted, then lowered to half-mast.

The tabloids, eager to deflect blame for the paparazzi chase, hammered on the theme of absent royalty. The Queen and her family had no time to grieve. Though it was wrong for the press to push her into a public display of sorrow, rising frustration left her no choice. Under intense pressure, the Queen returned to London on Blair's advice.

Andrew and Edward went out first from Buckingham Palace, testing the crowd's mood. The Queen and Blair watched anxiously on television. Would the people turn on them? Spit, shout, shove? After all, the palace had been bombarded with angry calls. But when the Queen, Philip, and Charles returned with the two boys, the crowd softened. The tension broke. Had the senior royals cynically used Diana's grieving sons to win over the baying crowd, to protect themselves and the institution? It certainly felt like it.

William and Harry later questioned the move, admitting they felt 'numb' and overexposed to the public so soon after their mother's death, reflecting on the intense scrutiny and emotional challenges they faced. William recalled, 'It was like nothing I'd ever experienced before. It was very alien to be part of something that was so public, but we were just trying to do what was expected of us.'[133]

It was decided that the Queen would address the nation.

Palace officials initially set it for 4 p.m., but Blair's advisor, Campbell, pushed for a live broadcast during the evening news for maximum impact. The Palace responded, 'The Queen does not do live.' But Blair insisted. When her tribute to Diana arrived at Downing Street, it felt cold, so Campbell made a few tweaks, adding phrases like 'as a grandmother' to give it warmth. The final speech at 6 p.m. on 5 September was a PR masterstroke. The Queen's tribute was warm and admiring, even though she never said she loved her.

'No one who knew Diana will ever forget her. Millions who never met her but felt they knew her will remember her,' the Queen said. 'I, for one, believe there are lessons to be drawn from her life and the extraordinary reaction to her death.' Her words, designed to soften public anger, went a long way towards healing the divide.

On 6 September 1997, a hush fell over London as the masses gathered for Diana's funeral. William and Harry walked in solemn step behind the cortège. It was a long, heavy walk. Crowds sobbed and wailed; thousands upon thousands lined the route. Step by step, they walked alongside their father, their grandfather, Philip, and Diana's brother, Earl Spencer. Losing her was not private for her sons. The world's grief overshadowed theirs, making their sorrow feel small.

In the years that followed, the brothers questioned the wisdom of putting them through that traumatic ordeal of walking in the procession. In a 2017 interview, Harry called it a 'very long, lonely walk', saying no child should ever be made to do it.[134] In his memoir *Spare*, he shared that many people, including their uncle, Charles Spencer, were horrified by the idea. There was even talk of William walking alone, but Harry refused, knowing his brother would have done the same for him.

Earl Spencer's eulogy to his sister at Westminster Abbey pulled no punches: 'She needed no royal title to continue to generate her particular brand of magic,' he said, angering the Queen, his godmother, in the process. Applause rolled into the gothic abbey. The Queen paid her respects in her own way. As Diana's cortège passed the palace, she stood with members of her family and bowed her head. Diana had not gone quietly as she vowed; she had received a state farewell in all but name, leaving the royals subdued, yet unbroken. As Diana's legacy soared, however, Charles knew that his own path forward and some form of retribution would be steep.

Princess Diana's death was a seismic moment in the Queen's reign, making it clear that the monarchy had to adapt to the public's emotional needs while continuing to uphold its traditional responsibilities. Diana's compassion and star power remained undimmed; her memory etched in millions of hearts. A beacon of hope and fearless advocate, she championed causes others avoided. Yet, behind the dazzling smile was a woman yearning for something simple: to be seen and valued by her husband. Despite all she gave to the Royal Family, she often felt unappreciated; a longing for recognition that was heartbreakingly never fulfilled in her lifetime.

At the Royal Golden Wedding that autumn, the Queen reached out to the public. During her 50th anniversary dinner, she acknowledged the nation's shifting mood: 'I have done my best, with Prince Philip's constant love and help, to interpret it correctly in the years of our marriage and my reign. Together, as a family, we shall continue to try.'

The Royal Family, shaken and scarred, rallied around its matriarch, the Queen Mother, who, at a hundred, had become the first royal to reach such a milestone. She had first stood on the palace balcony in 1923 after her wedding, her family whole and imperial. Now, diminished by scandal and thinned by tragedy, they stood beside her to mark her centenary – her survival, and theirs.

The Queen Mother's final visit to the Castle of Mey in Scotland was filled with quiet longing. With her health fading, she desperately wished to see the Barnacle and Pink-footed Geese on their annual migration. Each day, she asked her housekeeper, Nancy, if there had been any sign of the geese, but the skies remained empty. On her final day, as she was about to leave, her wish came true. A vast flock soared over the castle in perfect timing; it was a spectacular fly-past. Her face lit up with joy; she had seen them one last time. She passed peacefully in her sleep of natural causes on 30 March 2002, aged 101, at her home, Royal Lodge in Windsor Great Park, with her daughter Elizabeth at her side.

The Queen Mother had watched the British Empire fade, and seen her family's popularity shrink, knowing that the glint of a heroic age kept them standing. For the public, there were three royal stars in the previous hundred years. The former Prince of Wales, Edward, who became the Duke of Windsor, and Diana, Princess of Wales, both burst and fell; hoisted by their own petard. Only the Queen Mother held steady, stoic, defiant, seeing it all through to the end.

The respected long-standing courtier, Lord Charteris, a guardian of the Crown who died in 1999, saw little hope in a future King Charles. Instead, he wished for the impossible. 'I've known the Queen now since November 1949,' he said. 'Simply for the sake of the monarchy, it is my firm view that the Queen should live forever.'[135]

CHAPTER 14

THE PROUD MEDDLER

He [Prince Charles] would readily embrace the political aspects of any contentious issue he was interested in . . . He often referred to himself as a dissident working against the prevailing political consensus.

MARK BOLLAND, 2006

In the days after Diana's death, Prince Charles's reputation lay in ruins. Public anger burned and his popularity hit rock bottom. He knew he could not be seen with Camilla – not yet anyway. He turned inward and focused on the only role that mattered – being a father. He cancelled engagements and cleared his schedule. He chose to stay close to William and Harry wherever possible; he was determined not to fail them, the way he had failed Diana. Years later, in 2023, Harry recalled in his book *Spare* a quiet dinner with his father. A rare moment of honesty. Charles looked across the table and said, 'I suppose it's my fault. I should have got you the help you needed years ago.' Harry clearly did not forget that. It was not everything, but it must have meant something.

Seven months after Diana's death, Charles took William and Harry on what was supposed to be a low-key private skiing trip to

Canada, hoping for some bonding time. But public appearances in Vancouver drew mixed reactions. Overwhelmed by the attention, William pushed back, and the press highlighted concerns about their public exposure so soon after the loss of their mother. Were the boys being used to bolster their father's battered image, his detractors asked?

Charles, meanwhile, told his staff that he remained resolute about Camilla. His spin-doctors let it be known that her role in his life was 'non-negotiable'. With crisis management and PR expert Mark Bolland's help, they carefully managed her introduction into public consciousness. Key milestones included the leaked story about Camilla and William enjoying a convivial meeting, as well as her appearing at events alongside Charles, such as that first staged photo-op of them leaving London's Ritz Hotel on 28 January 1999, after Camilla's sister Annabel Elliot's fiftieth birthday party.

It was their coming-out shot. After years in the shadows, the couple went public; shoulder to shoulder, headline ready. The message was crystal clear – this is real, get used to it. Eventually, on 9 June 2000 at King Constantine of Greece's sixtieth birthday party at Highgrove, Camilla had her first publicly acknowledged meeting with the Queen. A brief, polite encounter, which marked the start of a royal thaw after years of frosty distance.

The noise around Diana's death, however, was relentless. For her sons, it ripped open old wounds. They hated the attacks on their father. A year on, they called for an end to the 'Diana industry'. 'Constant reminders create nothing but pain,' they said in a statement. But Dodi's father Mohamed Fayed would not let go. He continued to push his wild unsubstantiated claims: Diana was pregnant, Philip ordered the hit, and the secret service made it happen.

On 2 October 2007, the final inquest into Diana's death opened at the Royal Courts of Justice, led by Lord Justice Scott Baker. Ten years after the crash in Paris, the court finally faced the storm of rumours, conspiracies, and questions that had never gone quiet. Scott Baker chose not to summon Prince Philip. Instead, his private secretary, Brigadier Sir Miles Hunt-Davis, took the stand. Fayed's testimony was long, angry – and empty. No proof. Just noise.[136]

Lord Justice Scott Baker called in the big gun: Sir Richard Dearlove, ex-head of MI6. Behind closed doors, Sir Richard shot down Mohamed Fayed's 'absurd allegation' that Prince Philip, Prince Charles, MI6, and Tony Blair plotted Diana and Dodi's deaths. 'It is completely off the map,' he said. Asked flat-out by Ian Burnett QC if he was aware that MI6 had ever assassinated anyone during his time with the Service from 1966 to 2004, Dearlove did not blink: 'No, I was not.'

Sir Richard told the inquest that MI6 had 'no interest whatsoever' in Diana and Dodi's romance. Surveillance? Bugging? 'Outside the function of the service,' he said. There were no MI6 files on Fayed, the Ritz, or Henri Paul. A rogue operation? 'An impossibility.' As head of MI6, he signed off every action needing Foreign Secretary approval – break-ins, stolen docs, the works.

Sir Richard, who served as 'C' from 1999 to 2004, also dismissed ex-agent Richard Tomlinson's claim of an MI6 plot to kill Slobodan Milosevic, though he admitted a low-level Balkan plan was 'killed stone dead'. As for David Shayler's allegation of a plot to assassinate Gaddafi? 'Not true,' he said, flatly.

Discredited but defiant, ex-MI5 intelligence officer Shayler had claimed publicly that MI6 paid to stage Diana and Dodi's fatal crash – just as, he alleged, they had tried with Gaddafi, using a 'surrogate'. Jailed in 1998 for leaking MI5 secrets to the

Mail on Sunday, he was convicted under the Official Secrets Act in 2002 and served six months. By 2007, he had declared himself the Messiah. His partner, ex-MI5 officer Annie Machon, echoed the theory in her 2005 book, *Spies, Lies and Whistleblowers*. She claimed MI6 did not want Diana dead, but injured – fearing her martyrdom if killed.

After a six-month hearing, and twenty-two hours of deliberation, on 7 April 2008 the inquest coroner ruled that Diana's death was due to 'grossly negligent driving', partly blaming the paparazzi who had chased the Mercedes driven by an intoxicated Henri Paul.[137]

A decade after her death, Harry retraced Diana's final route at 65 mph, the speed of her car in those last moments. He wrote that both he and William wanted the crash reinvestigated and they wanted the paparazzi jailed. But, he said, 'the powers that be' stopped them, though he never named names. Her sons read everything. They pored over the inquest. Harry even got the court dossier, and inside there was a pixelated image of their mother dying. The impact was brutal. 'I was astonished he was sent that,' said a close source. 'You couldn't see her face, but it was an image of her dying. Who could have possibly thought that was a good idea?'[138]

In 2002, five years after Diana's death, Elizabeth II's Golden Jubilee began on a sombre note. On 9 February, she lost her sister, Princess Margaret, who died aged seventy-one at King Edward VII's Hospital, London, after suffering a stroke. A few weeks later, the Queen Mother died too, her passing leaving Charles heartbroken. In a televised address, Charles called her 'the most magical grandmother'.

Doubts about Charles as the future king kept piling up. In the Queen's Jubilee year, he was hammered for his lavish lifestyle and controversial takes on GMOs (genetically modified organisms). The public winced at reports – never confirmed – that his valets squeezed exactly one inch of toothpaste onto his brush, pressed his pyjamas daily, ironed his shoelaces, and ran his bath to a precise temperature.

It all fed a portrait of pampered detachment. Polls showed growing support for Prince William leapfrogging his father as the next direct heir to the throne. For Charles and his team, the headlines stung. Their conclusion was quite clear: winning over the public would not come easy.[139]

At seventy-six, the Queen shut down talk of abdication. 'That's something I can't do,' she told Archbishop George Carey; words he later shared, clearly with her blessing.

Charles, too, was asked about the Crown. In a *60 Minutes* interview, he did not dodge – but did not lean in either. 'You don't necessarily want to be king . . . I think it's better not to think too much about it.'[140]

Still mourning her mother and sister, the Queen threw herself into duty. Her Golden Jubilee tour began with a sweep across the UK, capped on 3 June by the unforgettable 'Party at the Palace'. Queen guitarist Brian May blasted 'God Save the Queen' from the roof of Buckingham Palace. Charles then took the stage, saluting her as 'Your Majesty . . . Mummy', and called his mother a 'beacon of tradition and stability'.

The next day, she attended a national service of thanksgiving at St Paul's, joined by 2,500 guests – including forty-seven royals. At the Guildhall lunch that followed, she spoke from the heart, calling herself 'overwhelmed and deeply moved' by the public's warmth. She honoured Philip's 'invaluable contribution' and thanked her children, especially Charles, for their love and 'unstinting help' in a year shadowed by loss.

A 'river of gold' marked her journey along The Mall opposite the palace as 400 children waving gold streamers went with the Queen and Prince Philip to the royal box on the Queen Victoria Memorial. Charles and his sons, William and Harry, took thirty minutes to walk from St James's Palace, engaging with the crowds on their way. The jubilant parade followed, featuring 20,000 marchers, including floats, choirs, military representatives, and children from the Commonwealth nations in their national costumes.

In her Golden Jubilee speech, the Queen said it plainly: 'I cannot lead you into battle. I do not give you laws or administer justice, but I can do something else – I can give you my heart and my devotion to these old islands and to all the peoples of our brotherhood of nations.'

The celebrations closed with the Royal Family on the palace balcony as Concorde and the RAF Red Arrows roared overhead in BAE Hawk T1 jets, trailing red, white, and blue. A skyborne salute to the Union Jack – and to Elizabeth. Public support soared. A *Mail on Sunday* poll named the Queen as Britain's most respected figure. Her standing, once shaken by Diana's death, was fully restored.

Then a year later, Diana's former butler, Paul Burrell, echoed her *Panorama* line when he announced, 'There were three of us in this marriage: the Princess, myself and the secrets we shared.' In his tell-all book *A Royal Duty*, he cast himself as Diana's closest confidant – the man who knew it all. The most explosive claim was a handwritten note from Diana that read: 'This particular phase in my life is the most dangerous – [someone] is planning "an accident" in my car, brake failure and serious head injury in order to make the path clear for Charles to marry.' It was dynamite. And it poured fuel on the conspiracy fire that never quite went out.[141]

William and Harry condemned Burrell's actions as 'a cold and overt betrayal' of Diana. Amid the frenzy, the *Mail on Sunday* pursued a sex scandal story involving Charles, backed only by a sworn statement from his ex-valet George Smith and with no solid evidence, igniting a media frenzy regardless. The story centred on claims by Smith, an assistant valet, and deeply troubled Falklands war veteran, from October 1995. During a drive to Highgrove, he broke down and told staff member Elizabeth Burgess that a senior royal aide had raped him. Smith, who struggled with PTSD, substance abuse and mental health issues, also alleged he had seen a sexual incident involving Prince Charles.

By then, Smith was recovering at the Priory Hospital in Roehampton, south-west London, for treatment related to his alcohol dependency and mental health issues, funded by Charles. With a tape recorder in hand, Diana secretly visited him, with her fiercely loyal personal assistant Victoria Mendham, and captured his muddled allegations. She later confronted Charles about them in 1996.

The matter might have stayed buried, but Diana's tragic death in 1997 changed everything. After she died, Burrell was seen taking a mahogany box of her belongings, including letters and the tape of Smith's claims. He was subsequently charged with the theft of 310 items, worth about £5 million, alleged to have been stolen from Diana's home before her death. When the Queen disclosed that Burrell had previously told her he had taken some items for safekeeping, the trial collapsed. Burrell had then dropped hints about a final 'secret' that could shake the monarchy, fuelling wild speculation.

When George Smith's sex scandal claims finally gained media traction in 2003 in the *Mail on Sunday* and other newspapers, strict UK libel laws kept many of the details unpublished, though they were implied through suggestive reporting. This forced the Palace to act, and without specifying the claims, it said Smith's accusations had been investigated several times, including by the police and were unfounded. Still, the damage was done. Smith's allegations, no matter how tenuous, had split the royal mask. While his 'secrets' stayed buried, the Crown came under scrutiny like never before.

New allegations, denied by the palace, then surfaced against Michael Fawcett, Charles's trusted servant, around the same time. He was accused of selling royal gifts improperly and using the funds for personal gain. Fawcett was also said to have accepted lavish benefits from wealthy donors in exchange for favours, suggesting he had excessive influence within the prince's household.

Charles ordered an internal probe in March 2003, the Peat Inquiry, in a bid to exonerate him and his office of wrongdoing. But how could it be taken seriously? It was led by Sir Michael Peat, an honourable man but also Charles's principal private secretary – his most senior aide. Before that, Peat had been Keeper of the Privy Purse for the Queen; in other words, he was an inherent part of the system. The legal oversight was provided by Edmund Lawson, QC, a distinguished barrister known for his expertise in criminal law.

When the report dropped, it dismissed all the claims. But the inquiry found there was rot in the system, sloppy books and weak oversight. It declared that Fawcett had broken rules too. He had accepted royal gifts, but no crimes were nailed down. Fawcett resigned, making headlines, but then came back as a consultant. The press went on the attack.[142]

Charles's fitness to rule came under fire – again. Lord Wedderburn, a sharp legal mind and Labour peer, did not mince words. If nothing changed, he warned, Charles as king could spark a storm big enough to shake the monarchy itself. He was not alone. The pressure group Republic pushed the MP Brian Iddon to raise the alarm in Parliament. An early day motion hit the books, pointing to murky finances in the Duchy of Cornwall.[143]

Whenever Charles came under fire over the Duchy, he did not reflect on the privilege of having inherited a vast estate; instead, he privately lamented that it was only worth around £1 billion, and situated in less fashionable south-east London around Kennington, rather than in prime areas like Belgravia. By contrast, in 2016 his old friend the late Duke of Westminster, Gerald Grosvenor, passed on the Grosvenor Estate, then valued at around £9 billion, to his son Hugh, aged twenty-five, instantly making him one of the wealthiest men in Britain.[144]

Charles's tendency to involve himself in politics was another cause for concern, upsetting many politicians. A monarch is expected to remain above party politics; neutral in public, leading without overstepping constitutional limits. While the role includes approving laws, wars, treaties, and honours (except for personal awards like the Royal Victorian Order), this is meant to be ceremonial – a formality, not a forum for opinion. But as heir to the throne, Charles always had opinions: plenty of them and often strong ones. And he rarely kept them to himself.

Charles's political meddling raised alarm bells. As king, for example, would he have backed Tony Blair's ill-conceived Iraq War push, like his mother did? Many doubted it. 'It is hard to imagine,' some said, given his deep knowledge of the Gulf and ties to Arab leaders.

In a 2006 High Court case against the *Mail on Sunday*, Charles's former aide Mark Bolland called him 'a dissident working against the prevailing political consensus'. The comment came in a written statement that painted a prince unafraid to rattle cages.

Charles was no fan of Blair's closeness to George W. Bush during the 2003 Iraq War. He thought Blair had squandered a chance to build Arab consensus, leaning instead on the 'terrifying' Bush administration. Behind closed doors, he called Blair 'Bush's poodle' and slammed his lack of foresight – criticism voiced well before the war began.

Bolland had left Charles's service in 2003, but his testimony offered a rare look inside. He showed a man walking a tightrope; heir to the throne yet pushing limits. 'The prince's expressions of his views have often been regarded with concern by politicians,' Bolland said, noting frequent pushback from rattled officials.

Privately, Charles slammed Blair for ignoring intelligence that challenged the US–UK case for war and for brushing off Arab advice. He called Western-style democracy in Iraq a 'pipe dream', doomed by tribal loyalties. He urged cultural understanding and rejected the West's hawkish mindset. 'Charles foresaw the futility. Why didn't the politicians?' one confidant asked.

To the prince, the root of terrorism was the unresolved Israel–Palestine conflict; the 'real toxin'. He believed that embracing true Islam and tackling that crisis could defuse the rage. 'Remove the poison, and you remove the cause,' he often said. He mocked Blair as 'Our magnificent leader' and sided with Robin Cook, who resigned as Leader of the Commons in protest over flimsy claims of weapons of mass destruction and no UN mandate. Charles saw the war as naive, illegal, and driven by blind allegiance, those close to him said.[145]

As Prince of Wales, Charles had spent years building strong ties with Gulf rulers, with frequent visits to the UAE, Oman, Saudi Arabia, and Jordan. Critics pointed to human rights abuses, but he saw the relationships as vital for the defence of the realm, especially with US focus elsewhere.

Charles's support for Palestinian rights and push for West–Islamic understanding drew considerable fire. Some called him anti-Jewish or anti-American. He became a polarising figure. Known for his 'interventions', Charles once said, 'I don't see why politicians should think they have the monopoly of wisdom.' By the 2000s, diplomacy had left him jaded, so had the tabloids. He called them 'organs of depravity and deception', saving his harshest words for the *Mail on Sunday*: 'poisonous'.[146]

The solo overseas tours when he was heir became what Charles called a 'kaleidoscopic confusion' – a blur of meetings with caricature-like leaders promoting boring, unsustainable projects, while he lamented the modern architecture flashing past his convoys. Travelling at the Foreign Office's behest, he was often following in the wake of visits by the UK prime minister, and he grew frustrated by disjointed conversations with dreary politicians, rarely able to get a word in edgeways. When he visited India, he bemoaned the military and politicians' institutional paranoia, suspecting his motives at every turn.[147]

His warnings were ignored, adding to the frustration about his role. He often joked about his tours, comparing himself to the French singer Maurice Chevalier and thinking, 'Ah, yes, I remember it well,' when faced with familiar faces and tired old stories. In November 2001, in Riga, Latvia, sixteen-year-old Alina Lebedeva protested NATO by striking him with a carnation. Unharmed, he called for leniency and later joked about bearing scars from the crazed assault of a carnation-wielding Bolshevik.[148]

Charles was never going to be a passive observer. In February 2004, he visited Iraq, Iran and Saudi Arabia, after the invasion, engaging actively rather than just watching from afar. At Saddam Hussein's former Basra Palace, he met troops whose humour and resilience impressed him – surprising the prince with chocolate cake and biscuits. During a meeting with coalition officials in southern Iraq, he was incredulous to learn that one man had been placed in charge of tourism. Pressed further, the official clarified that he meant, hopefully, future tourism.[149]

On the same mission, Charles took a Hercules into Iraq. He had last visited Tehran in 1975 with Lord Mountbatten, en route to Nepal for King Birendra's coronation. Mountbatten had left delighted by the Shah's generous gift of caviar. Returning in 2004, he found the city shabby and subdued under strict religious rule. Excited to meet President Mohammad Khatami, a reformist leader (1997–2005), Charles later confided that Khatami faced an impossible task reconciling reforms with Sharia law. Their brief conversation, through an interpreter, touched on Islam's view of the West, but was frustratingly cut short just as it became intriguing. Following their discussion, Prince Charles travelled to Bam to observe earthquake recovery efforts.[150]

Charles's political 'interventions' flared back into view in 2015 with the 'black spider memos' – letters to ministers marked by his loopy handwriting and forceful tone. Rob Evans of the *Guardian* pushed for their release, backed by the newspaper's lawyers. He argued the public had a right to see how the prince tried to sway policy. Attorney General Dominic Grieve warned that disclosure could damage Charles's future neutrality as king.

Despite resistance, twenty-seven letters were released in May 2015 after a tribunal upheld the Supreme Court's ruling. The *Guardian* hailed it as a win for press freedom. But the letters were mostly dull, covering his insights on architecture and conservation. The legal battle cost taxpayers over £496,000, with £96,000 going to the left-leaning newspaper.

The case reignited questions about what kind of king Charles would be. Asked if he would keep campaigning as monarch, he replied, 'No, I'm not that stupid. Being sovereign is a separate exercise.' He shrugged off claims of meddling: 'If that's meddling, I'm proud of it,' calling his actions apolitical.

As king, he vowed to stay within constitutional bounds, acting only with ministerial backing – a promise he has kept.[151]

CHAPTER 15

SACRED VOWS

They [Charles and Camilla] have overcome Becher's Brook
and The Chair and all kinds of other terrible obstacles.
They have come through, and I'm very proud and wish them well.
My son is home and dry with the woman he loves.

QUEEN ELIZABETH II, 2005

The morning of 10 February 2005 was mild – 52°F (11°C) – as headlines hailed yachtswoman Ellen MacArthur's solo circumnavigation of the globe in seventy-one days. She returned to Falmouth a national hero. Some papers led with the Identity Cards Bill clearing its third reading in the Commons. Then came a dramatic twist. By afternoon, the London *Evening Standard* broke the news: Prince Charles was engaged to Camilla Parker Bowles. The story swept the front pages.

Confident in their scoop, the *Evening Standard* skipped Palace confirmation, wary of leaks. Editor Veronica Wadley, backed by Head of News Ian Walker, chose to 'publish and be damned'. They were right. The first edition hit with the headline: 'Charles to wed Camilla in the Spring'.

Clarence House panicked. Caught flat-footed, they rushed out a statement confirming the date. The paper's gamble paid off – it won the London Press Club's 'Scoop of the Year'.[152]

The episode laid bare just how unprepared the Palace was for both the announcement and the wedding. Legal rules forced the wedding to take place at Windsor Guildhall, as using the Castle would have meant opening it to public weddings. Public reaction was split. Diana's shadow still loomed.

Behind closed doors, William and Harry were not on board. They urged Charles to reconsider.[153] Harry, especially, struggled. He saw Camilla as 'the wicked stepmother':[154] the woman who had wrecked his mother's life.

But Charles's mind was made up and the boys came to accept the marriage, albeit grudgingly. It was tolerance, not affection, for the woman their mother had despised. In public, they played their part. William offered his 'delight' at their father's happiness. Harry called Camilla 'a wonderful woman' and claimed, 'William and I love her to bits.'

At a pre-wedding photocall at Klosters, in Switzerland, BBC royal correspondent Nicholas Witchell asked how they felt about the wedding. Charles snapped, 'I'm very glad you've heard of it,' then muttered to his sons, 'Bloody people. I can't bear that man. He's so awful.' The microphones placed in the snow at the royals' feet had caught it all. It marked another low in Charles's fraught relationship with the press – a resentment rooted in years of tabloid cynicism, especially during his bitter split from Diana.

The Queen and Philip did not attend the Guildhall ceremony, but later joined the Service of Prayer and Dedication at St George's Chapel, officiated by the Archbishop of Canterbury, Dr Rowan Williams, who had ruled out the possibility of a church wedding for the royal couple given the Church of England's cautious stance on remarriage after divorce. The date, first set at 8 April, was switched to the following day to allow Charles to represent the Queen at Pope John Paul II's funeral.

Charles and Camilla viewed the ceremony as a chance to atone for their past, publicly acknowledging their roles in each other's marital failures. They chose the sternest prayer of penitence from the 1662 Book of Common Prayer for their marriage blessing, beginning with, 'We acknowledge and bewail our manifold sins and wickedness.' At the reception, Charles thanked his 'dear mama' and praised his 'darling Camilla' for her unwavering support and humour. Camilla, serene in an Anna Valentine dress and a golden Philip Treacy headpiece, was triumphant.

Queen Elizabeth had the last word, likening Charles and Camilla's complex relationship to the Grand National, the world-famous horse race that took place on the same day, signalling her approval. She announced, 'Hedgehunter has won the race at Aintree,' and joyfully welcomed her son and his bride to the 'winners' enclosure' at Windsor. Many cheered; others were close to tears. For the prince, the day marked the end of his long loneliness. His soulmate was finally by his side, and while they still had much to prove to the public, it felt like a victory for love. Camilla's father, Major Bruce Shand, aged eighty-eight and ailing, delayed seeing a doctor until after the wedding. Desperate to see his daughter remarried, he sought help four days later, only to be diagnosed with pancreatic cancer, passing away fourteen months later.

Clarence House suggested Camilla would be titled 'Princess Consort', yet the *Evening Standard* boldly contradicted this. The 180-year-old newspaper's front-page scoop on the engagement accurately predicted she would become Queen Consort and reported she would not use the title Princess of Wales, out of respect for Diana, despite being entitled to it. Instead, she would be styled HRH The Duchess of Cornwall; a strategic choice to minimise backlash. Despite vague Palace briefings and unreliable leaks, the *Evening Standard* was ultimately vindicated.

The Queen was understandably relieved. After all, her uncle Edward VIII had been forced to renounce the throne for a divorcee, shaking the monarchy to its core. Now, the rules had changed, society had evolved, and the future king could marry the woman he loved. The monarchy had dodged a bullet. The Queen knew it, and so did Charles. Diana's devotees remained silent, quietly honouring her memory by laying flowers at the gates of Kensington Palace on the anniversary of her death instead.

Ultimately, they found redemption, but at a cost. Diana and Harry certainly felt sacrificed. Commander Patrick Jephson, LVO, Diana's former private secretary, offered a starkly different view. Speaking on Channel 4's *Queen Camilla: The Wicked Stepmother*, aired in December 2024, he remarked, 'Cynicism runs through the entire story. When the history of Charles and Camilla is written, it won't be seen as a glittering episode in the British monarchy. It will be the opposite – tatty, tawdry. A story of opportunism and extraordinary cruelty for those caught under the wheels of their inexorable, inevitable love story.'

Love won in the end. Through jeers, scandal, and scrutiny, Charles and Camilla held their ground. In April 2025, they celebrated twenty years of marriage in Rome, the Eternal City. A far cry from the drama of their beginnings, their bond now tells a different story: one of resilience, transformation, and mutual respect.

As a newspaper reporter, I was the first to break news of Charles's proposal, a move that once shook the monarchy. Today, it barely raises an eyebrow. The couple have grown into independent forces: united, yet self-sufficient. During Charles's cancer battle, Camilla stayed steady, tending to her own passions while supporting him. Their strength lies in their balance: together, but never tethered.

If Charles believed that after the wedding, he was home and dry and now in for a comfortable ride in the image stakes, he was wrong. On 7 July 2005 London experienced the devastating 7/7 suicide bombings, which sparked a surge in Islamophobia. In response, Charles expressed unwavering support for interfaith harmony and criticised the attackers as having 'nothing to do with true faith'.

Despite backlash and accusations of being a 'secret' Muslim by blinkered critics, he maintained that extremism is not exclusive to any one religion. His commitment to dialogue between faiths deserves credit. It has been a consistent theme throughout his life; emphasising commonalities and the importance of understanding in addressing religious tensions.

Soundbites from his speeches were taken out of context, claiming to show Charles's 'conversion'. In one entitled 'Islam and the West' from way back in 1993, he said, 'Islam can teach us today a way of understanding and living in the world which Christianity itself is poorer for having lost.' Bizarrely, this was quoted as proof he had abandoned his Christian faith.

In a 1997 article for the *Middle East Quarterly*[155] entitled 'Prince Charles of Arabia', scholars Ronni L. Gordon and David M. Stillman suggested that the prince had secretly converted to Islam, citing his public statements on Islamic law and the status of Muslim women. They concluded that if Charles continued his admiration for Islam and criticised British culture, his reign would lead to a 'different kind of monarchy'.

Despite the hostile atmosphere after the 7/7 attacks, Charles faced down his critics. Risking a backlash, he wrote a controversial commentary in the *Daily Mirror*. 'Some may think this cause is Islam. It is anything but. It is a perversion of traditional Islam. Islam preaches humanity, tolerance, and community, as do Christianity, Judaism, and all great faiths . . . Offended by good relations between faiths, extremists seek to tear apart our multicultural society.'

He flirted with various religions over the years, showing a particular admiration for the Orthodox Church and often retreating to the monasteries of Mount Athos in northern Greece. While some speculate about his faith, those close to him insist he has always stayed a practising Anglican. Back in 1994, he told his biographer Jonathan Dimbleby that he wanted to be seen as a 'Defender of Faith' when he was crowned, causing controversy. When it came to it, after all the speculation, at his coronation on 6 May 2023, Charles III took an oath to be 'Defender of *the* Faith', affirming his role as the Supreme Governor of the established Church of England.

To mark her eightieth birthday, Queen Elizabeth decided to celebrate with her immediate family on a private cruise of the Scottish Isles aboard the *Hebridean Princess* in July 2006. Unlike the royal yacht *Britannia*, retired in December 1997 after forty-four years, the former car-ferry-turned-luxury-vessel had only one dining room, meaning royals and staff had to muck in. When informed that staff would have to eat after the Royal Family had finished to avoid a clash, the Queen showed her instinctive consideration for others, insisting that both groups dine together, albeit on opposite sides of the room. Royals and staff even shared the breakfast buffet. While the Queen and Prince Philip were content with the arrangement, Prince Charles, who joined the voyage two days late, was less than pleased. 'There is a hierarchy, and he likes to stick to it, he is very Edwardian, upstairs downstairs, like that,' said a senior Household source.

The *Hebridean Princess*'s smaller size allowed it to access coves and beaches that the *Britannia* had been unable to reach, giving an excited Prince Philip the chance to plot a course to visit locations he had long wanted to explore. At one remote beach, the royal bodyguards, Dick Griffin and Tim Nash, arrived ahead of the party to carry out a reconnaissance, and encountered a family already relaxing there. Politely asking for their cooperation, they ensured the family respected the royals' privacy. The family complied, even as they later saw Charles discreetly changing out of his wet trunks with a towel wrapped around him after swimming. No photos were taken, and it was as though the royals had never been there.

Afterwards, the Queen sent one of her protection officers over to the family with a gift in gratitude for their respect. The father of the group accepted it graciously, though he remarked with disbelief that no one would ever believe what had just happened.

For the Queen and her family, the trip was not solely a celebration but also a rare chance to enjoy moments of relaxed privacy, reminiscent of the joyful times they had shared aboard the *Britannia*. Its decommissioning in 1997, the same year as Diana's death, had been a poignant loss for Her Majesty, who held a deep emotional attachment to the vessel, often describing it as the one place where she could truly unwind. Critics noted that she had not shed a tear over Diana at her funeral, but at the ceremony retiring the royal yacht on 11 December 1997 in Portsmouth, she was seen welling up, marking one of the rare occasions she displayed public emotion.

*

Prince William had kept his big news secret, even from the Queen and his father, making private plans with Catherine for their future. On 16 November 2010, he telephoned the Queen to announce that he and Catherine were now officially engaged. She was delighted. When asked by the press, Charles joked that the pair had been practising long enough.

On 9 December 2010, as Charles and Camilla travelled to the Royal Variety Performance, their car was attacked during student protests over tuition fee hikes. Protesters shouted, 'Off with their heads' and 'Tory scum', splattered the car with paint, cracked a window, and banged on the vehicle. Though unharmed, the visibly shaken couple, particularly Camilla, faced a rare and intense public confrontation, reflecting the anger over the controversial fee increases. Former royal protection officer Inspector Ken Wharfe criticised the security decisions, calling the use of a Rolls-Royce 'a challenge the crowd couldn't resist' and 'nothing short of stupidity', likening it to 'waving a red flag in front of a bull'.[156]

The Palace announced William and Catherine's wedding for 29 April 2011, at Westminster Abbey, a joyful event that would at last overshadow the sorrow of Diana's funeral in 1997. Privately, Charles was surprised, even 'a little irritated' that William had proposed to Catherine using the same 12-carat Ceylon sapphire and diamond ring from Garrard's 1981 catalogue, that he had presented to Diana on their engagement.[157]

The couple appeared unflappable as they exchanged vows, with William placing a band of Welsh gold on Catherine's finger. As they left the abbey, the Queen remarked it was 'amazing'. Catherine asked William, 'Are you happy?' He replied, 'I am so proud you're my wife.' A beautiful couple, happy and in love, they stood for a fresh start for the monarchy.

The next day, now the Duke and Duchess of Cambridge, the newlyweds flew off for a honeymoon at Charles's Welsh retreat, Llwynywermod, his 192-acre estate in Carmarthenshire, where they enjoyed a blissful few days at the restored eighteenth-century farmhouse. It was made even better that their secret escape and its location was never discovered or written about by the press.[158]

William then returned to his Royal Air Force duties, with the Palace spinning the line that the couple had not had a honeymoon as he was too busy. The couple issued a statement expressing gratitude for the support on 'the most wonderful day of our lives', with Catherine adding, 'I'm glad the weather held off. We had a wonderful day.' Their wedding was estimated to have helped generate an estimated £2 billion for the UK economy and was a global media sensation, enhancing 'Brand Britain' – as well as Brand Windsor – ahead of the Queen's Diamond Jubilee celebrations the following year.

Prince Philip hoped to stand alongside the Queen for the key Diamond Jubilee events, but the Thames River Pageant on 3 June 2012 took a toll on his health. In the freezing rain, the ninety-year-old stubbornly refused to sit, meaning the Queen, then eighty-six, had to stand too. Both had been reluctant to sit in the two red velvet-covered 'thrones', sticking to the monarchical principle prioritising visibility over personal comfort. Soon after, Philip was hospitalised for a bladder infection.

The next day brought the Diamond Jubilee Concert at Buckingham Palace. Charles paid a heartfelt tribute to his mother, starting with 'Mummy', which drew loud applause. He joked about the weather, then mentioned his father in the hospital, prompting cheers from the crowd. Turning to the Queen, he said, 'Your Majesty, a Diamond Jubilee is unique. Some of us have celebrated three with you. This is our chance to thank you and Father for your selfless service.' Charles's performance won praise in the newspapers.

The four days of celebration concluded with the Queen standing on the palace balcony, joined by only five family members: Charles, Camilla, William, Catherine, and Harry. It was a clear indication of the direction in which the monarchy was heading. The Duke of York, the Princess Royal, and the Earl and Countess of Wessex were notably displeased by the decision. There was a shared view among them that if Prince Philip had not been in hospital, it would never have been allowed to happen.

Philip rallied and made a comeback for the London 2012 Olympic Games, but his absence during the Jubilee events had sharpened focus at the palace. At ninety-one, it was clear he could no longer keep up the same pace. Charles and senior aides recognised that both his parents needed to slow down, allowing the younger generation to step in.

There were discussions of Charles taking on a 'Shadow King' role to give the Queen more private time with Philip, though the Palace insisted she would never abdicate or agree to a regency. Instead, the Queen would now be more selective in her duties, with younger royals stepping up and representing her more often.

The younger royals – particularly William, Catherine, and Harry – had already shown their star power during the Olympics, enthusiastically wearing Team GB T-shirts and rallying behind the athletes. Now, they were set to become even more prominent. Earlier in the year, Harry's well-received Jubilee visits to Jamaica and Brazil had also convinced many that he could be an asset to the 'Firm'.

Then two weeks after the Olympics, shocking photos were published on the website TMZ and in the *Sun*, showing 27-year-old Prince Harry naked apart from a wristwatch and a necklace, standing in front of a young woman who was also naked, after playing a game of strip billiards in his Las Vegas hotel suite. The press had a field day. Harry complained that it was an invasion of his privacy, but later apologised, saying he had let his family down. Despite Harry's misstep in Las Vegas, royal advisers still saw promise in him.

On 3 December 2012, William and Catherine capped off the Jubilee year by announcing they were expecting their first child. The news surprised even the Queen and Charles, as William had kept the pregnancy secret until Catherine was hospitalised with acute morning sickness. Charles captured the mood perfectly, expressing his excitement at becoming a grandfather.

When asked about the pregnancy as he was boarding HMS *Belfast* in London, where he was meeting Sir Ranulph Fiennes to wish him well on his latest Antarctic exhibition, Charles told reporters, 'I'm thrilled, marvellous. A very nice thought of grandfatherhood at my old age if I may say so. So that's splendid. And I'm very glad my daughter-in-law is getting better, thank goodness.'

Britain was in the grip of a heatwave when the royal baby Prince George was born on 22 July 2013. Exhausted but beaming, Catherine appeared with William at her side, showing off their son to a cheering crowd, while the Queen later travelled to Kensington Palace to meet her great-grandson, and direct heir, in a dark-green Bentley.

CHAPTER 16

THE EPSTEIN CONNECTION

I didn't sweat at the time because I had suffered what I would describe as an overdose of adrenalin in the Falklands War when I was shot at and I simply . . . it was almost impossible for me to sweat.

PRINCE ANDREW, DUKE OF YORK, 2019

On 9 September 2015, Queen Elizabeth became Britain's longest-reigning monarch – 63 years and 216 days. For her, it was business as usual. She marked the day by opening the Scottish Borders Railway with Prince Philip and Scotland's first minister Nicola Sturgeon at her side. In Parliament, Prime Minister David Cameron called her reign 'truly humbling'. True to form, she stayed modest: 'A long life can pass by many milestones, my own is no exception, but I thank you all for your kind messages.' She showed no sign of strain, but the weight of all that happened in her final years would test even her resolve.

No one predicted the disgrace that would later engulf her third child, Andrew – once the Queen's golden boy. In his twenties, he was the monarchy's blue-eyed charmer. Charles joked he had 'the Robert Redford looks of the family'. The nickname 'Randy

Andy', once playful, would age very badly. Linked to women such as *Dynasty* star Catherine Oxenberg, he earned a playboy reputation in his younger days. He was tipped to marry actress and model Koo Stark, but the romance fizzled out after her role in the risqué film *Emily* drew heat from both the press and Palace.

When Prime Minister Margaret Thatcher sent a Task Force to reclaim the Falklands in May 1982, Andrew went too as a Royal Navy lieutenant and helicopter pilot aboard HMS *Invincible*. Some said a royal prince should not go. The Queen stood firm: 'He's a serving officer. He must go, like the rest.' For royal PR, it was gold. Andrew flew Sea Kings on search-and-rescue and anti-ship missions. He came back a hero. Recalling the war, he said, 'We saw the ship hit, and [HMS] *Invincible* fire her missiles – a spectacular sight, but terrifying from where I was.' The Queen met him on the quay, both a proud mother and sovereign. Three decades later, the shine was gone. He had gone from hero to zero.

Prince Andrew and Sarah Ferguson had known each other since childhood, but it was Princess Diana who rekindled the spark in 1985. Diana, a friend of Sarah's, played matchmaker – inviting her to a gathering at Windsor Castle. Sarah and Andrew clicked, and things moved fast. He proposed in February 1986. They announced their engagement in March 1986 and married on 23 July the same year at Westminster Abbey.

The marriage did not last. Andrew's long stints at sea wore their relationship thin, and in 1992 it finally broke amid claims of fierce rows and infidelity. While on holiday in Saint-Tropez, Sarah was photographed in a compromising moment with her financial adviser, John Bryan. The *Daily Mirror* splashed the images of him kissing her feet – intimate, scandalous, and impossible to ignore. The news hit while she was at Balmoral with

© PA Images / Alamy Stock Photo

Before the wedding, Charles already had doubts. 'I desperately wanted to get out', he confessed. Diana's mood swings unsettled him; she feared he still loved Camilla. Yet on 29 July 1981, the fairytale rolled on. Crowds filled London. The pretty English girl became HRH The Princess of Wales, radiant in pearls and tulle. It looked perfect. But cracks were already showing.

© Tim Graham / Getty Images

© Anwar Hussein / Getty Images

Together they raised William and Harry. But by the time Harry was born on 15 September 1984, the marriage was broken. He drifted back to Camilla after Harry was born – a relationship Diana had long suspected. *Right:* Diana and Harry accompany William on his first day at Eton College.

Above: Princess Diana's death stunned the world. As crowds mourned outside Buckingham Palace, the Queen emerged – silent, solemn – to view the flowers. In Her Majesty's televised tribute at 6 p.m. on 5 September 1997, she praised the princess, saying: 'No one who knew Diana will ever forget her.' It steadied the Crown, and the country.

Right: On 10 February 2005, the author, Robert Jobson broke the scoop in the *Evening Standard*: Charles would marry Camilla. The wedding took place on 9 April. The Queen and Prince Philip skipped the civil ceremony but attended the service of prayer and dedication at St George's Chapel.

© Storms Media Group / Alamy Stock Photo

© Newsphoto / Alamy Stock Photo

William proposed to Catherine in October 2010 on a private trip to Kenya, using Diana's sapphire ring. Their engagement was announced on 16 November. They married on 29 April 2011 at Westminster Abbey.

© UPI / Alamy Stock Photo

On 22 July 2013, as Britain sweltered in a heatwave, Prince George was born. Exhausted but radiant, Catherine stood beside William to introduce their son to cheering crowds. The Queen later arrived at Kensington Palace in a dark-green Bentley to meet her great-grandson – and future king.

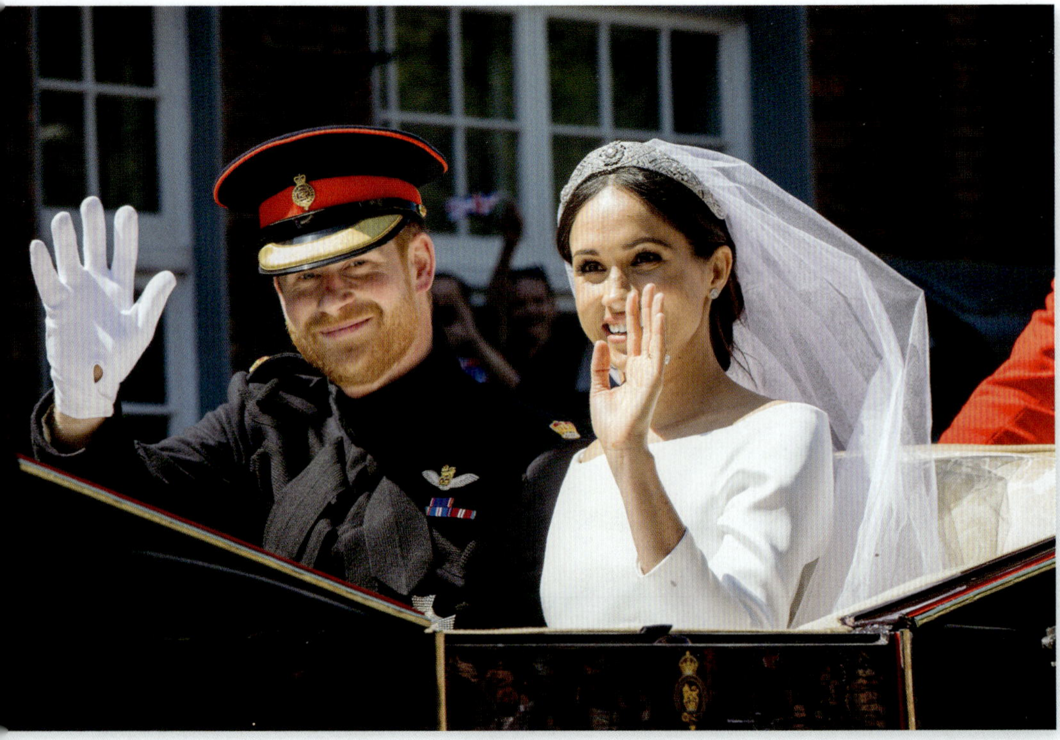

© David Betteridge / Alamy Stock Photo

On 19 May 2018, crowds filled Windsor as Harry married Meghan at St George's Chapel. Celebrities mingled with royals. TV host Oprah Winfrey was among them. It felt like a fairytale. But tensions followed. In March 2021, the couple's Oprah interview rocked the monarchy.

© Associated Press / Alamy Stock Photo

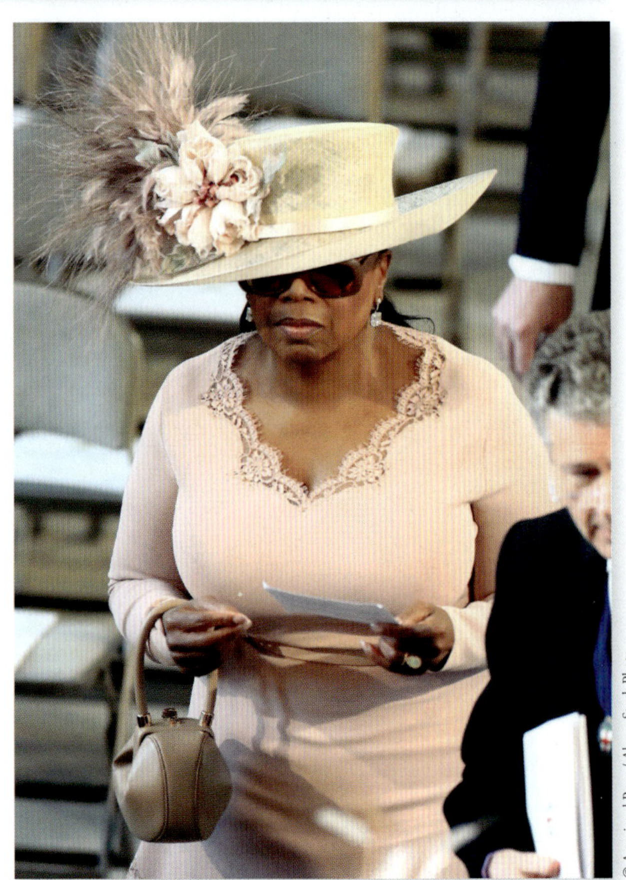

© WPA Pool / Getty Images

On 17 April 2021, the Queen sat alone as Prince Philip's coffin entered St George's Chapel, Covid rules keeping grief at a distance. After the service, Harry and William met their father. Charles pleaded, 'Please, boys, do not make my final years a misery.' It made no difference.

© PjrNews / Alamy Stock Photo

© Media Drum World / Alamy Stock Photo

On 8 September 2022, Buckingham Palace announced that Queen Elizabeth II had died peacefully at Balmoral aged 96. Her funeral marked history as well as the first public reunion of William and Harry since the split. Alongside their wives, Catherine and Meghan, they faced the crowds of mourners together.

Charles, in the golden supertunica, was crowned on 6 May 2023 at Westminster Abbey by the Archbishop of Canterbury, Justin Welby. William knelt in his Garter Robe and pledged loyalty. Prince George stood nearby as Page of Honour. In the third row, Harry watched, present but sidelined.

© Suzanne Plunkett / Getty Images

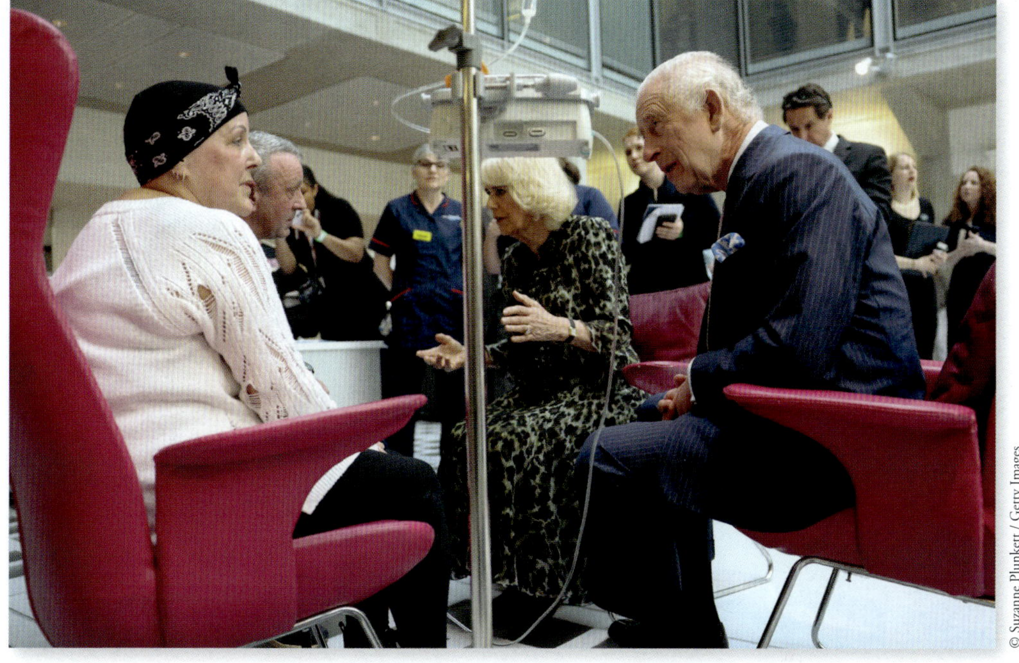

Two months after his cancer diagnosis, King Charles returned to public life on 30 April 2024 with a visit to University College Hospital's Macmillan Cancer Centre. Joined by Queen Camilla, he met patients and shared his own experience, 'It's always a bit of a shock when they tell you', he said.

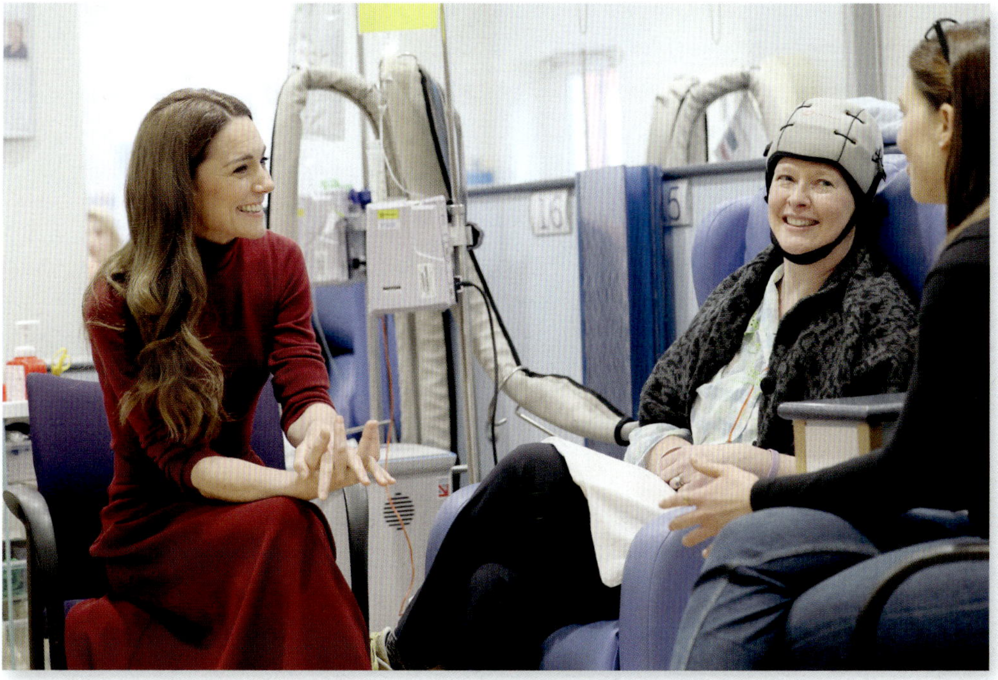

© Chris Jackson / Getty Images

In January 2025, Catherine, the Princess of Wales, made her first solo appearance since completing chemotherapy – visiting the Royal Marsden, where she had received treatment. She spoke candidly about the 'shock' of her diagnosis and her relief at being in remission.

Queen Elizabeth II stands at the centre of the Buckingham Palace balcony during Trooping the Colour 2019, surrounded by senior royals including Charles, Camilla, William, Catherine, Harry, and Meghan. One of the last pictures before the family's public royal rift began.

Changing of the old guard. The Royal Family gather on the Buckingham Palace balcony for the 80th anniversary of VE Day, May 2025. The absence of the late Queen Elizabeth after her death in 2022, Harry and Meghan, and Prince Andrew marks a visible shift in the shape – and future – of the Windsor legacy.

her children, a guest of the Queen. Humiliated, Sarah packed her bags and left the royal retreat in disgrace.

The Yorks finally divorced in May 1996 but maintained a close relationship. Post-divorce, they won praise for the way they raised their daughters Beatrice and Eugenie together. Others questioned their odd lifestyle, stuck living together out of routine, need, and old feelings. But in his private life Andrew soon slipped back into bachelor mode. He dated a string of women and became a fixture on the social circuit.

Andrew left the Royal Navy and took on a new mission, as the UK trade envoy. The post was official but not ministerial. No pay, just access. Appointed in 2001 by the Department of Trade and Industry, he was tasked with flying the flag for British business – selling exports, chasing investment, and shaking hands. His royal title opened doors, especially in the Gulf, Asia, and boom markets. He lived large, with deals by day and parties by night. But the flash came at a cost: dubious friends, blurred lines, and rising heat.

Andrew's taste for massages on the road was no secret – always female, always attractive, by his request. On a business trip to New York, he asked an aide to book an in-room massage. When the therapist arrived, a larger woman, he cut it short within minutes and sent her away immediately.[159]

The Epstein scandal flared in 2010, when Prince Andrew was photographed strolling through Central Park with the disgraced financier and convicted sex offender Jeffrey Epstein – after Epstein's release from prison. Andrew later claimed their meetings were rare, but records showed otherwise. They met numerous times, starting in 1999, and Andrew stayed at Epstein's homes in New York, Palm Beach, and the Virgin Islands. In 2000, Andrew even hosted a party for Epstein and his girlfriend Ghislaine Maxwell at Sandringham, apparently for her thirty-ninth birthday. Staff were stunned to discover the bathrooms were stocked not only with toiletries, but poppers, lube, and condoms.[160]

In 2000, Andrew and Epstein partied with Donald Trump at Mar-a-Lago. A year later, Andrew was photographed lounging with topless young women on a yacht trip with Epstein to Thailand. Andrew's bond with Ghislaine Maxwell deepened too. They were regulars at parties and weddings – even a 'hookers and pimps' themed bash.

Jeffrey Epstein's world began to crumble in 2005 with allegations of sex abuse, but despite an arrest warrant in 2006, he showed up at Princess Beatrice's lavish, 1920s-themed eighteenth birthday party at Windsor Castle. This was not a casual friendship. In 2008, Epstein struck a plea deal and served thirteen months in jail. Unwisely, Andrew stayed in touch. The 2010 Central Park photo of him walking with the convicted felon lit a firestorm.

By 2011, under mounting media heat, Andrew stepped down from his government role as UK Trade Envoy. That same year, Virginia Giuffre – then called Virginia Roberts – a survivor of Epstein's sex trafficking ring, first accused Andrew of abuse. He denied ever meeting her.

Roberts had endured years under Epstein's control. When she turned nineteen, he had lost interest; she was 'too old' in his eyes. To break free, she convinced him to pay for massage training in Thailand. But it was a cover. She met her future husband Robert Giuffre and fled to Australia, leaving Epstein behind for good.

Her claims gained wider public attention in 2015, when she named Andrew in court documents as someone to whom she was trafficked by Epstein. She alleged that the duke had sex with her when she was seventeen. An email exchange showed Andrew seeking Maxwell's advice, writing, 'Got some specific questions to ask you about Virginia Roberts.' Maxwell responded, 'Have some info. Call me when you have a moment.'

From then on Andrew clung to his familiar line: 'no recollection'. Palace spin and friendly voices cast doubt on a photograph showing him with his arm around Giuffre at Maxwell's London home. But on the BBC's *Panorama*, Giuffre stood firm. The photograph was real, she insisted. She had handed the original to the FBI in 2011. 'There's a date on the back from when it was printed,' she added, unshaken and unwavering.

In 2019, Giuffre's allegations resurfaced with sharper detail. She specifically described three encounters with Andrew.

The first: 10 March 2001, after dancing at Tramp nightclub, and ending at Maxwell's London home. Andrew denied it, claiming he was at Pizza Express in Woking with Princess Beatrice attending a children's party. But a witness placed him at Tramp. The second: Epstein's New York mansion. Giuffre said they had sex, and Epstein paid her $400. Andrew again denied it, citing official duties, though an aide admitted there were 'gaps' in his schedule. The third: Epstein's private island, Little St James, where Giuffre alleged there was an orgy involving Andrew, Epstein and young girls – some appearing underage. Andrew denied all of it. Later, some claims were struck from US court records.

Epstein's flight logs showed Andrew flew on his private jet multiple times between 1999 and 2005. Channel 4 *Dispatches* has reported that Giuffre was in London on the date she alleges she was trafficked to Andrew. They also revealed that Epstein met the Duchess of York and her daughters in Nassau in 1998. Sarah later admitted to accepting £15,000 from him – eighteen months after his conviction – to help with her £5 million debt. She called it a 'gigantic error of judgment', expressed regret, and promised to repay the money. She also acknowledged meeting Epstein on several occasions and described her actions as a 'huge mistake'.[161]

Andrew's troubles deepened after Epstein's apparent suicide on 10 August 2019 in a New York jail. The death set off a storm, with missing footage, inattentive guards, and rising cries of a cover-up. Amid the fallout, Andrew issued a statement. He expressed sympathy for Epstein's victims, condemned exploitation, and signed it simply, 'Andrew'. It was the third Palace statement that month. Behind the scenes, he had privately assured both Prince Charles and the Queen of his innocence. But by now palace courtiers were growing uneasy. The walls were beginning to close in.

In 2019, Virginia Giuffre went public again, with a press conference, NBC's *Dateline*, the works. She accused Andrew of sexual abuse and urged him to 'come clean'. Again, Andrew denied it, but finally admitted he had made a 'mistake' meeting Epstein in 2010 after his conviction.

Under mounting pressure, he agreed to a BBC *Newsnight* interview. His private secretary, Amanda Thirsk, backed the move, hoping it would clear his name. Afterwards he told the Queen it went well. It had not. The interview aired on 16 November. It was a total disaster.

His awkward answers, like his 'Pizza Express' alibi, claiming he could not sweat and saying he did not recall meeting Giuffre, made things progressively worse. The backlash was brutal and ruined what was left of his reputation. The public and press tore it apart. Within days, charities and businesses dropped him. Andrew's royal role was finished.

Historian Sir Anthony Seldon warned the interview had damaged the monarchy. SNP MP Hannah Bardell called it 'sickening', slamming Andrew for showing no remorse towards Epstein's victims. As public outrage exploded, the Royal Family closed ranks. Prince Charles, on tour in New Zealand, made urgent late-night calls to the Queen. The institution was in crisis mode. Charles insisted that Andrew had to be cut adrift.

The Queen acted swiftly to protect the monarchy, although she was still a devoted mother.

The Palace issued an announcement on 20 November 2019 saying Andrew was stepping back from public duties voluntarily, with the Queen's permission. In reality it meant he ceased public engagements and official roles as a working royal. As it was being issued, Her Majesty put on a brave face. Simultaneously she arrived at an engagement to present an award to Sir David Attenborough for *Blue Planet II* at Chatham House in central London. She smiled broadly as the revered natural historian and filmmaker greeted her. Dressed in a pink suit, she marked her seventy-second wedding anniversary apart from Prince Philip, who stayed at Sandringham. For the next two years Andrew and his legal team fought to clear his name, but despite all the bluster in January 2022, as pressure intensified due to Giuffre's lawsuit moving forward to a US court, the Palace power brokers decided enough was enough.

But before Buckingham Palace announced Andrew's loss of military titles and patronages on 13 January, the Queen arranged to have a private one-to-one meeting with him to soften the blow. Senior courtiers, however, intervened. They insisted on being there.

When Andrew arrived, he was confronted not just by his mother, but also by Sir Edward Young, her private secretary, and Sir Michael Stevens, Keeper of the Privy Purse. The two senior courtiers told the Queen it was imperative that they witnessed the conversation. It was a painful moment for both mother and son. Andrew understandably felt blindsided, though this was far from her intention, as sources close to her confirmed.

The Falklands War veteran was stripped of using HRH in official settings, all honorary military roles, and royal patronages, including Colonel of the Grenadier Guards, in a decision unambiguously decreed from the very top.

Cast out, he was barred from wearing the uniforms, insignia, or regalia tied to these honorary roles and could no longer be addressed by their titles. Humiliated, he was left with only the South Atlantic Medal for the Falklands War and his royal jubilee medals; an emotional downfall for the once-prominent proud prince.

A few weeks later in February 2022 on the advice of his legal team, Prince Andrew settled out of court with Virginia Roberts Giuffre for an undisclosed amount, reported to be around £12 million. The deal included a donation to her charity but no admission of liability. Andrew expressed regret for his Epstein ties, praised the survivors' bravery, and pledged to combat trafficking, but denied abuse.

Critics argued it stalled accountability, while shielding the Royal Family from deeper embarrassment. But the move did little to restore his standing, instead leaving many questions unanswered. The *Guardian* commented on the wording of the settlement, noting its careful distancing from any admission of responsibility: 'See how careful it is to put distance between an acknowledgement of Roberts Giuffre's pain – and any responsibility he may or may not have had for it.'

With the settlement agreed, the palace spin-doctors shifted focus to the Queen's Platinum Jubilee, celebrating her seventy-year reign. Courtiers had little time for Andrew, now a much-diminished figure, and did not hold back in briefing the press against him. He was absent from public events in June due to the Epstein fallout. Initially, he was expected to attend some private family events, but just before the celebrations, he tested positive for COVID-19, which conveniently further limited his participation. His absence ensured the spotlight remained firmly on the Queen.

Andrew's royal life was over, though he would not retreat quietly. The Queen stood by him, loyal to the end, even having him escort her at Westminster Abbey for the memorial service for Prince Philip in March 2022, a rare public moment for the prince. In her final days, she kept him close, shielding him as palace insiders continued to push for his total exile. She confided her support to a trusted confidant, 'You have to remember, he is my son.' With the Queen's death, he lost his strongest ally.

Andrew had held onto his residence at Royal Lodge, a Grade II listed house in Windsor Great Park, since 2002, secured with a 75-year lease. This irked Charles, who had once hoped to claim for himself the property that his beloved late grandmother had called home.

Once, when Charles needed a place to change before a polo match, he called at Royal Lodge, after it had undergone a £7.5 million makeover. Charles admired the tasteful design, except the dining room, where Andrew's touch was unmistakable. He had no idea, however, that Andrew had turned their grandmother Queen Elizabeth's bedroom, where she had died, into a cinema room.[162]

Andrew agreed to pay £1 million upfront for the Royal Lodge lease, with £400,000 annually for upkeep. But when King Charles cut his allowance and security funding to tighten royal spending, Andrew faced mounting financial strain. His Royal

Navy pension and investments fell short. Hoping Middle East ventures would pay off, he requested more time to prove he could meet his obligations.

Negotiations between the brothers became quite heated after the Queen died. During one meeting at Windsor Castle, attended by representatives on both sides, Andrew reminded Charles that his mother had given it to him to use and he intended to stay put, no matter what. What Andrew did not know was that after Charles became king, he even toyed with the idea that it would be a perfect residence for his wife, Camilla, should he predecease her.

Instead, he quietly purchased a £3 million property next to Queen Camilla's beloved Wiltshire retreat, Ray Mill House, in March 2025 to prevent it from being turned into a noisy wedding venue. Camilla had treasured her private sanctuary for thirty years, and buying it spared her from any future disruptions and gave her the privacy she desired.[163] Eventually, Andrew negotiated a deal with the King, allowing him to stay at Royal Lodge on adjusted terms.

Despite pressure from Prince William and senior advisers to distance Prince Andrew, in December 2023, King Charles, moved by compassion for his disgraced brother, invited Andrew and his ex-wife Sarah to the Sandringham Christmas gathering. Andrew was included in private family events, and even joined the royals on their public church walk, engaging with the crowds.

Scandal seemed to cling to Andrew. On 12 December 2024, a special tribunal led by Mr Justice Bourne upheld the Home Secretary's decision to bar a Chinese businessman – then anonymised as 'H6' – from the UK on national-security grounds. Judges said H6 had won an unusually high degree of trust from a senior royal and that, given Andrew's circumstances, such access could be misused. The Home Office case pointed to H6's links with the Chinese Communist Party and its United Front Work Department and warned his relationship with Andrew could be leveraged.

Court papers and reporting showed how close the access had become: H6 was invited to Andrew's 60th birthday in 2020 and was authorised to help scope an investment initiative aimed at Chinese partners. An aide, Dominic Hampshire, encouraged that role; internal documents recorded discreet meetings and the duke's vulnerability at the time. Andrew's office later said contact ceased once officials raised concerns; H6 denied being a spy. The Special Immigration Appeal Commission later confirmed that the anonymised 'C Initiative' in the judgment referred to Pitch@Palace.

The *Daily Mail* later claimed that China viewed Andrew as a 'useful idiot', with ties dating back to 2001 when he became the UK trade envoy. His visits to China had increased after 2010 under David Cameron's pro-China agenda, including trips hosted by the CCP-linked CPIFA. Critics accused him of aiding Beijing's goals via his Pitch@Palace business project, though supporters called it routine diplomacy aligned with government trade policy.[164]

H6, later identified as Yang Tengbo, expertly infiltrated British high society. Posing as a pro-UK businessperson, he gained access to top institutions, visited palaces, co-owned a business with Britain's 'most connected woman', helped expand the King's alma mater to China, and invested alongside Lady Barbara Judge in British industry. Tory MP Tom Tugendhat described Andrew succinctly, saying, 'He's been an idiot for many years.' Few within or outside the Royal Household would dispute that assessment.[165]

The Duke and Duchess of York decided to skip the 2024 Norfolk Christmas celebrations to avoid further embarrassment for the King. Instead, they stayed at Royal Lodge. But they were back in the fold, making a joint appearance alongside the Royal Family at the Easter Sunday service at St George's Chapel, Windsor Castle, in April 2025.

Virginia Giuffre eventually settled on a remote farm in Neergabby, fifty miles north of Perth, Australia, with her husband and three children, running SOAR (Speak Out, Act, Reclaim) to support victims of sex trafficking. After Ghislaine Maxwell was convicted in 2021 for recruiting and grooming girls for Epstein, Giuffre warned, 'It's definitely not over.' But all the years of fighting took their toll.

In March 2025, in a bizarre incident, Giuffre posted on social media that she had only days to live after a crash with a school bus, but police dismissed it as 'minor'. Her family said she was 'banged up and bruised' by the accident and she worsened in the weeks that followed. On 25 April 2025, Virginia Giuffre was found dead by suicide at her farm, aged forty-one. Her family said she 'took her own life after a long battle with the scars left by her abusers.' Despite his repeated denials, Prince Andrew's reputation remains tarnished by the Epstein connection. Giuffre's tragic end sealed Prince Andrew's fate casting a permanent shadow over his denials. Her death became the final word in a royal scandal he had hoped would fade. The undisclosed settlement now looked like silence bought, not vindication. Sympathy swung to her, and with it, public judgement. The Palace remained quiet. Andrew had no defence left – only disgrace.

CHAPTER 17

TIME'S UP

Maybe people know this and maybe they don't, but the term 'Megxit' was or is a misogynistic term.

PRINCE HARRY, 2021

At 11 p.m. on 31 January 2020, it was done. Britain left the European Union. This sovereign island nation, part of Europe's collective governing framework since 1973, now stood alone again. Four years earlier, the *Sun* newspaper had stirred controversy by claiming the Queen had backed 'Brexit' – a blend of 'Britain' and 'exit' – but Buckingham Palace swiftly denied it. Her true position remained a mystery. When the 2016 referendum came, 51.89 per cent voted to leave the European Union.

Charles, then still heir to the throne, privately called the decision 'madness', blaming it on voter ignorance. His remarks, to his close circle, reflected his deep unease with the decision. 'They didn't know what they were doing,' he confided to a friend. On this issue, for once, at that moment he was out of step with the nation.[166]

As Britain grappled with the Brexit fallout, Meghan Markle

stepped onto the royal stage. Within a few years, this beautiful actress would shatter long-standing traditions, bend rules, and shake the monarchy to its core. The new phrase 'Megxit' entered the lexicon; maybe not the *Oxford English Dictionary*, but every tabloid headline about her.

The spark of it all? A blind date with Charles's second son, Harry, in July 2016. The prince was smitten instantly with the American actress, a divorcee three years and six months his senior. The stars aligned when they met, he said. She claimed she barely knew anything about the royals and his world, hoping only for a man in the UK who was kind. Who knows the truth, but she knew enough about the British royals to have asked a friend to take a photo of her outside the palace as a tourist several years earlier.

Even before Meghan's arrival on the scene, Prince Harry had gained a reputation as a rogue royal. He spoke bluntly about the futility of his role in William's shadow. 'Willy was the Heir; I was the Spare,' he wrote in his memoir years later, noting the term was not media spin, it came from his family. 'I was there for backup, distraction, or, if needed, spare parts, kidney, blood, bone marrow,' he claimed. 'It was made clear from the start.'[167]

In 2002, when Harry was seventeen, the now-defunct *News of the World* had dropped a bombshell: Harry's cannabis abuse and underage drinking. The headline, 'Harry's Drugs Shame', caused a media firestorm.

The *News of the World* also claimed that Harry been banned from his local pub, the Rattlebone Inn, after getting drunk and insulting a French chef who worked there, calling him a 'f***ing frog'. Harry's underage drinking had alarmed Charles's protection officers, who, uneasy with the pub's illegal, after-hours lock-ins, tipped off the local police and warned Highgrove staff to steer clear of the place.[168]

In his memoir *Spare*, Harry later clarified his drug abuse, denying smoking weed at Highgrove but digging himself in deeper by admitting to cocaine, cannabis, and magic mushrooms elsewhere. He said that he had tried cocaine as a teenager but claimed it 'wasn't very fun, but it made me feel different'. He admitted smoking weed at Kensington Palace, and said he hallucinated on magic mushrooms. It was his way, he said, to escape reality.[169]

When the *News of the World* labelled Harry a 'drug addict', Mark Bolland, Charles's savvy PR man, instinctively knew he needed to act fast for the sake of the monarchy and Charles's reputation. While Harry dismissed the drugs claims as 'basic teenage stuff', the palace PR man struck a cloak-and-dagger deal with the tabloid's editor, Rebekah Wade (later Rebekah Brooks), a friend whom he and his partner Guy Black had holidayed with.[170]

Between the pair of them, a back story was spun to shield Prince Charles. The new narrative cast him as a devoted father, who sent his wayward son Harry to rehabilitation at Featherstone Lodge, in Peckham, south London, a facility for drug dependency. The move drew praise: Addaction called it 'swift and effective', and Tony Blair commended Charles for handling it 'responsibly and sensitively'. The Press Complaints Commission, led by Bolland's partner Guy Black, defended the coverage as being in the 'public interest', but cautioned against overreach. The Clarence House PR team then shut down further questions, declaring firmly, 'This is a family matter and now closed.'

Understandably, Harry was furious. He felt he was being used to polish his father's image. Yes, he had visited the rehabilitation centre, but it had happened weeks earlier for charity work with his aide and friend Mark Dyer alongside him, not his father. The tabloid spin, he said, had turned him into a pawn in a squalid game. Later, in *Spare*, he called it a 'total stitch-up' and wrote that he felt 'thrown under the bus'.[171]

The Palace had created a tidy narrative: Charles, a responsible single father, tackling his teenage son's reckless behaviour. Clever spin, Harry called it. Speaking to ITV's Tom Bradby years later, it still irritated him. Harry said bluntly: 'There comes a point when members of the family get in bed with the devil to salvage their image. The moment it's at my expense, I draw the line.'[172]

Then in January 2005, the *Sun* splashed a photo of Harry in a Nazi uniform on its front page under the banner headline, 'Harry the Nazi'. The damning image showed him in a German Afrika Korps outfit, swastika armband and all, holding a drink and a cigarette. He was wearing it to attend a friend Richard Meade's 'colonial native' fancy-dress party near Highgrove. When the photo was leaked to the press, the backlash was immediate. Harry called it a foolish mistake and issued a swift apology.

Years later, in his memoir *Spare*, he revisited the scandal, trying to shift some of the blame onto William and Catherine. He claimed the pair encouraged him to wear the outfit and 'howled' with laughter at the costume. Did they force him to dress that way? Of course, they did not. His pathetic excuses only deepened the controversy.

In 2009, Harry faced fresh outrage after a self-shot video appeared of him referring to a fellow army officer cadet as 'our little P*ki friend'. The racist slur, revealed by the *News of the World*, sparked public fury. Harry was pressurised into apologising again, but insisted the remark was made 'without malice'. The

Army sent him to equality training, but the incident left another dent in his public image.

His escapades continued. In August 2012, Harry's trip to Las Vegas had ignited a scandal when those naked photos were leaked of him playing strip billiards with friends and strangers. The *Sun* had published the photos, sparking a debate on press freedom versus privacy. Over 3,600 complaints flooded in, but the beleaguered PCC refused to act without Harry's formal complaint. The Palace stayed quiet, pointing out that Harry was about to be deployed to Afghanistan for his second tour of duty.

Despite the odd clash with the paparazzi, Harry soon rebuilt his image, over time becoming the most popular member of the Royal Family in opinion polls. He founded the Invictus Games for wounded, injured and sick military service personnel in 2014, before leaving the Army on 19 June 2015, after serving for ten years and rising to the rank of captain. He then made solo official visits to Australia and New Zealand, and followed up with a tour of the Caribbean in November 2016, where he received rave reviews, showcasing his human and compassionate side.

Teaming up with William and Catherine, he helped to launch the Heads Together campaign to tackle mental health stigma. William focused on young men, Harry on veterans, and Catherine on children. The public loved it. But Harry later admitted the harmony between the three of them began to unravel when Meghan entered the picture.

When Harry told William and Catherine he was dating the *Suits* star Meghan Markle, their jaws dropped. William, a fan of the popular legal TV drama, seemed impressed and blurted, 'F**k off?' in disbelief. Ever since Diana's death, William had always looked out for his younger brother, so he naturally worried about Harry's whirlwind romance. When he voiced concern over its speed, Harry felt defensive and protective, perhaps seeing it as a betrayal. It marked the start of a rift between the brothers that never healed.

Meghan Markle, a staunch feminist and advocate for women's empowerment, who famously challenged a sexist TV advert at just eleven, embraced her biracial identity. With a white father, Thomas Markle Sr, and a black mother, Doria Ragland, she spoke openly about racism and the complexities of being of dual heritage; reflecting on how it shaped her life and public feeling even before meeting Harry.

Harry was in awe of Meghan and found her inspirational, captivated by her strength and fearless commitment to speaking out for what she believed in. She did not seem bothered about his royal status either, which he liked. She only asked if he was kind, before agreeing to date him. However, Ninaki Priddy, her friend since childhood, later claimed that Meghan always had her sights set on royalty, calling Harry her greatest prize.[173]

Weeks after their first two dates, Harry invited Meghan to Botswana, camping under the stars. Their love grew stronger away from prying eyes in Africa, a place Harry had embraced ever since he dated his Zimbabwean-born heiress girlfriend, Chelsy Davy.[174] By October, their secret was out, and Harry felt the need to defend Meghan from the over-intrusive press, issuing a statement condemning media harassment. After New Year's Eve in London, Harry whisked Meghan away to Norway to see the Northern Lights, planning every detail to the letter himself to make it perfect.

By early 2017, Meghan had met Catherine and her daughter Charlotte, and they got on well. In *Vanity Fair*, Meghan spoke of her relationship with Harry, declaring simply, 'We're in love.' Meghan then joined Harry at the Invictus Games in Toronto, sharing a public stage and a very public kiss. Weeks later, on 27 November, the loved-up couple announced their engagement with a photoshoot and interview with the BBC's Mishal Husain.

When asked by the press about Harry and Meghan's engagement, Catherine, who was on an official visit to the Foundling Museum, smiled and said, 'William and I are absolutely thrilled. It's such exciting news. It's a happy time for any couple, and we wish them all the best and hope they enjoy this happy moment.'

Privately, though, William was uneasy. He thought Harry was moving too fast and did not know Meghan well enough. Harry took this as an insult, and tensions flared. While William did not explicitly warn him against marrying her, Harry interpreted his comments as scepticism about his new girlfriend Meghan's fitness for royal life.[175]

Charles initially thought Meghan was good for Harry. She pressed all the right buttons, said the right things. He liked her, as did Camilla. But by the time of the engagement announcement, his enthusiasm seemed to have waned. When staff offered their congratulations, his response was notably restrained.

Meghan was seen by the public as a breath of fresh air, charming, smart and erudite. The feedback during her whirlwind pre-wedding tour with Harry was positive. Even the Queen's corgis seemed charmed, too. Meanwhile, William debuted a buzz cut, keen to reclaim the spotlight.

What followed rattled the monarchy. Outwardly, all seemed well. William was asked to be Harry's best man. But behind the scenes, Harry was tense, his moods erratic. Charles, footing the bill for the Windsor wedding, noted Harry's sudden deference, but wrestled with the volatile tempers of both sons, a painful echo of his years with Diana.

Then came the tiara trouble. Meghan wanted a specific tiara, but the Queen's trusted dresser, Angela Kelly, refused over concerns about its Russian origins. She settled for Queen Mary's diamond bandeau. Then William intervened, urging the Queen to restrict Diana's jewellery to Catherine, the future queen.

The stress was eating away at them. Harry and Meghan were getting treatments from celebrity acupuncturist Ross Barr, but staff noted that Harry stayed on edge, petulant and short-tempered. He even snapped at Kelly, leading the Queen to explain to Harry that the tiara could not be used by Meghan; it was not only a question of provenance, but also due to seniority. What had upset Harry is that Kelly had insisted he sign a form for the tiara, and he thought she was impertinent. She reportedly tore it up to calm him.[176]

'Angela was very special to Her Majesty,' a senior insider pointed out. 'When Her Majesty heard what had happened, she was very disappointed.' Rumours swirled that Meghan was demanding, but it was Harry, trying too hard to make everything perfect, who was the one making waves.

The press had dubbed William, Catherine, Harry, and Meghan the 'Fab Four', but cracks appeared at Sandringham in 2017. Charles praised Meghan as 'intelligent and nice', but warned Harry that money was tight, despite significant support. Harry was smitten with Meghan's confidence, but the Duke and Duchess of Cambridge seemed uneasy. Tensions flared when Meghan borrowed Catherine's lip gloss, leaving her grimacing. Later, William called Meghan 'rude', prompting her sharp reply, 'Take your finger out of my face.'

Pre-wedding tensions ran high. Meghan's 'baby brain' comment to Catherine, fresh from giving birth to Louis, upset the princess, and tears were shed over Charlotte's bridesmaid tights – though who cried is still debated. By the time William was confirmed as best man, relations had soured. Harry was tense and snappy.

Days before Meghan's wedding, her father Thomas was caught staging paparazzi photos. Meghan was reportedly 'disturbed' and 'disappointed'. Amid the fallout, Thomas announced via TMZ he would not attend the ceremony, citing a heart attack.

Thousands lined the streets in Windsor on 19 May 2018, cheering as the bride arrived in her stunning Givenchy dress; marking a magical day of love that united cultures and captivated the world. The nation rejoiced as Diana's son found happiness, welcoming a new Windsor member who promised change. Only Meghan's mother, Doria, stood for her family at the St George's Chapel ceremony with Charles walking Meghan down the aisle. Celebrities including Oprah Winfrey and David Beckham mingled with royalty, but Meghan stole the show. Dazzling in a Stella McCartney dress for the reception, she became an instant global icon. Yet, after their honeymoon, tensions emerged; rumoured family rifts and struggles with royal expectations hinted at challenges ahead.

Again, Meghan looked stunning in a custom Christian Dior gown during a reception at the British ambassador's residence in Rabat, Morocco, on 24 February 2019, part of her official tour with Prince Harry. However, her expensive wardrobe was raising eyebrows. The estimated £60,000 price tag drew the Queen's ire when she read about it in the press. She later let Meghan know that such an expensive outfit was an ill-judged choice.[177]

When the couple, now the Duke and Duchess of Sussex, touched down in Sydney on 15 October to embark on their first joint royal tour of Australia, New Zealand, Fiji and Tonga, the Palace announced that Meghan was pregnant. Initially seen as a modern asset to the royals, tensions soon surfaced. Stories circulated about Meghan's interactions with palace staff, labelling her as 'duchess difficult'. The honeymoon period with the media was short-lived, as headlines painted a picture of discontent within the Royal Household.

Their baby son Archie Harrison Mountbatten-Windsor, who was seventh in line to the throne, arrived on 6 May 2019. His birth marked a shift as Harry and Meghan broke tradition, skipping the hospital photo call and opting for a private introduction at Windsor Castle two days later, signalling their move away from royal norms. Again, their decision ruffled feathers in the palace and the press.

Inside Windsor's walls, fewer than twenty-five guests gathered for the royal baptism. They slipped quietly into the small chapel, hidden from the crowds pressing outside, hoping for a glimpse. But the gates stayed shut. 'We pay for them,' one disappointed voice muttered. 'They could've given us something.'

There was joy on the surface, but underneath it the brothers, once so close, were at loggerheads. Added to this, tension between Catherine and Meghan still simmered after the earlier bridesmaid dress spat. Well-sourced rumours swirled in the press, silence held, but the feud between the couples was a ticking time bomb.

Cracks had first surfaced in public on 28 February 2018, at the Royal Foundation Forum. Asked about family disputes, William admitted, 'Oh, yes.' Harry tried to deflect with humour, 'Healthy disagreements.' Pressed further, William's answer was, 'We don't know,' and his parting words hung heavy, 'We're stuck together for life.' Columnist Rachel Johnson of the *Mail on Sunday* saw trouble ahead. Meghan, passionate and outspoken, outshone William, unused to sharing the stage. 'She's joining a hierarchy,' Johnson warned, 'where everyone knows their place.' Meghan had never been one to follow the rules.

Within a year, the shiny Fab Four PR charade unravelled. By February, William and Harry had formally split their household, with spin doctors framing it as part of some master plan, which had been long in the making. More Palace spin: it was of course nonsense. Harry and Meghan had bluntly turned down a move next to the Duke and Duchess of Cambridge's lavish Apartment 1A in Kensington Palace. Courtiers claimed it was 'about timing', but again they struggled to make it sound credible. During drinks at William's grand home, Meghan was struck by the contrast to Nottingham Cottage, where Harry was then housed. 'Not jealousy,' a source said, 'but surprise at the size and disparity.'[178]

Harry and Meghan moved to Frogmore Cottage in Windsor, splitting their media operations from the Cambridges. The Queen had planned to buy it outright for them as a gift; like the arrangement she had made for the Duke and Duchess of York over Sunninghill Park when it was completed in 1990.[179]

Soon demands came for a complete £2.4 million overhaul of the property, transforming Frogmore Cottage into a single-family home from five separate units, before moving in 2019. The upgrades included modernising its infrastructure, new heating systems, updating electrical wiring, as well as personal touches such as custom kitchen designs and built-in bookcases. Initially funded by the Sovereign Grant, the cost of the full renovation was reimbursed by the Sussexes in 2020 after stepping back as senior royals, to avoid public backlash.

Stories of staff conflicts and bullying persisted and were denied. In the office shake-up, William pulled rank, securing all the top-tier aides for himself and fortifying his team. Harry and Meghan began to drift. Under scrutiny, Meghan felt compelled to deny the bullying claims that surfaced in *The Times*, with her lawyer Jenny Afia publicly defending the Duchess on the BBC, though acknowledging the experiences of others. Allegations persisted, fuelled by their former press secretary Jason Knauf's formal complaint in 2018. William, worried yet estranged from Harry, felt unable to approach his brother to defuse the crisis.

Charles may well have wanted to intervene and knock some sense into his two sons, but he chose to stay out of their escalating quarrels. He hoped that silence might lead to eventual healing. 'He hates direct confrontation,' a close source revealed. He remained hopeful they would see the bigger picture, but in hindsight, his hands-off approach only deepened the rift.

Charles had more pressing issues on his mind. In July 2018, Clarence House courtiers were rattled by the inquiry into the prince's one-time friend, the disgraced former bishop and convicted paedophile Peter Ball, former Bishop of Gloucester. He was required to make a submission in which he expressed his 'deep personal regret' for trusting Ball, even as old letters revealed his fierce defence of the criminal, dismissing accusers as 'ghastly' and 'fraudulent'. In 2015, Ball's deceit was exposed and he was jailed for thirty-two months for abusing eighteen young men, leaving Charles to claim he had been 'misled' and to cut all contact with him after the trial. It highlighted starkly the risks of his role, with critics condemning the prince's glaring lack of judgement as his old letters supporting Ball resurfaced to haunt him.

His questionable associations had threatened to land Charles in trouble before. As a young man, he had seen the South African-born writer Sir Laurens van der Post as a sage and mentor and was drawn to his spiritual ideas. But revelations of fraud and scandal later shattered van der Post's image. He was exposed as a fraud, who had embellished his military record, misrepresented his work with the Kalahari Bushmen, and fathered a child with a fourteen-year-old girl under his care. His legacy shifted from sage to scandal.

The eccentric TV personality Jimmy Savile, later exposed as a predatory paedophile, was also a familiar background figure. In the 1980s, Savile bizarrely advised the Royal Family on public relations and even Charles and Diana's marriage, drafting guidelines for their team. Charles, unaware of his crimes, often sought his counsel on charity and public image. Even after Diana's death in 1997, the prince kept Savile on his guest list, ignoring warnings from senior aides about the depraved abuser. At a black-tie dinner Charles hosted at Birkhall, Savile showed up wearing a shiny shell suit paired with a black bow tie,[180] a sharp reminder of the prince's misplaced trust, which was only shattered after Savile's death in 2011.

By autumn 2019, Meghan and Harry were already privately reshaping their place in the monarchy's future. Then Harry went nuclear. Their southern Africa tour, initially flawless, saw Meghan feted in South Africa. It began on a high note, with Meghan making a well-received speech about empowering women in Nyanga township, twelve miles south-east of Cape Town. Then back in the city, with their baby son Archie, the couple shared smiles alongside Archbishop Desmond Tutu.

Harry's solo part of the trip to Angola, Malawi, and Botswana highlighted his charity work, but beneath the polished photo ops, cracks were beginning to show. In Malawi, he snapped at a Sky royal reporter, Rhiannon Mills, when she asked a simple question.

Hours later, he dropped a bombshell: a public statement accusing the British tabloids of a 'ruthless campaign' against

Meghan, particularly during her pregnancy and while raising their newborn son. Harry declared his wife had endured months of daily vilification, and he could not stay silent any longer. It was an extraordinary course of action while on an official tour, backed by taxpayers' money and the British Foreign Office.

Meanwhile, while filming *Harry & Meghan: An African Journey* with ITV's Tom Bradby, Meghan laid bare her struggles under the royal spotlight. She claimed the constant negative press had left her isolated. She expressed her vulnerability, adding oddly, it had been a 'very real thing to be going through behind the scenes.' When Bradby pressed to clarify her feelings, she said, 'Thank you for asking, because not many people have . . . I'm not really okay. It's been a struggle.' Her raw pain was unmistakable. While some admired her honesty, others criticised the timing, as the couple had just visited a disadvantaged township. For Meghan, the message was clear: 'It's not enough to survive. You have to thrive.'

She went on to say she had tried to adopt a British stiff upper lip, but the emotional toll was too heavy. 'I really tried,' she said, 'but what that does internally is probably really damaging.' Despite Bradby's suggestion that fame comes with inevitable media pressure, she pushed back, saying few understood the weight of royal life. Yet amid the turmoil, she found solace in her family: 'I have the two best guys in the world.'

Without first consulting his father or brother, Harry stated publicly that he and William were 'on different paths', while still professing deep love for his brother, which confirmed the rift the tabloids had been writing about for months. Charles and William were incandescent. Perhaps sensing growing hostility within the family, Harry and Meghan skipped the traditional Christmas at Sandringham, opting instead to spend it at Mille Fleurs, a secluded mansion in North Saanich on Vancouver Island, in Canada. They spent the holiday enjoying hikes and private family time with their son Archie. Canadian prime minister Justin Trudeau welcomed them, tweeting, 'You're among friends, and always welcome here.'

When Harry returned, he privately told Charles that he and his wife wanted a new, semi-detached setup: half in, half out of the Royal Family. They wanted to be able to make their own money too, effectively cashing in on their royal status. Presumptuously, they assumed that given their apparent popularity, the Queen would back them. She did not.

The scandal blew up on 8 January when journalist Dan Wootton broke the exclusive story in the *Sun* saying Harry and Meghan were heading back to Canada and were considering their royal role. Hours later, the Sussexes confirmed the story on their Instagram, announcing plans to step back from senior royal duties, and to split their time between North America and the UK. The statement had been made without the Queen's approval. The monarch and Charles were furious. William felt betrayed. It started a Fleet Street frenzy. The following day Wootton wrote, 'Harry and Meghan last night announced they will be quitting as senior Royals,' the *Sun* headline used the expression 'Megxit' for the first time on the front-page headline.

The Sandringham summit in January 2020 marked a turning point for the British monarchy. In the Long Library, where the Queen had delivered her first ever televised Christmas address, under tight security she joined Harry, Charles, William, and their private secretaries, to confront the fallout of the Sussexes' decision to step back from royal life. Meghan, who stayed in Canada, was reportedly set to join via video call, but technical issues kept her out, although she stayed in close contact with Harry.

The crisis summit addressed whether Harry and Meghan could balance royal duties with financial independence, while keeping their HRH titles. The Queen, sympathetic of Harry's struggles as the spare, echoing the difficulties of her sister Margaret, offered support but held firm. Harry's idea of splitting time between North America and his royal obligations clashed with the monarchy's need for unity and dignity. The answer from the top was clear: no halfway role was possible They were either in or out.

Her Majesty's ruling deepened the existing tensions in the family, particularly between Harry and William. Prince Philip, once a mentor to Harry, was so angered by what he saw as a threat to the family's cohesion that he stayed away. William, still seething over his brother's actions, arrived composed but distant. Discussions were emotional. Harry was forced to concede far more ground than he anticipated, in exchange for his and Meghan's 'freedom'.

The Queen's statement after the ninety-minute meeting was measured. She expressed regret at the couple's decision but recognised Harry and Meghan's desire for independence. A transition period was agreed upon, with final details left to be sorted. For Harry, it was a hard lesson. For the monarchy, it was a defining moment; one that underscored its unyielding structure and the personal cost of stepping away from it.

The deal meant Harry losing his patronages and military titles, including being Captain General of the Royal Marines, which stung him. He had assumed that significant role in 2017, succeeding Prince Philip who had held it for sixty-four years, succeeding his own father-in-law, George VI. At the handover to his grandson, Philip's words were sharp: 'Don't f**k it up.' Sadly, he did. Harry held the role for just three years and two months.[181]

On 19 January, it was confirmed: the Sussexes would drop their HRH titles and become financially independent. From that point on, their colours were nailed to their own mast. Harry, then sixth in the line of succession (now his father is king, he is fifth), no longer had a royal role – no duties, no honorary titles, no active responsibilities. Meghan too had zero constitutional importance. Her title came with her marriage and is purely symbolic.[182] Harry felt he had no other choice but to leave. In a parting shot, he made their feelings clear, taking yet another swipe at the royals: 'Service is universal.'

The growing distance between Harry and William was unmistakable during the Sussexes' final royal engagement on 9 March at the annual Commonwealth Day service at Westminster Abbey. They returned to Vancouver and five days later the couple moved to California. Harry called it his 'freedom flight'.[183]

They bought a $14.5 million home in Montecito, but their apparent dream of a quiet life quickly dissolved. They were ready for payback and to cash in big time. To fund their extravagant lifestyle, they started work on securing multi-million-dollar deals with Netflix and Spotify, leveraging the royal ties they had agreed not to use.

Back in the UK, suddenly everything changed. On 23 March 2020, Prime Minister Boris Johnson announced the UK's first COVID-19 lockdown in a sombre televised address. The public was ordered to stay home; only essential shopping, medical needs, limited exercise, and key work were allowed.

For three months, the nation held its breath as scientists raced to develop a vaccine. Schools and businesses shut, gatherings were banned, and travel was curbed. Amid the chaos, the Queen became a steadying figurehead, a symbol of calm in crisis.

Her televised 'We'll meet again' speech on 5 April was a

reminder of wartime resilience. She spoke of sacrifice and hope, reassuring the nation: 'We should take comfort that while we may have more still to endure, better days will return, we will be with our friends again; we will be with our families again; we will meet again.'

Both Charles and William caught COVID-19. William kept his diagnosis quiet, but as heir, Charles went public – first in March 2020 with mild symptoms, then again in February 2022. The second time, he was at Clarence House, preparing to head to Highgrove for the weekend. When he could not travel to his country retreat, he was incandescent. Frustrated, he even threatened to drive himself down the M4. Alarmed royal aides, fearing a rule breach, hid his car keys. Eventually, he cooled off and stayed put in London, sticking to the government guidelines until symptom-free.

In November 2020, William and Catherine shared a rare personal message after the death of their beloved English cocker spaniel, Lupo. On Instagram, they wrote: 'Very sadly last weekend our dear dog Lupo passed away. He has been at the heart of our family for the past nine years and we will miss him so much – W & C.'

The Queen tested positive for COVID-19 in February 2022, experiencing mild symptoms but carrying on with light duties. Some questioned how closely the royals followed the rules, but for most people, she remained a symbol of calm in a world upended. Restrictions were lifted, then returned. November saw new lockdowns; January brought more deaths. The virus pressed on. Through it all, the Queen stood unshakeable, speaking little but radiating resilience and quiet strength. In a shattered world, she remained the constant.

CHAPTER 18

THE FALLOUT

Meghan and Harry beg for privacy,
but are hungry for attention.

THE *NEW YORK POST* HEADLINE FOR AN ARTICLE BY COLUMNIST MAUREEN CALLAHAN, 2020

What followed shook the monarchy to its core, with some even questioning its legitimacy and long-term future. Far from Harry and Meghan stepping back quietly, tensions continued to simmer between them and the Royal Family. On 7 April, just weeks after their dramatic exit, the Sussexes launched Archewell – a new foundation named after their son, replacing the banned 'Sussex Royal' brand.

In May 2020, HarperCollins announced *Finding Freedom: Harry and Meghan and the Making of a Modern Royal Family*, by Omid Scobie and Carolyn Durand, a biography promoted as offering an insider account of the Sussexes' departure from royal life. It reflected Harry and Meghan's one-sided view. At first, the couple denied involvement, but court documents later revealed Meghan had authorised a friend to brief the authors, aiming to counter her father Thomas's public claims.

The royal couple hoped their new home in Montecito would

be their haven; a quiet, leafy escape from royal life and tabloid glare. Their mansion with nine bedrooms, a library, gym, spa, cinema, wine cellar, guest house, tennis court and pool, set in a seven-and-a-half-acre estate, offered enough space for the royal couple to stretch out. Far from the palace, but not from the spotlight, it became their haven – perfect for philanthropy, media deals, and curated freedom.

Before they left Britain, arrangements were made to by the Queen and Charles to cover security costs for Harry and Archie for a year, part of a broader understanding within the family. Charles also offered to assist with household bills and living expenses while they settled in. Even so, Harry found the shift into his new life difficult to navigate. During her final Christmas at Sandringham, the Queen was irritated when Harry phoned during her cherished 5 p.m. afternoon tea – a daytime ritual she considered sacrosanct. He was not put through. Harry reached her the following day. After hanging up, she sighed in front of staff, 'More money.' Even the Queen, it seemed, had grown weary.[184]

September brought another bombshell: a multi-million-dollar Netflix deal for the Sussexes to produce content that would 'inform but also give hope'. At the same time, they agreed to repay the £2.4 million in taxpayer funds spent renovating Frogmore Cottage, the Windsor home gifted for their use by the Queen in 2019.[185]

Then came a deeply personal moment. Meghan, writing in the *New York Times*, revealed she had suffered a miscarriage in July. Her raw account of 'almost unbearable grief' drew widespread praise for its honesty.

But with each big announcement – like their December Spotify deal, also worth millions – public cynicism deepened. Many in the UK accused them of cashing in on the royal name they had supposedly left behind. Fleet Street called them out as hypocrites, claiming it was not privacy they had sought – but profit.

On Valentine's Day, Harry and Meghan announced they were expecting their second child. The Queen, Charles, and William shared in the joy – but the harmony was short-lived. News quickly followed of the couple's plans for a tell-all interview with Oprah Winfrey, just as Prince Philip, aged ninety-nine, was hospitalised with an infection and a heart procedure. The Palace played down the seriousness.

In California, bizarre tabloid rumours swirled that Meghan had ambitions for the 2024 US presidency – a far-fetched notion that drew swift backlash. Critics scoffed: how could a former C-list actress with no political background and zero qualifications for high office seriously aim for the White House? She had struggled with the demands of royal public service, so how would she handle leading a nation? The speculation struck a nerve, marking a sharp shift in public mood. Sympathy for the once-adored couple was fading on both sides of the Atlantic.

Even American papers, once sympathetic, started to turn. The *New York Post*'s columnist Maureen Callahan captured the mounting scepticism, hinting that the Sussexes' pursuit of big money had eroded their carefully crafted image. 'It's only been ten months since Prince Harry and Meghan Markle announced they were leaving the British Royal Family in search of "privacy" – yet they have never been so much in our faces, sanctimoniously and hypocritically telling us how to live and who to vote for, all while signing a reported $100-million deal with Netflix.' The tide had begun to turn, and the couple's every move came under intense scrutiny.

The Sussexes' needed to reclaim the initiative. They did.

On 11 February 2021, Meghan won a high-court privacy case against the *Mail on Sunday*, the judge ruling in her favour over the publication of a private letter to her estranged father. Meghan called out 'illegal and dehumanising practices,' adding, 'for these outlets, it's a game. For me and so many others, it's real life, real sadness.'

A week later, Buckingham Palace confirmed that Harry and Meghan would not return as working royals, ending the one-year review period.

In a strange interview with television host James Corden, Harry discussed his son's first word and Zoom calls with the Queen, while defending the Netflix royal historical drama *The Crown* as 'fictional'. Claiming he had not walked away from royal duties but stepped back for his mental health, he declared, 'My life is public service.' It was only a prelude to what followed.

As the couple readied for the airing of the Oprah Winfrey tell-all interview, *The Times* reported that Meghan had mistreated royal staff, allegedly reducing several aides to tears, leading to resignations and strained confidence. Meghan's team said she was 'saddened by the attack on her character'. She was now ready to explode the monarchy's carefully curated image. The attack was devastating and from within.[186]

Television trailers for Oprah hinted at Meghan's claims of mistreatment. When it aired on the US network CBS on 7 March 2021, it was the most explosive royal interview imaginable, delivering 'truth bombs' that shook Buckingham Palace. Accusations of racism, family rifts, and mental health struggles painted a bleak picture of royal life. Its scheduling also sparked controversy as the interview aired during Prince Philip's hospitalisation, dividing opinions on its timing and purpose. Unapologetic, Meghan told Oprah, 'I don't know how they could expect that, after all this time, we could still just be silent' accusing 'The Firm' of perpetuating 'falsehoods' about them.

Oprah faced a backlash for not challenging the claims, while Meghan called speaking out 'liberating'.

An audience of 17 million people in the US alone and millions more globally watched Meghan unleash her bitterness, firing at anyone in her path: Charles, William, even Catherine, and the so-called 'men in grey suits' at the palace. It was a spectacle, gripping for viewers but agonising for the Royal Family. Meghan's most shocking claim during the two-hour-long divisive rant was that life as a royal had driven her to have suicidal thoughts. Visibly emotional, she said, 'I just did not want to be alive anymore. And that was a very clear and real and frightening constant thought.'

Then came her bombshell allegations of racism at the palace. Although she didn't name names, she spoke of troubling royal conversations about her unborn son's skin tone – remarks Harry later framed as 'unconscious bias'. She also alleged the family denied Archie a title and security, partly due to concerns over his skin colour. 'When I was pregnant, there were conversations about how dark his skin might be,' she told Oprah. Surprisingly, the interviewer again did not press for specific details. Why would she? She knew she had the headlines in the bag, and her viewing figures would soar.

When he joined the conversation, Harry looked uneasy. He consciously avoided eye contact with Oprah, shifting awkwardly in his chair. At times he contradicted Meghan, muddling the timeline of the racist remark. 'That conversation, I'm never going to share,' he said. Yet, he added that it was 'awkward' and came early on, along with talk of Meghan needing to keep acting because there was not enough money for her. He then ruled out the Queen and Prince Philip as culprits, creating even more confusion.

Then came the blow that echoed Diana's infamous BBC *Panorama* interview. 'I was trapped, but I didn't know I was trapped,' he claimed. 'My father and my brother, they are trapped. They don't get to leave.' Harry spoke too of the family's rigid mindset, 'This is just how it is. This is how it's meant to be. We've all been through it.' But for him, there was a 'race element' too, something new, unforgiving and unforgivable. Harry then revealed the sad truth of his broken relationship with his father. It was gut-wrenching.

Why had he felt compelled to walk away and tell all? 'My biggest concern was history repeating itself. What I was seeing was far more dangerous because of race, social media, and the relentless press,' he said, drawing parallels to his mother Diana's trauma and tragic death. Many felt his pain. For Harry, the media triggered his grief. Meeting Meghan had prompted him to process his loss, seek counselling, and channel anger through boxing, just as his mother had done through taking up kickboxing. Emphasising his protective instincts, he went on, 'I'll always protect my family. Meghan's experiences are always on my mind. It's not paranoia – it's about preventing history from repeating.'

William was furious. He reached out to friends and insisted that he did not feel trapped; with his blessing, they in turn told the press. William knew and embraced his path, both the burden and the honour. Harry's words cut deep. Speaking for William, and so incorrectly, was infuriating to him. The brotherly bond was shattered, and trust gone. William believed his brother had lost his way, especially after Meghan's claim about Catherine making her cry. The racism accusation was the final blow, a total betrayal. As the Queen and Charles stayed silent, William could not.

Under pressure, the Palace released a statement from the Queen: 'The issues raised, particularly that of race, are concerning. Whilst some recollections may vary, they are taken very seriously and will be addressed by the family privately.' In his book *Courtiers*, journalist Valentine Low of *The Times* later reported that the original draft of the statement had been softer. William and Catherine, however, had pushed for stronger wording, insisting it reject much of the claims in the Oprah interview. According to Low it was Catherine herself who coined the memorable phrase 'recollections may vary', reminding everyone involved that 'history will judge this statement'.[187]

But the stain of racism had already taken hold and it could not be washed away. Four days after Harry and Meghan's interview, William stood firm on a visit to a school in Stratford, east London. The Palace press officer on duty had instructed the press gathered behind a steel barrier: no questions. But *Sky News* reporter Inzamam Rashid was there to do his job. He called out, 'Is the Royal Family a racist family, sir?' William, masked for COVID, did not flinch. 'We are very much not a racist family,' he said, not looking back. Asked if he had spoken to Harry, the prince replied, 'No, I haven't spoken to him yet, but I will.'

Days after William had spoken with Harry, Gayle King revealed on CBS that the brothers' conversation was 'not productive'. William was sideswiped. The leak felt like yet another betrayal.

Chaos followed. The Palace faced growing pressure after being accused of harbouring racism. Silence was no longer an option. Harry and Meghan's claims drew sympathy and the *Guardian* added to their allegations – unearthing documents showing that royal staff had banned 'coloured immigrants or foreigners' from clerical roles into the late 1960s. The damage was real. The Sussex saga exposed deep divisions in the Royal Family and reignited questions about the monarchy's relevance, inclusivity, and ability to modernise. For the Queen, in the twilight of her reign, it was a bitter pill to swallow.

Then a few weeks later, Prince Philip died, leaving the Queen heartbroken and the Royal Family in mourning.

After retiring from his official public duties in August 2017, aged ninety-six, Prince Philip had chosen to live quietly at Wood Farm, a five-bedroom cottage on the Sandringham Estate in Norfolk. Away from the cameras, he spent his time reading history books and biographies and painting watercolours, and inviting close family and friends to stay.

During the COVID-19 lockdowns, he moved back to Windsor Castle, where he and the Queen spent precious time together, giving her a 'new lease on life'. Cared for by a few select servants in a secure group known as 'HMS Bubble', the couple settled into a routine, sharing afternoon tea most days, which delighted the Queen. Philip made his final public appearance on 22 July 2020, standing straight-backed and immaculately dressed on the steps of Windsor Castle as he passed on his role of Colonel-in-Chief of The Rifles to Camilla, the Duchess of Cornwall.

He had become increasingly frail. After his release from hospital following a heart procedure on 16 March 2021, Philip returned to Windsor Castle. He was lethargic, sluggish, and did not want to leave his room, which worried the Queen. She sent for his close companion Penny, the Countess Mountbatten, hoping her presence would help him to regain his 'zest for life' they all so loved. He did rally a little, but it was short-lived.

In his final conversation with Philip on 8 April 2021, just hours before his death, Charles tried to discuss arrangements for his father's upcoming 100th birthday. Speaking louder for his nearly-deaf father, he said, 'We're talking about your birthday, and whether there's going to be a reception!' Philip shot back, 'Well, I've got to be alive for it, haven't I?' Charles laughed, 'I knew you'd say that!'

Philip died peacefully the following day at Windsor Castle, with the Queen by his side. The Palace announced the news at noon, with Her Majesty expressing profound sorrow. After his passing, she entered his rooms for the last time. Despite his royal title, Philip lived simply – his single bed, where he died, was in his large bathroom.[188]

When the arrangements for his funeral were underway, the Queen made it clear that Countess Mountbatten should be there. COVID restrictions or not, she would be one of the few mourners inside St George's Chapel. It was a significant gesture, a quiet nod to Philip and Penny's bond – years of friendship, trust, and loyalty. Her presence said more than words.

Like many fathers and sons with strong beliefs, Charles and Philip had clashed over the years, but as Philip grew older, they had mellowed and found common ground on the monarchy's future, religious issues, and the environment, both valuing interfaith dialogue and honest conversation to strengthen communities. Charles's closer bond with his father was clear in his televised tribute to his 'dear papa', describing him as a 'much loved and appreciated figure', and a 'very special person'.

Charles's sorrow was profound and visible as he led Philip's coffin to St George's Chapel on the Land Rover his father designed. The Queen arrived by car, while Charles stood with Anne in a solemn tribute. Inside, the Queen sat alone, due to the COVID lockdown guidelines, and Camilla squeezed Charles's hand.

After the service, the family walked back to the castle. Harry walked alongside William and Catherine, and she dropped back to give them a chance to talk. Commentators saw it as a subtle sign of reconciliation. In fact, moments later, at a fraught meeting after the funeral, Charles stood between his feuding sons, William, and Harry – reunited in grief but not in spirit. When William said he had no idea why Harry and his wife had quit Britain, Harry was flabbergasted. Charles pleaded, 'Please, boys, do not make my final years a misery.' Sadly, it was ignored.[189]

Philip's death was more than a personal loss – it left the Queen without her most trusted ally in managing the ever-demanding courtiers. Without him, she faced their rigid schedules and constant pressures alone. Once, when she was keen to fly to Balmoral to feed her corgis already sent ahead, she was told she had to stick to a fixed airtime slot. Fed up with the inflexibility, she snapped, 'Tell them I want a different time slot. I am the Queen, after all.' She got her way and the dogs got fed and had their walk with her on time, so as not to upset their routine.[190]

Meanwhile, the royal race relations storm gathered momentum. Historic missteps came to light. In December 2017, Princess Michael of Kent had caused outrage by wearing a 'blackamoor' brooch to a palace Christmas banquet that Meghan attended. Critics called it racist. The princess apologised, claiming it was a gift she had worn often before.

Online speculation wrongly targeted Charles over the Archie skin colour remark, with some dredging up a 2001 case as apparent proof of bias. Elizabeth Burgess, a former Black secretary to Charles, had accused his staff of racial discrimination, alleging that valet Michael Fawcett used a racial slur towards her. She had filed a tribunal claim for constructive dismissal, but it was rejected for lack of evidence.

In reality, Charles has long been an advocate for diversity within the Royal Household, and a senior royal aide dismissed the racism claims outright: 'It goes against everything the Prince of Wales believes in. He sees diversity as a strength. It's rich coming from Harry, who needed defending after his Nazi uniform and that racist remark when he was at Sandhurst in 2009.'[191]

In fact, by 2023, ethnic minority representation at the palace rose from 8.5 per cent to 9.7 per cent, with a target of 14 per cent by 2025. As of July 2024, 14 per cent of the Prince and Princess of Wales's staff came from ethnic minority backgrounds, a sign of steady progress.

On 4 June 2021, Harry and Meghan welcomed their daughter, Lilibet Diana, honouring the Queen's childhood nickname. Some saw it as a peace offering, but controversy erupted when the BBC reported the Queen had not been consulted, contradicting the Sussexes' version. Harry insisted he had her blessing, but Buckingham Palace stayed silent, declining to confirm either side. The Sussexes' lawyers called the BBC report 'false and defamatory' and threatened legal action – but no lawsuit followed.[192]

The Queen first learned of Lilibet's name from the morning press, and was so incensed at the afront, she threw the paper to the floor, startling her staff. Later, during one of the Sussexes' final UK visits before her death, they skipped a planned tea in the Oak Room without notice. She had requested a special cake. By 5.15 p.m., with no word, she told staff to clear it all away. The Queen met her great-granddaughter Lilibet only once, during the Platinum Jubilee.[193]

William and Harry called a brief truce in July 2021, standing side by side in Kensington Palace's Sunken Garden to unveil a statue of their mother on what would have been the late Princess Diana's sixtieth birthday. For a moment, they smiled and laughed, joined by her siblings – a flash of the bond they once shared. But once the cameras stopped rolling, the closeness faded just as quickly.

A year later, the royal racism saga flared up again. In November 2022, Lady Susan Hussey, Prince William's godmother and a senior royal aide close to Charles and the late Queen, was forced to resign amid allegations of racism, sparking a media frenzy. Activist Ngozi Fulani claimed Hussey had asked racially insensitive questions about her heritage during a royal reception at the palace. The Palace immediately called the remarks 'unacceptable and deeply regrettable', apologised to Fulani, and reaffirmed its commitment to diversity.

Lady Susan stepped down from her role as Lady of the Household and staff were reminded of inclusivity policies. Privately, the King and others were upset at the speed at which William 'threw Lady Susan under the bus,' close sources said.

Later, two senior royals were named in the Dutch edition of the book *Endgame* – King Charles and the Princess of Wales – as the figures who allegedly questioned Archie's skin colour. The author, Omid Scobie, widely seen as sympathetic to Meghan, alleged the names appeared due to an early, unapproved manuscript being sent to the Dutch publishers. The publisher, Xander Uitgevers, rejected that claim. The English edition omitted the names, citing legal reasons. The Palace said it was 'considering all options', but the King and Catherine remained silent. The damage, however, was done.

The racism claims soon rang hollow. Even Harry, during his *Spare* publicity tour, denied that he or Meghan had ever accused the family of racism – blaming the media for twisting their words. Charles had spent years championing diversity, a mission he continues as king. Catherine, though typically reserved, was said to be 'deeply saddened' and insisted she had 'nothing to do with it'. With zero tolerance for racism, she kept her composure, walking tall at the Royal Variety Performance in a showstopping £1,288 gown. As ever, she rose above the noise.

Toxic trolls calling themselves 'The Sussex Squad' emerged from the shadows – a spiteful, faceless crowd. On social media, they hurled abuse at William and Catherine and targeted anyone who dared question Harry or Meghan. It did not stop there. They lobbed baseless accusations into the void, hoping something might stick. In the darker corners of the web, some of it did.

Catherine is no 'Stepford-like royal wife', as Scobie claimed in *Endgame*. She is a force; driven, dutiful, and unafraid to speak with purpose. As the Princess of Wales, her mission is clear: shaping young minds and championing children's mental health. It is her legacy in the making, and one she will carry as Queen Consort. She understands the strength in silence. It has not been an easy journey. Even Princess Anne, no stranger to press battles herself, especially in her youth, has acknowledged the pressure Catherine faces. 'It's always worse for the younger royals,' she said. 'No social media in my day. It has made things harder.'

Catherine faced baseless rumours, including speculation about a rift with her aristocrat friend Rose Hanbury, Marchioness of Cholmondeley, tied to unfounded gossip about her closeness to William. She never responded, but her presence alongside Rose at a private dinner during the Houghton Festival in August 2023 quietly put the talk to rest. Steady and self-assured, the Princess of Wales remains focused on family, duty, and service. Her *Together at Christmas* carol concerts at Westminster Abbey reflect her quiet commitment to supporting William and King Charles in delivering lasting change.

Catherine remains devoted to the man she met and fell in love with at university nearly twenty-five years ago, and the feeling is mutual. William often watches her with quiet admiration, his gestures subtle but telling. During a walkabout in Birmingham in April 2023, a woman complimented her burgundy dress. Without hesitation, William smiled and said, 'She always looks stunning.' The clip went viral. 'There's a man who loves his wife,' one fan wrote. Another added, 'He's not wrong.'

CHAPTER 19

THE FLIGHTS OF ANGELS

Time and again, we were struck by her (Queen Elizabeth II) warmth, the way she put people at their ease, and how she brought her considerable humour and charm to moments of great pomp and circumstance.

FORMER US PRESIDENT BARACK OBAMA, 2022.

As Elizabeth II marked her Platinum Jubilee in 2022, Charles took the lead in the proceedings. Behind the scenes, she now leaned heavily on him, quietly hiding her reliance on a wheelchair and determined not to show weakness. Aware of cracks within the Royal Family, she moved to steady the institution. Calling for unity, she urged her family and the nation to look forward with 'confidence and enthusiasm'.

Since becoming the Duchess of Cornwall, Camilla had worked hard to repair her image and earn public acceptance. At first, critics had questioned her dedication to royal duties and even some aides doubted her commitment. In planning meetings, 'TBC' beside an event with Camilla was joked to mean 'To Be Cancelled'. But she proved the doubters wrong again. She threw herself into causes such as literacy, the fight to eradicate domestic violence, and animal welfare. Her approachable demeanour and devotion to her personal causes endeared her to many who had once reviled her.

In her Jubilee message, the Queen now laid out her wishes plainly, leaving no room for doubt: 'And when, in the fullness of time, my son Charles becomes king, I know you will give him and his wife Camilla the same support that you have given me; and it is my sincere wish that . . . Camilla will be known as Queen Consort.' With that, the seal was set. The woman once scorned as a royal mistress was now crowned in spirit.

A family celebration marked the moment. Who was missing? Harry. The shift was stark. Camilla, once the outcast, now stood as a symbol of stability, welcomed by the Queen with warmth. Harry, once the cherished prince, had become the outsider. Their roles had reversed, the monarchy's tide turning with them.

When she had been locked in discussions with William and Charles about Harry and their advisers, Queen Elizabeth described Harry's behaviour as 'quite mad'. She made it clear to those close to her that privately she felt let down by the Sussexes' departure, which she saw as short-sighted and a missed opportunity.

The Queen had warmly welcomed Meghan, viewing her dual heritage, beauty, and communication skills as assets to the family. When it all fell apart, she publicly wished the couple well in California, but in private, tired of the drama, she eventually ordered Harry's calls be redirected to his father. Charles, however, tired of his errant son's ranting, eventually stopped taking Harry's calls after he swore at him and demanded funds. 'I'm not a bank,' he declared to his circle. One concern loomed large for Charles and his senior team: what would happen when the money ran out? It soon became awkward for long-serving staff, who knew Harry well, to be left making polite excuses when Charles would not come to the phone.

In her twilight years, Elizabeth also faced mounting strain, not least from her troubled second son, Andrew, who repeatedly sought her help in regaining public duties after losing his patronages over the Epstein scandal. In April 2022, Harry and Meghan had a brief, tense meeting with Charles and another with the Queen, a reminder of the family's deepening divisions.

In May 2022, Charles and Camilla set off on a three-day tour of Canada for the Queen's Platinum Jubilee. It got off to a rocky start before take-off. At Beaconsfield Services, located off Junction 2 of the M40 motorway in Buckinghamshire, Camilla's jewels were stolen after three royal aides left the bag, labelled 'HRH The Duchess of Cornwall', unattended in an unlocked car. A local gang struck when one aide stepped away for a cigarette while the other two were inside getting coffees. MI5 were scrambled and quickly tracked the thief via CCTV, and the jewels were recovered within hours. No charges were filed, no police report was ever made, and the incident was buried to avoid embarrassment. 'The press never found out, which amazed everyone,' a senior source later said.[194]

The Sussexes attended the Queen's Platinum Jubilee under restrictions, with Netflix crews banned from palace access. They faced some boos from the crowd when they entered St Paul's Cathedral. The celebration featured street parties, Trooping the Colour, and a Diana Ross concert, ending with the Queen's balcony appearance. Charles honoured her with a heartfelt tribute, thanking her for a 'lifetime of selfless service' and playfully mentioning her love for the Derby.

The Queen, frail and tired from her condition and earlier appearances, was urged by Charles to wave from the Buckingham

Palace balcony for history's sake. A military-style plan ensured she arrived unseen in a wheelchair. Holding her walking stick, she stood alongside Charles, Prince George, and the family, smiling as fireworks erupted to 'God Save the Queen'. It was her final public salute to her people.

Charles, now paterfamilias of the family, quietly readied himself for kingship. When hosting investitures at Windsor, he stayed over and occasionally dined with his mother. She in turn increasingly turned to him for advice, and sometimes to take her place when she was not feeling up to carrying out engagements.

Her days were quiet, often lonely, with few visitors beyond regulars like Andrew, his ex-wife Sarah, and their daughters. Loyal footmen Paul Whybrew and Ian Robertson tended to her needs, while William, now living at Adelaide Cottage nearby, offered some company. She often spotted him and his family in the park from her window, though his rigidity occasionally frustrated her.[195]

On one occasion on 15 July, even William, whom the Queen told those close to her she feared might become a 'celebrity monarch' rather than a dedicated and dutiful one, left her feeling disappointed, inside sources said. She was feeling particularly frail that day, facing issues with keeping control, and asked him to stand in for her at the official opening of Thames Hospice's new twenty-nine-bed facility by Bray Lake, near Windsor. She had a particular connection with it through a retiring staff member who had looked after the budgerigars at the Royal Aviary, and she did not want to let anyone down. When William cried off, citing fatherly duties, she is said to have been irritated and scoffed wasn't that what nannies and policemen were for?

Ever the stalwart, she went anyway and asked the Princess Royal to go with her. The forty-five-minute engagement was the last she carried out. During the visit she devoted some time speaking to a woman who was expected to live no more than forty-eight hours.[196] It would be the last engagement she ever carried out in England.

Afterwards Queen Elizabeth headed to her beloved Scotland, finding quiet refuge in Craigowan Lodge, longing less for Highland walks and more for stillness and peace – and the chance to say a few final goodbyes. She arrived in late July, knowing it would be her last visit. One morning, uncharacteristically vexed, she asked staff to summon grocer George Strachan, whose family had faithfully served the Royal Family at Balmoral for generations. Breaking her strict rule of no breakfast guests outside family, she made herself available. She simply wanted to say goodbye: a quiet gesture of loyalty and grace, so quintessentially her.[197]

On 9 August, the Queen left Craigowan Lodge and formally arrived at Balmoral Castle for her final summer stay. The traditional welcome was held in private; by now her mobility issues made public ceremony impossible. Still, ever dutiful, she carried out her final constitutional acts on 6 September: bidding farewell to Boris Johnson and inviting Liz Truss to form a government. Her parting words to Truss were simply, 'I'll see you again next week.'

Two days later, her health declined sharply. The Princess Royal stayed constantly at her side. Charles, hosting a dinner at Dumfries House, East Ayrshire, was urgently summoned. Before boarding the helicopter for the 150-mile journey to Aberdeenshire, he paced and muttered, 'It's all going to change.' It did – within hours.[198]

Charles had been quietly preparing for this moment since the loss of his father. After Prince Philip's death, the Queen's health had declined rapidly. One by one she lost those closest to her: racing advisor Sir Michael Oswald, confidante Ann Fortune FitzRoy, Duchess of Grafton, and childhood friend Lady Myra Butter.

During her final year she stoically battled multiple myeloma, a form of bone marrow cancer, but it eventually claimed her. The diagnosis was later confirmed by former prime minister Boris Johnson in his 2024 memoir, *Unleashed*, something that is understood to have irritated King Charles, who often found the flamboyant politician exasperating.[199]

At 6.30 p.m. on 8 September 2022, the Royal Family website posted a black-and-white portrait of Queen Elizabeth II with a simple statement: 'The Queen died peacefully at Balmoral this afternoon.' Sir Edward Young, her private secretary, noted that she 'slipped away' and suffered 'no pain' – unaware of anything.[200] Her death certificate later revealed she had passed at 3.10 p.m., aged ninety-six.

Earlier, after watching his mother decline at her bedside, Charles had left Balmoral for his nearby Scottish home Birkhall. Seeking solace, he had been foraging for wild mushrooms when told the end was near and rushed back to his mother's side. Sadly, he arrived a few minutes after her passing. One of the first symbolic acts was the removal of the Sovereign's ring, which was then given to Charles, who was now the king. Her 3-carat round-cut engagement ring was passed to Princess Anne; an intimate gesture of love and trust shared between mother and daughter.[201]

Dr James Glass, the Queen's apothecary, recorded Her Majesty's cause of death as 'old age', thus preserving her health's privacy: for the moment, anyway. The newly appointed prime minister Liz Truss was informed of the Queen's death at 4.30 p.m. Angela Kelly, her personal assistant, was so overcome with grief after paying her respects she was helped from the room by two footmen. They wisely did not feel Princess Anne would welcome her presence, or that of other servants, where her mother had taken her last breath.

At Elizabeth II's accession she had been the Queen of thirty-two nations, reduced to fifteen by the time of her death. Over 170 prime ministers had served her across the Commonwealth, and she had marked silver, golden, diamond, and platinum jubilees. She had walked through history, including state visits to China, Russia, and Ireland in 2011, which she regarded as particularly significant, as it marked the first visit by a reigning British monarch since Irish independence and was seen as a powerful gesture of reconciliation.

She had met five Popes and thirteen of the last fourteen American presidents, from Truman to Biden; only Lyndon Johnson missed the list.[202] She rarely confided in anyone, a complete and self-contained woman. For most, she was the only monarch they had ever known. When her death was announced to millions it felt like the end of an era, the close of the Elizabethan age. The nation mourned their matriarch, bereft.

With grief etched into his lined, weary face, King Charles III delivered a heartfelt farewell to his beloved mother. In his first televised address as monarch on 9 September 2022, he ended with a deeply poignant tribute: 'To my darling Mama, as you begin your last great journey to join my dear late Papa, I want simply to say this: thank you. Thank you for your love and devotion to our family and to the family of nations you have served so diligently all these years. May "flights of angels sing thee to thy rest".'[203]

Quietly and without fanfare, Angela Kelly, who had been the Queen's trusted dresser, was flown south after Her Majesty's death and bluntly told to hand over the late Queen's belongings and jewellery to a senior figure in King Charles's circle. Her time at court was over. Once a powerful presence, who had the Queen's ear, she was swiftly sidelined. Within months, she was asked to vacate her grace-and-favour Windsor home. Charles honoured his mother's wishes by securing her a new place in the Peak District, near her family, but it came with a tight non-disclosure agreement, reportedly silencing any plans for a third book of her memoirs.

The King later tasked the Queen's trusted footman, Paul Whybrow, who famously appeared with Her Majesty and her corgis in the James Bond filmed skit for the 2012 Olympics, with reviewing all her correspondence, including her exchanges with the legendary Hollywood star Douglas Fairbanks Jr. He was ordered to send anything potentially embarrassing to be vetted by the King. Whybrow was given a generous retirement settlement and, unlike Ms Kelly, allowed to live in retirement on the Windsor estate.

Queen Elizabeth had been ninety-six, but her death still hit Charles hard. He grieved deeply, though those close to him said he shifted into 'autopilot', holding back the tide of emotion; restrained and controlled. It was the only way to carry the weight of the crown.

The new monarch and Camilla, now Queen Consort, returned to Buckingham Palace to cheers of 'God save the King'. On 10 September, history was made with the first televised proclamation at St James's Palace. Though he had once weighed taking the title King George VII, Charles chose to reign as Charles III.

On his tour of his kingdom's capitals before the state funeral, Charles, weary and irritable, snapped at staff over a missing pen box. William and Camilla stayed calm as the Garter King of Arms proclaimed him king, marked by trumpet fanfare and gun salutes across London. In Belfast, a leaking pen drove Charles to mutter, 'Oh, God, I hate this pen,' before storming off.

Amid the grief, William and Harry called a truce in the so-called 'battle of the brothers'. Palace spin-doctors let it be known that William had invited Harry and Meghan to join him and Catherine at Windsor to view the floral tributes. The Sussexes held hands, but the tension between the two couples was palpable as they were filmed speaking to the crowds. Catherine later admitted to a member of the family, 'It was one of the hardest things I'd ever had to do.' At least one person in the crowd turned their back on Meghan.

On 11 September, The Princess Royal Anne and her husband Vice Admiral Sir Tim Laurence accompanied the Queen's coffin 170 miles to Edinburgh, where farmers saluted with tractors and crowds lined the route. She curtseyed as the casket entered Holyroodhouse. The next day, kilted soldiers from the Royal Regiment of Scotland bore the coffin to St Giles' Cathedral, where a Service of Thanksgiving was held for the Life of Her Majesty the Queen. The ceremony honoured her deep connection to Scotland and allowed the Scottish public to pay their respects. King Charles and his three siblings later held a vigil for ten minutes around the coffin. Earlier that day in London, King Charles had addressed MPs at Westminster Hall, and honoured his mother's 'selfless duty', vowing to follow her example and nearly tearing up as 'God Save the King' was sung.

The late Queen's final journey to England was on an RAF C-17, with Anne calling it an honour to accompany her coffin. Over 250,000 mourners paid respects as Queen Elizabeth lay in state at Westminster Hall.

The state funeral on 19 September at Westminster Abbey was a solemn and grand affair, with soldiers marching, music swelling, and her family and staff trailing her coffin. The crowd wept, marking the end of something vast and unrepeatable. Her final farewell drew royals and world leaders, with hundreds of thousands lining the streets to Windsor, with 97,000 along the Long Walk alone. In a private service at St George's Chapel, her coffin joined Prince Philip's in the King George VI Memorial Chapel, marked by a black marble stone bearing a Garter Star and their names.

The Queen was dead, and the nation and Royal Family continued to mourn, but unfazed, Harry kept firing shots at his family. The couple's Netflix series, titled *Harry & Meghan*, premiered on 8 December 2022. The documentary was released in two parts, with the first three episodes debuting on 8 December and the final three episodes following on 15 December. The series was excruciating for the King, William and Royal Family members to watch, airing so soon after the Queen's death.

The documentary shared private moments, including Harry receiving a text from William after the Oprah interview. Harry also accused William's office of briefing against him and Meghan, fuelling criticism that the couple aired too many family grievances. Meghan's exaggerated curtsy reenactment for the Queen, which she compared to a scene from 'Medieval Times, Dinner and Tournament', an American dinner theatre, was widely criticised as mocking and disrespectful, upsetting many viewers. Additionally, unearthed footage from Meghan's role in the TV show *Suits* showed her performing a curtsy, leading some to question her claims of unfamiliarity with the gesture.

On *60 Minutes*, the popular US news magazine programme on CBS, Harry expanded on claims that the Palace leaked stories to protect more senior royals. His assault on his family was relentless. In January 2023, Harry released his memoir

Spare, offering raw insights into his life, including his struggles with his role as the understudy, his grief over Diana's death, and his strained relationship with William and Charles. It was an instant bestseller, selling over 1.4 million copies in the first day across all formats in the US, Canada, and the UK, setting a record for the fastest-selling non-fiction book. Global sales in the first week exceeded 3.2 million copies, netting a fortune for Harry, who reportedly received an advance of at least $20 million (£17 million).

Now Harry had Camilla in his sights. His final salvo was aimed squarely at Camilla. He suggested she had leaked stories to the press and even named senior press figures, including respected Fleet Street editor Geordie Greig, accusing them of helping to reshape Camilla's image at his own expense. An astute editor, Greig calmly addressed this. 'I've been named as close to Camilla,' he said. 'There's exaggeration in his [Harry's] claims. Camilla's always been professional, even reticent. Imagine what she could say!' said the respected *Independent* and former *Daily Mail* and *Mail on Sunday* editor-in-chief. Writing about when William met Camilla for the first time, he said, 'Stories began to appear everywhere about her private conversations – none of which came from my brother. Of course, they could only have been leaked by the one other person present.' For Charles, this direct slur against his wife was a step too far.

The memoir also notably included claims of a physical altercation between Harry and William. He wrote, 'He grabbed me by the collar, ripping my necklace, and knocked me to the floor. I landed on the dog's bowl, which cracked under my back.' It left the younger sibling cut, stunned and his ego bruised, apparently.[204]

Family members were not overly surprised by the rough

and tumble but did not entirely side with William about the story either. Even senior aides are known to tread lightly around the older prince, mindful of his mood swings before raising sensitive issues. Insiders describe him as occasionally 'difficult to handle', a contrast to his composed, family-man public persona. Palace sources recall an incident when William was once overly assertive with his father, echoing traits of his mother's fiery temper, which Charles often faced. The conflict, however, stemmed from William completely misinterpreting a situation, which floored Charles.[205]

While Harry's memoir became a bestseller and huge money-spinner, its publication deepened the already strained family rift. Despite professing love for his family, along with the Netflix interview it deepened the Royal Family's mistrust of the rogue prince, with fears that any private talks conducted with him could surface publicly. Charles, weary of the fight, chose silence, refusing to respond to his son's lurid claims. Insiders whispered it was Harry, not Meghan, leading this reckless charge. To many, the ex-soldier had not only betrayed his family, but his king and his country.

As Harry and Meghan forge a new path in California, the distance from his royal roots grows starker. 'I would like to get my father back. I would like to have my brother back,' he said. But Harry admitted that at that moment neither side would 'recognise' the other. The monarchy marches on, while the divide deepens, and reunion seems increasingly unlikely.[206]

King Charles focused on shaping his reign with purpose, determined to modernise the way the institution is run. He signalled to senior aides that change was coming, calling the Royal Household 'top heavy' – too many high-paid chiefs, not enough lower-ranking staff renumerated fairly. He dubbed

Buckingham Palace, mid-way through a £369 million, decade-long refurbishment, as the 'people's palace'. Aware that time may not be on his side, the new king moved quickly. His first Christmas broadcast, a tribute to his late mother, drew 10.7 million viewers – the most-watched royal message of the century.

CHAPTER 20

VIVAT REX CAROLUS!

To know that we have your support and encouragement . . . has been the greatest possible Coronation gift, as we now rededicate our lives to serving the people of the United Kingdom, the Realms and Commonwealth.

KING CHARLES III, 2023

King Charles sat in St Edward's Chair on 6 May 2023. The crown was heavy. He was annoyed, because William had been a few minutes late, busy filming for his social media about the big day. Now his son and heir dutifully knelt in his Garter Robe and pledged loyalty. Prince George, a Page of Honour for the day, stood nearby, steady and silent. William kissed his father's cheek. He knew William had not wanted to robe-up but bowed to his father's will. In the third row, Harry watched on, close enough to see but playing no part. Charles kissed the Coronation Bible and took the Oath. Behind the screens, the holy oil touched his skin.

Dressed in George VI's red velvet surcoat, Charles changed into a white tunic for the sacred ritual, then donned the golden supertunica and sword belt. He received the regalia and led the homage with William and the Archbishop of Canterbury. After the two-hour ceremony, the newly crowned monarch stepped outside to a cheering crowd. Gun salutes rang across the UK. Once vilified, King Charles and Queen Camilla, were met with warmth, their coronation surpassing all expectations.

There had been some gripes. His Majesty's decision to have a smaller service and to not invite all the hereditary peers, including some non-royal dukes, baffled and upset them, with some calling it a snub. Given their historic role in such ceremonies as part of the same hereditary system as the royals, they had a point. Unlike his mother, Elizabeth II's coronation in 1953, which included around 850 peers, his crowning prioritised modern inclusivity. With only 2,250 Abbey seats, the King invited celebrities and politicians instead, along with charity workers and NHS staff.

There was even talk of drafting at least one black page 'for optics', but that was overruled as too contrived. Instead, the eight Pages of Honour were Prince George, Lord Oliver Cholmondeley, Nicholas Barclay, and Ralph Tollemache attending the King, with Queen Camilla being attended by her grandsons Gus and Louis Lopes, Freddy Parker Bowles, and her nephew Arthur Elliot, all of whom had close family ties to the royal couple.

While reducing numbers made sense, entirely sidelining the nobility and ignoring their contributions to public service and tradition, it raised awkward questions about the monarchy's own hereditary nature. A modest but wider representation of hereditary peers would have struck a better balance, some argued, preserving tradition without overshadowing progress and diversity.

Prince Harry's solo appearance at the coronation set tongues wagging. Meghan stayed behind in California to mark Archie's fourth birthday. There were whispers of a brief peace talk with the King, but there was no sign of a thaw between Harry and William. From a distance, he watched his brother take centre stage. At that historic moment Harry looked adrift; present, but no longer at home.

On the King's instructions, it was a more modern, inclusive ceremony, dropping many traditional elements and drawing widespread public support, with some protests and only a few arrests. Multi-faith leaders attended, reflecting the King's inclusive vision. The Ascension Choir, an eight-member gospel ensemble, especially assembled to perform at the coronation, made history as the first gospel choir at a coronation, fulfilling Charles's desire to incorporate diverse musical traditions into the event.[207] Scholars proclaimed, 'Vivat Rex Carolus!' as Charles vowed to serve.

The Royal Family returned to Buckingham Palace to be greeted by cheering crowds. Despite the rain, tens of thousands lined the route, celebrating the historic day. Meanwhile, Harry quietly left by car for Heathrow to catch a flight back to the US without joining his father and the rest of the family for the balcony appearance.

The next day, on 7 May, Windsor Castle hosted a star-studded Coronation Concert, where William honoured his father by giving a speech on stage, praising him for his lifelong dedication to service and environmental causes. He acclaimed Queen Elizabeth II too, saying she would be a 'proud mother'. Lionel Richie lit up the concert with his hit songs 'Easy' and 'All Night Long', his star power undeniable. Katy Perry dazzled in a gold gown, belting out her hits 'Roar' and 'Firework' to the delight of 20,000 fans, even getting Princess Charlotte to sing along. The night blended tradition and flair, hosted by Hugh Bonneville, with other major stars like Andrea Bocelli adding to the spectacle.

Lionel Richie, a Prince's Trust ally, was invited to stay at Windsor Castle after the show, prompting Katy Perry and her team to demand the same treatment. The palace bigwigs eventually relented, but Perry's entourage caused a stir by partying late into the night, straying into restricted areas.

The coronation celebratory weekend ended with 'The Big Help Out' volunteer drive. Designed to inspire community service and bring people together, the initiative saw thousands participating in charitable activities across the UK. A grateful Charles pledged a modern reign, blending tradition with a forward-looking vision.

Even before his accession, anti-monarchists had questioned Charles's fitness to reign. With Elizabeth II's passing, they felt it was the perfect time to demand constitutional change. It was a matter that the Princess Royal addressed in her own inimitable style, in a rare interview on *CBC News* in Canada. Ahead of Charles's coronation, she reflected on the monarchy's future amid public scrutiny, as well as the protests. Speaking candidly, she dismissed concerns about the institution's relevance.

'We [The Royal Family] don't, in many respects, need to deal with it. It is the monarch that is the key to this. And the constitution that underpins the monarchy,' she said, emphasising the wider Royal Family's supporting role. 'What we do, we hope, contributes to the monarchy . . . conveying continuity of service and understanding.' Pressed on the monarchy's long-term future, the Princess Royal firmly defended its value. 'I believe there is a genuine benefit from this particular arrangement – the constitutional monarchy – and I think it has good long-term benefits. That commitment to long term is what the monarchy stands for.'

Giving a fascinating insight, Princess Anne also spoke about what the public could expect from King Charles now he had stepped into his new role. 'We've been very lucky. My mother was queen for a very long time,' she said. 'For my brother, this is something he's been waiting for, and he's probably spent more time thinking about it.' As for what to expect from the new king, she added, 'You know what you're getting because he's been practising for a bit, and I don't think he'll change.' Anne's straightforward remarks were a reminder of the monarchy's emphasis on stability amid modern challenges ahead. After the coronation, King Charles III's approval rating rose to 63 per cent, up six points.

Some close to the Crown have grown uneasy over what they described as a creeping 'sloppiness' within the palace. They highlighted shabby cover-ups that have rattled even seasoned courtiers. Whispers suggest the King has been ill-served by senior aides who have let standards slip since the passing of Queen Elizabeth and Prince Philip. Since Charles's accession, the household has weathered a string of scandals – some involving staff misconduct, others hushed up but known at the top. Behind closed doors, serious questions are now being asked about privilege, responsibility, and who is truly keeping the palace in order.

In November 2023, one of the royal servants was stopped for alleged shoplifting at the upmarket Fortnum & Mason store in London. Despite a valuable diamond bracelet being found in her bag, somehow, they escaped punishment by the luxury department store, which holds a precious royal warrant. Security staff observed them removing the security tag from the bracelet before attempting to leave via a side exit. Intervention by another royal servant prevented a formal arrest when they persuaded the servant to open their bag after store detectives had apprehended them.

Another royal servant, who was oblivious to what was going on, had been sharing a drink with the royal aide in the store's basement wine bar before the alleged theft occurred. The accused aide, previously monitored by store staff for allegedly taking make-up samples during an earlier visit, was caught on security cameras taking the bracelet from the store's beauty section. As she tried to exit through a side door, security staff had intercepted her.

Fortnum & Mason, favouring discretion, warned the aide she would be banned from the store but allowed her to leave without charges. She reportedly claimed it was a misunderstanding, but there was no doubt as the theft was captured on film. No charges were filed, reportedly due to concerns that prosecuting a royal aide could jeopardise the store's Royal Warrants, first granted in 1910. Despite the gravity of the incident, the aide faced no police or disciplinary action and retained her position within the Royal Household. Her colleagues expressed 'surprise and disappointment' over the episode, describing her as 'utterly faithful' to the royals.

Fortnum & Mason, founded in 1707 on candles that had been recycled from the Royal Household, and known as the late Queen's favourite store, had a long-standing relationship with the Royal Family. Buckingham Palace and the store declined to comment on the matter when asked by the *Mail on Sunday*. The case also highlighted broader concerns over rising shoplifting in the UK, with Fortnum's reportedly relying on private detectives due to diminished confidence in police action.

The King and Queen were informed, but the servant kept her position, with palace sources citing mental health considerations when the *Mail on Sunday* contacted the Palace in November 2023. The individual, however, continue to travel on overseas tours. The shocking incident was reported by the newspaper as a front-page story without naming the servant.[208]

In September 2024, the *Mail on Sunday* revisited the story, reporting that another royal servant, whom they did not name, had complained to their trade union about being 'sidelined' at work in the palace following the shoplifting incident involving a palace colleague, who again they did not name. According to a report by the paper's respected chief reporter Ian Gallagher, although the servant was totally uninvolved and unaware of their palace colleague's attempted crime, they claimed their knowledge of the event had 'negatively impacted [their] career'. They claimed they had been marginalised, with duties they anticipated performing for senior royals assigned to others.[209]

The hypocrisy of the cover-up was exposed in December 2024, when the King stripped several companies of their Royal Warrants, including the renowned British confectionery brand Cadbury, founded by John Cadbury in 1824 and a warrant holder since 1854. Ethical reasons and links to Russia were cited among the reasons that firms lost their warrants. Critics within the household, where the shoplifting incident was openly discussed among other staff, labelled the move 'totally hypocritical' – contrasting it with the leniency shown to the favoured royal servant.

The shoplifting incident came at a time when High Street retailers were grappling with a surge in crime, with around 670 shoplifting cases going unsolved in the UK daily, and an estimated 245,000 shoplifting thefts left without suspects in 2024 alone. Fortnum & Mason was honoured with two new Royal Warrants in 2024; one from His Majesty King Charles III and another from Her Majesty Queen Camilla. It marked the first time in twenty-eight years that the store had received new warrants, underscoring its longstanding relationship with the Royal Household, which spans over three centuries and thirteen monarchs.

Queen Camilla was spotted Christmas shopping at Fortnum & Mason just before Christmas 2024. During her visit, Queen Camilla picked up a £13.95 tin of cinnamon and orange tea, honouring the royal tradition of shopping at Fortnum & Mason. She paid for it.

Around the same time, a palace maid was arrested after a fight at an All Bar One cocktail bar following a Christmas party for Buckingham Palace staff. The *Sun* reported that trouble flared when up to fifty servants arrived for a pre-arranged party after palace drinks. It spiralled 'out of control' with police officers called after 'glasses were hurled, and punches thrown'. A housemaid aimed a punch at the manager, smashed glasses, and was arrested.

The altercation led to the maid spending a night in custody and receiving a fine. Reports of widespread drug use among Royal Household staff further marred the palace's reputation. One maid had to resign amid allegations of cocaine use and other substance abuse, raising questions about the household's internal culture and oversight.[210]

Meanwhile on both sides of the Atlantic, public opinion continued to turn against the 'Duke and Duchess of Montecito', as Harry and Meghan were now mockingly dubbed by the press. In the UK, Conservative MP Bob Seely criticised Harry for 'trashing his family' and proposed legislation to strip the couple of their royal titles. Then their $20 million Spotify deal ended after just twelve episodes of Meghan's *Archetypes* podcast. Disgruntled Spotify executive Bill Simmons, who was the Head of Podcast Innovation and Monetization, labelled the pair 'grifters'[211] over their lack of content, raising doubts about the value of their brand. The Sussexes became targets of satire, including a *South Park* episode mocking their privacy claims. Critics also pointed out their hypocrisy, especially over private jet use amid environmental advocacy, fuelling perceptions of entitlement and tone-deafness.

In January 2025, as wildfires swept through Los Angeles, Meghan Markle reportedly postponed the launch of her Netflix series, *With Love, Meghan,* to focus on relief efforts. She and Prince Harry claimed to have opened their Montecito home to displaced friends and volunteered at the Pasadena Convention Centre. Their efforts drew sharp criticism from actress and filmmaker Justine Bateman, who slammed them in a post on X. She wrote, 'Meghan Markle and Harry are no better than ambulance chasers. What a repulsive "photo op" they achieved. They are "touring the damage"? Are the politicians now? They don't live here: they are tourists. Disaster Tourists.'

The 58-year-old Hollywood actress, known for *Family Ties* and *Desperate Housewives,* took to X to criticise the couple, who were seen in footage plainly dressed and speaking with victims and other helpers, as the death toll reached twenty-four. She wrote, 'Meghan and Harry are no better than ambulance chasers. What a repulsive "photo-op" they achieved. They are "touring the damage"? Are they politicians now? They don't live here; they are tourists. Disaster Tourists.'

Prince Harry's continuing legal battles with the British tabloids delivered one major courtroom win and one significant settlement. He secured £140,600 in damages from Mirror Group Newspapers in 2023 for unlawful information gathering, and in 2024, reached a substantial out-of-court settlement with News Group Newspapers. Together, the cases form the backbone of his campaign against press abuse – a break from the Royal

Family's traditionally cautious approach. His stance was said to have also strained his relationship with his father, who worried that if he initiated a reconciliation with his son, it could backfire and lead to him being dragged into Harry's drawn-out legal woes.[212] Harry confirmed this in a BBC interview in May 2025.

Harry's relentless attacks on his family had seemed unstoppable, until a sudden Palace announcement stopped him in his tracks.

CHAPTER 21

WORRYINGLY DECREPIT

As all those who have been affected by cancer will know, such kind thoughts are the greatest comfort and encouragement.

KING CHARLES III, 2024

King Charles often quipped to friends about reaching that 'worryingly decrepit stage' of life. He jokes too, in his own inimitable style, about it becoming a 'conglomerated miasma' of conflict and chaos. While jesting, they know he is half-serious.

When he was the Prince of Wales, he worried about his energy levels flagging. He sometimes struggled to keep his eyes open. In the 2018 BBC documentary, *Prince, Son and Heir: Charles at 70*, Prince Harry revealed that their father would often work late into the night, sometimes falling asleep at his desk. He mentioned that they would find him with papers stuck to his face. This was not due only to his busy work schedule, but the fact that he suffered from draining sleep apnoea.

Charles's life and energy levels improved dramatically after he started using a CPAP machine, introduced to him by Vice President Al Gore when he hosted him at Highgrove in 2006, to treat the condition where breathing repeatedly stops during sleep, causing fatigue and poor concentration. He now swears by the device that delivers steady air pressure to keep airways open, preventing disruptions. Although it does mean that Charles and Camilla sometimes sleep apart.[213]

Conscious of the probable brevity of his reign, the King often reflects on a lifetime of service: hundreds of overseas tours where he has been forced to endure the empty rhetoric of countless politicians with a diplomatic smile.[214] Many believe that Charles's legacy must include his more than half a century of duty as heir to the throne, and we must not assess him on what will probably be a relatively short reign alone.[215] Others think that given her enduring grace, Charles will inevitably remain in his late mother's shadow. Only time will tell. The King knows unquestionably, however, that he has no time to waste in the top job.

At Dumfries House, when asked about his love of painting watercolours, he sighed resignedly, admitting: 'I don't have time anymore.' Once soothed by the pastime, his brushes now mostly gather dust. The crown's weight allows no such refuge. In a world gripped by war in Ukraine, Russia, and the Middle East, he knows he cannot be a monarch cloaked in detachment, steering clear of worldly affairs.[216]

His path as twenty-first-century monarch is tightrope-thin: neither partisan, nor passive. In November 2023, he went to the UAE for the UN's COP 28 gathering at Expo City, Dubai. Respected among Arab leaders, while he was there he had several private meetings behind the scenes with leading figures in the region and lobbied for peace over the Israel–Gaza crisis. Decades of ties with the region's royal families may now begin bear fruit, not by force, but through careful, deliberate steps. He will not overreach, but silence in the face of a suffering world would betray him and the modern crown he represents.

With the transition and coronation now behind him, the King moved quietly but quickly, cutting through the clutter of an overstaffed Royal Household system. When he finally took the helm, he was surprised at the way Buckingham Palace was being run and demanded immediate change. His action plan was met with push back from the old guard of high-ranking courtiers and increasingly frustrated, he confided dismissively to friends about the palace, 'It's being run like a hotel, and not a very good one.'[217]

His Majesty felt thwarted at every turn. Enough was enough. Irritated by senior palace officials dragging their feet, his hot temper flared. He bluntly instructed the long-serving senior courtiers Vice-Admiral Sir Tony Johnstone-Burt, Master of the Household, and Sir Michael Stevens, Keeper of the Purse and Treasurer to the King, that he wanted change. Some of the senior figures in the top-heavy household, accustomed to the more sedate pace of the late Queen's twilight years when they had a freer hand, did not grasp at first that when the King flagged an issue, he expected action immediately, not excuses or lip service. 'Sure, he's lost his temper when nothing changed, when he returned and saw nothing had been done but eventually, they got the message,' said a senior source.[218]

Subtle changes followed. When the King was told in passing that treasured works of art had been put up on the walls in staff members' private quarters, he was aghast. He went on a room-by-room personal inspection at royal residences such as Sandringham, and instructed an inventory be made. Many of the equine paintings, favoured by the late Queen, were taken down and sent to storage. Beautiful paintings of Bedouin girls by famous Arabic artists and Roman ruins replaced them in the private royal residencies of Sandringham, Balmoral, and Windsor Castle.

The palace began to shift, not loudly, but unmistakably. His mark was there, quiet but undeniable. 'This isn't about financial cuts,' a senior insider remarked. 'It's about getting value for money and efficiency. Sometimes less truly is more.' Another source, referring to him cutting the number of family members dependent on his patronage, was blunter: 'The King isn't running a housing association for distant relatives.'

The eviction of Harry and Meghan from Frogmore Cottage, a Crown Estate property granted to them by the late Queen but unused since their move abroad, was only the start of the process. Their loss of a British base, announced soon after publication of Harry's memoir *Spare*, is described as the 'tip of the iceberg'. The message is clear: no freeloaders in the modern monarchy.

Horrified, the King blocked his brother Prince Andrew's bizarre request to pay £32,000 for spiritual Indian gurus to treat him while they were all staying at his home. It was something the Queen had previously passed through; for Charles it was a definitive 'no'. Several non-working Royal Family members, like his nieces Princesses Beatrice and Eugenie, were told unequivocally they would have to stand on their own two feet and pay their way.

Charles has also ordered his aides to tighten spending from both the Duchy of Lancaster and the Sovereign Grant. His priority? Smarter use of resources – like offering competitive pay and pensions to hire and keep top-tier staff. 'There have been staff cutbacks. That started straight away. The buzz phrase in the household now is "value for money",' said the senior source.

Several members of the extended Royal Family have enjoyed subsidised palace accommodation, with some having apartments being used by their children as 'London pads'. The inside source said: 'Over time, that is all going to change. Properties will be let at commercial rates going forward and to people outside the family. Where it is in a palace environment, they will of course be security vetted.' The King has set about reshaping the monarchy, so it is fit for generations to come. 'Too many advisers to advisers,' one insider remarked. 'That stops now. The Boss demands efficiency, real work, fair pay.' Another added, 'The old ways made no sense. Change had to come.'

Charles's reform agenda came to an abrupt standstill only seventeen months into his reign, derailed by a double health crisis that shook the monarchy to its core. On 17 January 2024, the Palace first revealed that the Princess of Wales was recovering from abdominal surgery. Hours later, it was announced that the King himself required treatment for an enlarged prostate. The public and press looked on with growing concern. Behind palace walls, Charles had been quietly enduring mounting pain. Months earlier at Birkhall, his condition had worsened so dramatically that a doctor was summoned. He was given morphine, fitted with a catheter, and taken to Aberdeen Hospital.[219]

By revealing specific details of his treatment, Charles had broken with the tradition set by his parents. Openness was the plan. Despite Queen Camilla urging more caution, the King wanted to lead by example; he wanted men over sixty to seek help, backed by stark medical data. The impact was swift. NHS web traffic on prostate issues soared after his announcement.

In California, Harry and Meghan, who had spent the last few months badmouthing the Royal Family, offered their 'well-wishes'. Few listened. Charles said nothing and Catherine did not respond either. The Sussexes had lost credibility; they no longer had the upper hand their popularity had once given them. A palace aide scoffed at their statement, calling it 'cynical'.

The pair had, after all, been slinging mud at the family and playing the victim just weeks before.

On 26 January, the King had his procedure in the London Clinic, the same central London private hospital as the Princess of Wales. While he was there, he visited Catherine in her room. Three days later, he left through the front door, smiling. In the meantime, she had slipped out of a back exit to escape being photographed by the paparazzi.

Life resumed until on 5 February the Palace dropped another bombshell. During surgery for a benign prostate issue, doctors had found something unexpected – cancer. After favoured Fleet Street editors had been alerted, the Palace issued a formal statement. It read:

> During the King's recent hospital procedure for benign prostate enlargement, a separate issue of concern was noted. Subsequent diagnostic tests have identified a form of cancer. His Majesty has today commenced a schedule of regular treatments, during which time he has been advised by doctors to postpone public-facing duties.

This time, details of the specific type of cancer were withheld. But after consulting top aides, Charles thought it imperative that he reveal his diagnosis to end rumours and to raise awareness of the disease and the importance of early detection. He started treatment at once. Of course, he was concerned, but he vowed to face it head-on.

First, he broke the news to his close family personally, including Harry, whom he telephoned with the worrying news. He was shocked and alarmed, so too was William. At the time, Charles was undergoing chemotherapy, and simply wanted peace and quiet. The last thing he needed was any drama. Without an invite, Harry took it upon himself to fly over to see his father from his California base. The King, who had planned to spend the weekend at his Sandringham Estate in Norfolk, was irritated when he was left kicking his heels until his errant son arrived.

Their meeting was brief, around thirty minutes. Charles, wary of prolonging it, had pre-arranged for the meeting to be interrupted, citing it was time for a medical procedure. Harry left soon after, but there was no procedure scheduled and never was. Instead, the King flew straight to Sandringham by helicopter, which had been waiting to take him. William stayed away. He had no interest in spending time with his brother.

A past concern with cancer and decades of work with charities connected with the disease gave the King a unique insight into what he was facing. He became more empathetic to those with the plight. He listened to Dr Michael Dixon, a seasoned NHS general practitioner and advocate of complementary medicine. He was appointed head of the Royal Medical Household in 2022, shortly after Queen Elizabeth's death, and oversees all Charles's health care. When his doctors recommended, he started eating lunch, something he has rarely done in his life. His chefs prepared spinach soup, his favoured dish. He also started to take regular afternoon naps.

Letters flooded in, thousands of them, overwhelming the King with their genuine warmth. 'They've reduced me to tears,' he told Prime Minister Rishi Sunak. It was not just polite applause, it was heartfelt; there was glitter on homemade cards and chocolate Smarties from children, and complete strangers pouring out their hearts with affection. Staff noted the impact on the man. This was a more emotional king, they thought, contrasting it with colder moments from his past. Some recalled that when a palace staffer, Katie Bland, was diagnosed with a lump in her breast, Charles had made an offhand aside that left several members of his staff feeling disheartened and disappointed.[220]

But the bad news kept coming. On 22 March, in a pre-recorded televised message, Catherine, the Princess of Wales, revealed she too had been diagnosed with the preliminary stages of cancer. Her doctors had advised that she start a course of preventative chemotherapy. She called it a 'huge shock'. Her voice steady, she vowed to fight. She stood tall, her words slicing through the quiet: 'At this time, I am also thinking of all those whose lives have been affected by cancer. For everyone facing this disease, in whatever form, please do not lose faith or hope. You are not alone.'

William was totally crestfallen. Later, he would call the experience 'brutal . . . the hardest year of my life' in a candid interview with *The Times* journalist Kate Mansey.[221] His father and wife were both stricken. A cruel blow for a man with three young children. He urged his father to slow down and listen to his medical team. He too wanted to cut his engagements back to ten for the year. The King refused that request. 'Think again,' he urged.

Charles rallied behind his 'beloved' daughter-in-law and spoke of her 'courage and resilience' – particularly poignant as he was also undergoing cancer treatment. Like William, he became a 'beacon of strength' to the princess. The two had a private one-to-one lunch at Windsor Castle, the day before Catherine's pre-recorded video was aired. There, they were able to offer each other support. After it was shown, Charles issued a palace statement saying he was 'so proud of Catherine for her courage in speaking as she did.'

When William finally went back to public duties, he was bombarded with questions about his wife's health at every turn. He said little but promised to 'look after' her. On his first public appearance after her cancer announcement, he gave a helping hand loading food and cooking in the kitchen at the food distribution charity Surplus to Supper, in Sunbury-on-Thames, Surrey.

Volunteer Rachel Candappa, aged seventy-one, handed two 'Get Well Soon' cards to the Prince addressed to the King and Catherine. He looked visibly moved, saying, 'Thank you, you are very kind.' When Ms Candappa told William to look after Catherine, he placed his left hand on her shoulder and told her, 'I will.' She said afterwards, 'He's human after all, remember he's royal, but apart from royal he's a husband, a father to the children, so he needs to look after her.' Alongside William, Queen Camilla also stepped up, taking on more duties and emerging as a steady force during a time of royal uncertainty.

Easter came and the doctors cleared the King to meet the public. But Catherine and William stayed away. Outside St George's, he stepped forward. 'Keep going strong,' one man shouted. Charles smiled. 'I obey my instructions,' he said with a glint in his eyes. Well, he did, kind of. After months of darkness, the light was at last beginning to return. On 15 May 2024, the King hosted a garden party at Buckingham Palace. The tea flowed, the band played, and the scones were perfect.

It was a celebration of Britain's creative industries – actors, directors and behind the scenes crew – 4,000 of them. Among them were luminaries such as Tracey Emin, Sir Lenny Henry, Kate Moss, Sir Ridley Scott, Maya Jama, and Louis Theroux. The King was not just upholding tradition, he was rewriting it. He looked sharp, very dapper, wearing a natty pink waistcoat with his grey morning suit, to match his wife Queen Camilla's outfit.

It was traditional, yes, but with subtle changes – like the garden party itself. Charles's fresh-look monarchy, inching forward.

During a visit to the University College Hospital (UCH) Macmillan Cancer Centre, in London, Charles appeared more open and candidly shared his reaction to the diagnosis, saying, 'It's always a bit of a shock, isn't it, when they tell you.' The King moved through the hospital, steady and smiling, his own health struggles set aside. In the foyer, he and the Queen made an impromptu walkabout, meeting patients who were standing behind ropes. His focus was clear: early testing saves lives.

Upstairs, in a room lined with pink-cushioned chairs, he listened as Asha Millen, aged sixty, shared her fight against bone marrow cancer. She asked how he was, and he replied, 'I'm well.' Nearby, Lesley Woodbridge, sixty-three, spoke of her sarcoma diagnosis. The King said little but listened intently. Queen Camilla was quieter still, slipping into side rooms, her words soft. She admitted to Roger Woodbridge, husband of cancer patient Lesley, 63, 'It's just so difficult.'

In the hospital's depths, they saw tomorrow: melanoma vaccines, lung cancer breakthroughs, CT scans offering hope. Before leaving, the royal couple walked among the crowd again, being handed a stuffed Jack Russell, books and cards, all exchanged for smiles. When the day ended, what remained were not just lifted spirits but a spark of hope, for awareness, for action, for change.

The late Queen Elizabeth's shadow still looms large, but steadily, the King has carved out his role as the nation's patriarch. He has never been one to idle. Even while being treated for cancer, he continues to work hard. For years, he fought to make a difference, to illuminate dark corners, to champion causes. Even though he now wears the crown, it has not bound him. He speaks his mind less, avoiding awkward conflict with his ministers, but his hand is firm, gathering minds to tackle the weighty matters of the day.

In the past, Charles spoke of a 'desperate desire' to restore greatness to Britain. That desire burns still. If anything in this fractured world, under Charles's stewardship the standing of the monarchy has held firm. His work and projects he initiated speak louder: uniting the Commonwealth, aiding island nations through the Blue Economy, and proving leadership is not about show. For him, it is all about impact.

The King, sure-footed, happily consults his son William now. He trusts him to do what is right. William, though, is clear: his life must balance duty and family. He and Catherine know their time will come as king and queen, but for now, they have drawn a line. To the late Queen Elizabeth, to courtiers, and now to the King, William has said the same. He and Catherine will do their share, but their children come first. Their eldest, Prince George, must grow into his role without its weight crushing him. 'He needs time,' said a palace insider. 'They want him to understand what's ahead but live as a boy first. Balance now will make him strong when his time comes.'

Catherine, too, has her priorities set. A former royal aide put it simply: 'She supports William and together they raise their children their way. They are their priority. Of course, her public duties matter, but family matters more.' Some sneer, calling it all terribly quaint and traditional. Catherine calls it essential. Family is her foundation, first, second, and third. She makes the school run, watches the plays, cheers at sports days. It is deliberate. Her parents were there for her, and that steadied her. 'She wants her children to feel that same security,' said another source.

For Catherine, the little things are not trivial at all; they are everything. In September 2024, in a polished video directed by Will Warr, she shared with the public that she had completed chemotherapy and that she hoped to stay cancer-free. While many found it moving, some critics slammed her for it. Queen Camilla, relieved at Catherine's recovery and very much with her tongue in cheek, joked with friends that it was 'like a shampoo commercial'.[222]

Once she was given the all-clear, William and Catherine made a big call for Prince George's future. At twelve, he is growing up fast and, at his own request, became a weekly boarder at Lambrook School in Bracknell, Berkshire, staying in a designated boarding house starting in autumn 2024, believed to be his final year there. He stayed there from Monday to Friday, living among his friends, and went home for weekends, a balance between independence and family. George, like his father, loves watching Aston Villa FC with his dad and playing football near Ascot too. A prince, but also a boy, finding his place.[223]

CHAPTER 22

ROYALLY MINTED

For decades Parliament has been far too lenient about the royal family's finances. This avaricious practice needs to end.[224]

NORMAN BAKER, 2023

The royal money men have often framed the cost of the monarchy to taxpayers as pocket change; equivalent to a first-class stamp in 2019 or a loaf of bread in 2023. But, of course, that just scratches the surface. Officially, the monarchy cost tax contributors £86.3 million in 2022–23, or £1.29 per person. This figure excludes the separate £34 million annual allocation for Buckingham Palace refurbishment. The royals continue to receive significant public funding, with the Sovereign Grant set to rise to £132 million in 2025–26 due to increasing profits from the Crown Estate, intensifying calls from critics of the monarchy for a comprehensive audit of royal finances.

These figures tell only one side of the story, and do not include huge hidden expenses. According to the anti-monarchist group Republic, the genuine cost may reach a staggering £510 million when the cost of protection is factored in. Meanwhile, the Crown Estate contributed a record £442.6 million profits for the Treasury in 2022-23, offsetting the monarchy's expenses, but leaving questions about the monarchy's net cost.

The actual cost has been a battleground for many years. Supporters claim the monarchy pulls in millions of pounds boosting tourism and 'Brand Britain'. The real figures, however, are elusive. Tourism reports show that 60 per cent of visitors come for royal sites, with Buckingham Palace high on the list. While it is clear they bring in crowds, particularly at moments of national celebration, how do you put a price on it? That is still anyone's guess.

Critics are quick to note that around ten million people flock to Versailles each year – making it one of the world's most visited landmarks. Originally a hunting lodge built by Louis XIII in 1623, the palace has outlasted the monarchy it once housed. France has not had a 'royal' ruler since Louis-Philippe I, of the House of Orléans, a cadet branch of the larger House of Bourbon, the ruling royal family of France, whose reign ended with the 1848 February Revolution and the birth of the Second Republic. He was followed by Napoleon III, the nephew of Emperor Napoleon I, who served as President of France from 1848–52 and then as Emperor of the French from 1852–70 before being deposed during the Franco-Prussian War.

All those years without a monarch – yet Versailles remains a magnet for tourists. By contrast, Buckingham Palace draws between 500,000 to 550,000 visitors annually, though it is worth noting the far more limited public access.

It is true that major royal events can deliver a short-term jolt to the economy, but the impact is often fleeting and mixed. The 2012 Diamond Jubilee bank holiday, for instance, cost an estimated £1.2 billion in lost productivity, while the 2022 Platinum Jubilee set the economy back £2.4 billion. Royal weddings like Harry and Meghan's in 2018 draw crowds and spending, but rarely translate into lasting economic benefit. Despite growing calls for transparency, royal finances remain notoriously opaque, shielded by age-old tradition, privacy laws, and special exemptions. Key expenses like their security and income from private estates remain frustratingly murky.

So, when Channel 4's *Dispatches* and The *Sunday Times* launched a five-month investigation their findings were a sobering reality check; and did not make easy viewing for the royals and their supporters. The programme, *The King, The Prince & Their Secret Millions*, aired on 2 November 2024 and exposed how the King's Duchy of Lancaster and William's Duchy of Cornwall estates bolster their considerable income, raking in £50 million from National Health Service hospitals and state schools. Embarrassingly, the probe exposed the huge earnings made by the two landed trusts from renting out land and buildings they own to public bodies.

One instance highlighted was an £11 million contract over fifteen years that grants an NHS hospital trust the use of a London warehouse to house its ambulance fleet. The investigation uncovered that the Duchy of Lancaster even tried to gain good publicity from the deal by releasing a statement that it was 'pleased to be of assistance' to Guy's and St Thomas' NHS Foundation Trust. The January 2023 press release painted a generous picture: the redbrick warehouse near Tower Bridge was a boon to the trust. Yet, it was charging them £829,348 in annual rent.

Since becoming the Duke of Cornwall on his father's accession, William has been meticulous in watching over the way the estate is run, staying until the end of Duchy finance meetings. 'He is right across it. And won't be bamboozled or have the wool pulled over his eyes,' said a source close to him.

The investigation revealed that the Duchy of Cornwall has quietly turned its vast estate into a cash machine. In Dorset, fire and county authorities were tied into longterm leases on land, as were state schools, while the Ministry of Justice now pays to occupy Dartmoor Prison for decades. The Royal Navy, too, funds jetties and ship moorings on Duchy shores. Even charities – from St John Ambulance to Macmillan Cancer Support, Marie Curie and Comic Relief – have rented garages and offices, giving one London block the nickname 'Charity Towers'. Negotiated under King Charles and now overseen by Prince William, these deals have netted the Duchy tens of millions of pounds.

Both ancient trusts, of course, work within the letter of the law. A spokesperson said in response to the television probe, 'The Duchy of Lancaster operates as a commercial company, managing a broad range of land and property assets across England and Wales. It complies with all relevant UK legislation and regulatory standards applicable to its range of business activities.' But that is missing the point. Critics argued that these deals cannot be morally right, especially for the man who is not only head of state, but head of the nation, as well as his son and immediate heir. It is understood that when aides pressed for more transparency on the running of the landed trust in 2024, Charles pushed back.[225]

The backlash was immediate. Popular left-leaning radio host James O'Brien, on his LBC show on 4 November, accused the King and Prince William of 'milking the country', criticising their financial practices and public funding. Broadcaster and author Libby Purves, writing in *The Times*, criticised King Charles and Prince William for profiting from public services. She labelled it a 'PR disaster' that even 'the staunchest monarchist will wince at', highlighting the controversial rents taken from the NHS, charities, and the military.[226]

Norman Baker, the former Liberal MP and Privy Councillor, a long-time critic of the monarchy he dubbed 'Europe's priciest', highlighted the tax breaks, voluntary income taxes, and the growing Sovereign Grant, which were all fuelled, he said, by palace lobbying. He demanded tax fairness, reforms to the two Duchies and perks, and greater media scrutiny, to challenge what he describes as the UK's 'last imperial monarchy'.

The monarch's personal wealth has also come under scrutiny in the past. The so-called 'Paradise Papers', leaked to the press in 2017, showed the late Queen Elizabeth II's private estate, the Duchy of Lancaster, had around £10 million in offshore funds, including funds based in Bermuda and the Cayman Islands. Some of this invested money was linked to a company accused of exploiting poor families through predatory rent-to-own schemes. It was not a good look.

Once again, no laws had been broken, but these revelations still raised eyebrows about the appropriateness of Britain's head of state benefiting financially from such arrangements, fuelling public criticism over financial secrecy within the monarchy.

A 2023 *Guardian* investigation exposed how unclaimed estates in Cornwall and Lancashire, from those who die without heirs, bolster funds for both duchies. Despite promises in the aftermath of the Second World War to direct such funds to charity, much of the money instead continued to go into the royal property portfolios. Incredibly this centuries-old practice, used by Edward VIII and George VI to amass wealth, continues today, raising fundamental questions about the morality of the practice. Critics argue it is time to end the royals' tax-free windfalls and allow proper transparency and scrutiny of their financial dealings.

Queen Victoria once paid tax, but by 1910, George V had secured exemptions, and by the 1930s, George VI paid none whatsoever. In 1992, but only after public uproar, Queen Elizabeth agreed to pay income tax and capital gains tax, and in 1993 she first monarch to pay it for sixty years. King Charles's fortune is still opaque, blending personal and national holdings. Estimated wealth spans Balmoral, Sandringham, the Duchy of Lancaster, vast art collections, stud farms, and a stock portfolio. While taxed on income and gains, inheritance tax does not apply to him.[227]

The cost of the monarch and the extended Royal Family has long been a sore point. The new deal started in 1993. Prime Minister John Major claimed the move was voluntary, not forced; Buckingham Palace denied the Queen acted under duress. The tipping point, however, came over who would pay the £36.5 million for the extensive restoration of Windsor Castle after a fire.

The north-east wing, including St George's Hall and the Private Chapel, required extensive restoration. The hall's roof was rebuilt with a medieval-inspired hammerbeam design, while the chapel, destroyed entirely, was reimagined within the hall's redesign. Completed in 1997, the project balanced historical accuracy with modern fire safety, funded partly by public tours of Buckingham Palace.

New rules left only Queen Elizabeth, Prince Philip, and the Queen Mother publicly funded. Sir Marcus Fox, a Tory grandee, called it a relief. Lord St John praised her wisdom. Historian David Starkey was less impressed. 'This fixes symptom, not the problem,' he said. 'The monarchy needs a purpose.' The controversial historian made a valid point that caught the Queen's and her courtiers' attention.

Since 2001, the Palace has flaunted its 'transparency' by

publishing costs. In 2003–04, they revealed publicly that the cost of Queen Elizabeth as sovereign was £36.8 million. Her personal fortune, however, was not disclosed. It was estimated to be in the region of £275 million, but this figure has never been confirmed. Royal records stayed sealed. William, who guards his privacy jealously, also keeps his income a closely guarded secret, rowing back on the limited transparency his father sanctioned over the running of his office, when he was heir to the throne.

As Duke of Cornwall, King Charles publicly disclosed his Duchy tax payments from 1993, while Prince William has opted for less transparency and has chosen not to publicly disclose the amount of tax he pays on his Duchy income, though it is understood he pays income tax at the standard UK rate after allowable deductions. His decision to row back on openness has sparked a debate amid the Duchy's £23.6 million income in 2023–24.

Writing in the *Sunday Times*, Craig Prescott, a lecturer in law at Royal Holloway, University of London, specialising in UK constitutional law and author of the new book, *Modern Monarchy*, wrote that perception is everything for modern royals, and an outdated Duchy threatens that, putting their public support at risk.[228] Criticism from respected quarters kept coming. A leader in *The Times* on 24 November 2024 was blunt, stating: 'It is hard to calculate how much the Royal Family costs Britain. Greater transparency is required.'

The Sovereign Grant now stands at £86 million annually. Security costs stay hidden. The Court Circular, a maze of royal duties, keeps citizens guessing too. By 2011, David Cameron's government secured 15 per cent of those profits for the monarchy. The Chancellor of the Exchequer George Osborne called it an economic link to the Crown Estate's performance, aiming to provide financial stability and align royal finances with economic conditions. Cameron later admitted the move had been overly 'generous'.[229]

Charity financing has not proved smooth for Charles, either. In 2021, his close personal aide Michael Fawcett, his long-term aide and loyal fixer, became embroiled in a messy 'cash for honours' style scandal. The aide allegedly promised honours and citizenship in exchange for sizeable donations to his boss's charities. Email trails and letters exposed deals tied to wealthy Arab sheikhs and restoration projects. The Prince's Foundation distanced itself, but the damage was done. With Charles coming under fire from the press, Fawcett stepped aside temporarily from his role as chief executive of the Prince's Foundation to allow for an investigation.

Fawcett's fall from grace centred on dealings with Saudi billionaire Mahfouz Marei Mubarak bin Mahfouz, a major donor to Charles's projects, including Dumfries House. In return, Fawcett allegedly offered him help with securing an honorary CBE (Commander of the British Empire) title and medal, and support for his citizenship bid. Unearthed emails revealed the arrangement and Mahfouz quietly received the honour at Buckingham Palace in 2016, officially for philanthropy. But investigators uncovered more: promises of royal favour, loftier titles, and fast-tracked citizenship in exchange for cash.[230]

The scandal pulled back the curtain on a network of wealthy Middle Eastern donors, where influence flowed as easily as money. Mahfouz stood at the centre, his honorary title symbolising the uneasy marriage of royal favour and deep-pocketed expectations. As scrutiny intensified, the Charity Commission and Scotland Yard launched investigations. Fawcett, once indispensable, became untouchable – even for Charles. The system came under the microscope, and the questions grew sharper: How many deals were struck? How far did the promises go? And crucially, what did Charles know, and when?

Under fire, Fawcett resigned in November 2021, after leaked letters revealed he had offered to help Mahfouz Marei Mubarak bin Mahfouz, a major donor to The Prince's Foundation and Saudi businessman, receive an honorary CBE from Charles in a private Buckingham Palace ceremony, not listed in the Court Circular. In 2017, when he was the Foundation's chief executive, Michael Fawcett, offered in writing to help secure Mahfouz an upgrade to a knighthood and support his British citizenship application – matters regulated under the Honours (Prevention of Abuses) Act 1925. Though Mahfouz has denied wrongdoing, an internal charity probe confirmed Fawcett had coordinated with fixers on the honours process. The revelations led to a Metropolitan Police investigation. But in August 2023, police concluded no further action would be taken. Falling on his sword took some of the heat off his boss, to whom he was devoted.

Scotland Yard and the Charity Commission launched separate probes and Charles categorically denied knowing anything about the alleged deal. The following February, Scotland Yard launched an investigation into the allegations, but in August 2023 they concluded their investigation, deciding to take no further action.

Charles kept a close eye on every detail of his Scottish project and retreat, though the public was told otherwise. Behind closed doors, Fawcett was his trusted confidant, his eyes and ears. The door always stayed firmly shut whenever he and Charles were in meetings. His advisers knew the risks. He may not have known every detail, but it happened on Charles's watch.

The scandal stained Charles's charitable empire, exposing

uncomfortable ties between wealth, honours, and royal influence. In the end, it was about power, access, and the price of blurred loyalty. Fawcett, faithful to the last, was cast adrift, the sacrificial lamb.

An inquiry by the Office of the Scottish Charity Regulator (OSCR) later cleared Fawcett of misconduct too. But the report did criticise poor governance and Fawcett's 'unacceptable' failure to brief trustees on serious risks, such as uninsured artworks worth over £100 million. It also revealed that Fawcett had been appointed to lead the foundation with no formal job description, effectively operating without oversight. Significantly, it found no wrongdoing by him or other charity officials.

As Fawcett was effectively cleared, Charles actively explored ways of bringing him back into the royal fold, but both Queen Camilla and Prince William – as well as his senior aides – strongly advised against it. Their intervention reportedly frustrated the King, but he reluctantly agreed.

Charles knew that without Fawcett, the Dumfries House project might have failed. He relied on his most loyal aide to make things happen. A great networker and deal closer, Fawcett knew all the right people and how and when they could help his boss; he would always go the extra mile. As a result, Dumfries House became the East Ayrshire region's second-largest employer, after the public sector, with over 200 staff contributing to its educational programmes and boosting the local economy.

Fawcett was a great facilitator. When Queen Camilla's daughter, Laura Lopes, was hoping to sell her house but struggling, he asked Lord David Brownlow to help, which he did. Brownlow, a trustee and later chair of The Prince's Foundation, supported the charity through his firm Havisham Properties, which between 2012 and 2017 purchased 11 homes in the Knockroon ecovillage near Dumfries House for around £1.7 million. In 2018, he was appointed a Commander of the Royal Victorian Order. The Wirth family, co-owners of the gallery Hauser & Wirth, have long-standing connections with the Royal Family, including a long-term rental property near Balmoral. Princess Eugenie worked at the gallery, and Ayesha Shand also built part of her career there.[231]

Anti-monarchy campaign group Republic uncovered that scores of military personnel are seconded to the Royal Household, costing taxpayers over £500,000 in 2023 for roles such as equerries and valets, support ceremonial, logistical, or advisory roles within royal operations. Many private secretaries over the years were seconded from the Foreign and Commonwealth Office.

Critics called it 'wasteful', but it was just the tip of the iceberg. Sources disclosed that two of Charles's three valets are Ministry of Defence-paid senior warrant officers. It emerged too that the Royal Logistics Corps is now used to transport the King's bags, once handled privately and much more cost effectively by Arterial Movers when he was heir.[232]

A Flag Sergeant, whose job is raising the Royal Standard wherever the monarch is present, is also bizarrely tasked with cleaning the Master of the Household and his deputy's shoes. While the Ministry of Defence defends these roles as necessary, many see the system as outdated indulgences funded by taxpayers.[233]

Throughout his life, Prince Philip was a military man to the core. While loving Charles dearly, the Duke often bristled at what he saw as his son's overindulgent lifestyle. He preferred to travel light and with a small entourage, just one aide and a police protection officer, with a suit carrier slung over his back. In stark contrast, Charles's large retinue and extensive luggage would leave his father unimpressed. When they travelled together on a royal flight, Charles would always let his father disembark first; that way he would avoid his critical eye and the inevitable rebuke, when he saw staff off-loading his mountain of luggage.

At Sandringham, a footman was tasked with bringing Charles's tightly packed ingredients for his special breakfasts in a big holdall, known as the 'breakfast bag'. Philip would question the need for this when the chefs on tap prepared meals that were, as he would put it, 'bloody good enough for the rest of us.' It was another example of idiosyncratic indulgence Philip could not abide. When at Balmoral he saw special cushions had been put out in the drawing room for not only Charles, who has suffered from chronic lower back pain for years, but for Camilla too, the straight-backed duke joked dismissively, 'Oh, don't tell me it's catching.'

Some staff and former aides admit King Charles sometimes shows traits of OCD. He has a fiery temper too and some describe how working for him can be like 'treading on eggshells'. In his book *Rebel Prince*, Tom Bower claimed that Charles travelled with his own toilet seat on official tours. During a 2018 walkabout in Brisbane, Australia, the prince personally dismissed the claim, saying, 'Oh, don't believe all that crap.' However, insiders suggest there is some truth to the story.[234]

At Craigowan Lodge, about a mile from the main Balmoral Castle, his servants would swap the cheap plastic loo seat that Charles could not abide for a wooden one during his stays, a quiet indulgence. Once, however, they forgot to change it back at the end of his stay, just ahead of Philip's visit there. So, an aide was sent back from Highgrove, a drive of 500 miles taking around nine hours by car, to replace the offending wooden lavatory seat with the original plastic one before the old duke arrived, avoiding an inevitable clash about it between father and son.[235]

Some past staff members say surviving under 'The Boss' – King Charles – requires a touch of sycophancy; those who fail to show the due deference that he expects to receive rarely stick around. Sir Malcolm Ross, one of the late Queen's most senior and long-serving courtiers, was stunned by the flood of weekend calls he received when he switched to become Charles's Master of the Household. He told other staff that he received more calls from the then prince in his first weekend than during his entire time working for the Queen. One such princely instruction was to remind staff to turn off the tap while brushing their teeth.[236]

A servant was once even scolded for running the bath too high, only to be reminded that seven cars were washed daily by the chauffeurs, perfectly illustrating the bubble Charles inhabits. Cars are constantly shuffled around the country for engagements. Even now the King is under the illusion that only one electric car is used, oblivious to the second pre-positioned due to the limited distance range of the vehicles. Insiders say he has insisted in the past on a one-night trip to Highgrove simply to see the wild meadow in bloom, never mind the chef, butler, valet, personal assistant and police convoy following along. One former servant said, 'It's one rule for him, another for everyone else.'[237]

Highgrove House, Charles's cherished retreat, reflects his love for organic gardening and entertaining. Its expertly designed gardens blend wild beauty with formal elegance, making it a perfect setting for hosting guests. Notable visitors often stay in the White Room, leaving behind plaques in the bathroom to mark their visits. Jools Holland, Billy Connolly, Emma Thompson, Spike Milligan, and Al Pacino have all left their mark. Comedian Jim Davidson was invited to stay after headlining a charity gig for the then Prince of Wales. He asked to bring his ex-wife along as she was a big royalist – only for a mix-up to land them in the same room overnight. His plaque reads: 'Jim Davidson stayed here with his ex-wife by royal appointment.' When one admiral who had stayed then sent one in, it did not make the wall.

Missteps over invited guests, however, were inevitable; photos with the wrong people with colourful CVs, meetings that aged poorly. One near miss involved Roman Abramovich, the enigmatic ex-Chelsea owner and Russian billionaire. Sir Michael Peat, Charles's senior aide, had arranged a meeting between the two men at Highgrove, but the Prince, who without their knowledge dubbed these wealthy donors 'Bond villains', got cold feet at the eleventh hour. Recommended to steer clear, he bolted to Camilla's Ray Mill House, leaving aides to explain his sudden 'unavoidable' absence to the bemused oligarch.

When Charles called ahead later to announce his return, he was furious when told that Abramovich and his entourage were still on site, having been given a tour of Highgrove's eclectic gardens. To avoid him, Charles used a side entrance.

Abramovich, under pressure from sanctions linked to Russia's invasion of Ukraine, sold Chelsea football club for £4.25 billion in 2022, under a UK government proviso that he would not benefit. Of the sale proceeds, £2.35 billion remains frozen in a UK account, earmarked for humanitarian aid in Ukraine but awaiting allocation.[238]

CHAPTER 23

THE SILENT THREAT

If people don't want it, they won't have it.[239]

CHARLES, THE PRINCE OF WALES ON THE MONARCHY, 1994

For years, left-leaning British writers, thinkers and politicians have pushed to abolish the monarchy, with little success. Critics from Thomas Paine to George Orwell called monarchy as outdated. In *The Rights of Man* (1791), Paine called it undemocratic by design. Orwell, even amid Britain's war with Hitler and the Nazis, dismissed it as an 'anachronism'. He died in 1950 still convinced Britain needed a radical social reset.

Among those who pushed for system change, the MP Tony Benn stood out. A staunch socialist and former Labour minister, he was forced out of Parliament in 1960 after inheriting the title Viscount Stansgate. He fought back, insisting democracy must outrank nobility. His campaign led to the Peerage Act 1963. Benn became the first to renounce a peerage, and then returned to the Commons, elected and unbowed. For him, power had to be earned, not inherited.

To Benn, the monarchy embodied privilege and stood in the

way of real democracy. He called for an elected head of state. In his famous 'Five Democratic Questions' speech, he urged anyone meeting a powerful person to ask them five questions, 'What power have you got? Where did you get it from? In whose interests do you exercise it? To whom are you accountable? And how can we get rid of you?' His 1991 The Commonwealth of Britain Bill in which he proposed abolishing the British monarchy failed, but the message endured.[240]

A lifelong critic of the Crown, Jeremy Corbyn did not push for abolition as Labour leader in 2015. Though openly republican – once calling the monarchy 'a load of nonsense' – he took the required parliamentary oath and later joined the Privy Council, swearing loyalty and secrecy to the monarch. That same year, he met Prince Charles at Clarence House. The two men, born only months apart, were cordial enough. The gardener-politician even earned royal favour by bringing Charles the gift of a jar of homemade jam, crafted from fruit grown on his London allotment.[241]

Commonwealth nations and former realms are steadily cutting ties with the Crown. Ghana, Kenya, and Nigeria led the way in the 1960s, followed by Guyana, Trinidad and Tobago, and Dominica in the 1970s. In 2021, Charles, as guest of honour, watched Barbados become a republic – fifty-five years after independence – by amending its 1966 Independence Order.

Now, Jamaica is planning a referendum to ditch the monarchy. Antigua and Barbuda aim for a similar vote within three years. Belize is phasing out royal symbols, including the monarch on its currency. Saint Kitts and Nevis is launching a commission to explore republicanism, with public consultations and constitutional reform underway.

Australia, Canada, and New Zealand show little urgency to

cut ties with the monarchy. Australia rejected a republic in 1999, and interest flickered after the death of Queen Elizabeth II, but quickly faded. Prime Minister Anthony Albanese shelved plans for a vote after the 2023 Voice referendum failed, citing economic priorities. King Charles and Queen Camilla's 2024 realm tour stirred some debate, but no serious push for change followed.[242]

Faith in William and Catherine took a hit during their troubled 2022 Caribbean tour. In Belize, there were planning blunders; in Jamaica, calls for reparations and a blunt message from Prime Mister Andrew Holness: William would never be king there. A photograph of the couple greeting Black children through a fence drew outrage – branded a 'white-saviour parody'. In the Bahamas, events were slammed as 'tone-deaf' colonial throwbacks. Already shadowed by Meghan Markle's racism claims and the Black Lives Matter movement, the charm offensive was badly out of touch. William later promised reform, but the backlash left a mark.

At the October 2024 Commonwealth summit in Samoa, King Charles addressed leaders as Head of the Commonwealth for the first time. With history heavy in the room, he said, 'I understand how the most painful aspects of our past still resonate.' Measured but firm, he stopped short of apology or reparations, instead urging reflection and unity: 'None of us can change the past, but we can commit to learning its lessons and righting enduring inequalities.' The message was straightforward: acknowledge colonial wounds but look ahead. Commonwealth leaders jointly echoed the call for 'truthful, respectful dialogue to build a future based on equity.'

In 2025, the monarchy stands at a crossroads. Its survival hinges on balancing tradition with modern expectations. At its best, it unites above politics; at its worst, it feels like a gilded relic – vulnerable to irrelevance and scandal. And even when the controversies are trivial, the damage seems to stick. Each headline chipping away at the brand.

Having rogue royals like Harry and Meghan firing shots from the sidelines with venom – just as Diana did – is deeply damaging to the institution. Harry's claim that his father and brother are 'trapped' may be just his view, but mud sticks.[243] Now royal in name only, the pair usually make headlines for the wrong reasons. In March 2025, Meghan's *With Love, Meghan* was slammed as a vanity project and a shameless grab for cash under the Sussex banner.

Harry did not fare better. That same month, he stepped down as joint patron of Sentebale, the charity he co-founded with Prince Seeiso of Lesotho to help children and young people living with HIV and AIDS in Lesotho and Botswana. Other trustees quit too after a bitter rift with the board chair Dr Sophie Chandauka, citing legal gridlock; she accused them of harassment, sexism, racism and cover-ups, leading to a Charity Commission review. For Harry, who spoke of his 'awakening' to race issues after falling for Meghan, the allegations were 'catastrophic', according to his mother's friend, journalist Richard Kay.[244] In August, The Charity Commission found no evidence of widespread bullying, harassment misogyny or systemic misconduct at Sentebale. But did identify governance weaknesses and mismanagement. Meanwhile, Harry's heavily redacted US visa records revived speculation over the past drug use that he detailed in his memoir *Spare* and stirred fresh questions about privilege and accountability.

In May 2025, Prince Harry got a £1.5 million wake-up call. A British judge rejected his demand for automatic, taxpayer-funded police protection in the UK. The ruling was blunt: no duties, no detail. He quit the job – he does not get the benefits. From Montecito, Harry raged. On the ruling, in a BBC interview, he said, 'I've had it described to me … this is an old fashioned, good old-fashioned establishment stitch-up. And that's what it feels like.' He blamed the Royal Household, and said he was 'devastated'. From now on every visit to the UK he made, if he wanted protection he would have to go through palace channels; they held the keys.

Harry was adamant. 'I never asked him (the King) to intervene – I asked him to step out of the way and let the experts do their jobs.' Yet there was no disguising the sting when he added, 'I don't know how much longer my father has.' He also spoke of forgiveness – 'I have forgiven my family for everything that's happened' – but made clear there would be no return. 'I can't see a world in which I would be bringing my wife and children back to the UK.' His security fears are not unfounded; he is a target due to his royal birth and the fact he served in the front line in the Army. But this was not simply about safety. It was about status. And the court made it clear: that door was closed.

The bombshell interview, in which Harry also let slip that he and his father were not speaking but he still hoped for reconciliation, came on the eve of the VE Day 80th Anniversary commemorations, thus overshadowing a moment meant to honour veterans and bring the nation together. For a king unlikely to see a Jubilee, this was a watershed moment as Charles led the nation in tribute to heroes past and present. Harry's timing felt off – deliberate, pointed, even.

The King ignored it. He delivered a pitch-perfect address, reading from his mother's wartime diary. It was raw, real, and deeply personal. A sovereign standing tall in the shadow of history, reminding the nation what service truly means. The RAF's Red Arrows had roared overhead earlier and crowds filled

The Mall as three generations of royals, most in military uniform, took the applause from the palace balcony. The Palace insisted it was all about the veterans, but make no mistake, this was a seminal moment for Charles too.

Supporters of the institution see continuity, tradition, charity, stability, tourism and national identity as positives. Critics see outdated pomp and ceremony drenched in British nostalgia – quirky, yes, but increasingly out of step, especially in realms like Canada, Australia and New Zealand, where a foreign-born monarch based thousands of miles away remains their head of state. Velvet robes and plumed hats at Windsor's Garter Ceremony may dazzle tourists, but to many, it is pure theatre. Even William, no fan of such meaningless nonsense, understands the reality: spectacle is not enough. Survival rests on public belief. The Crown must matter, and even more, it must be seen to serve and make a positive impact.

The Prince and Princess of Wales give monarchists reason to hope – modern-thinking, grounded and committed, yet loyal to tradition. Where missteps have occurred, they have moved to make amends, earning respect for striking the right balance. William and Catherine channel the same quiet strength of Queen Elizabeth and Prince Philip, but with a fresher, more relatable touch.

William connects through social media, podcasts, and celebrity interviews. He cheers on his football team Aston Villa FC with passion, sometimes with his son George at his side. He speaks openly about family life, unwinds with video games, and is not afraid to laugh at himself. Yes, he is privileged, but to millions he feels relatable. Like his love of football, he used to regularly play in five-a-side matches in Battersea Park, it is his authenticity that resonates. Known for his empathy and attentiveness, associated with his late mother Diana, William makes people feel heard.

He balances poise with quiet strength, supported by Catherine's steady presence. After her cancer they both became more religious. William regularly attends church to worship but does so as privately as possible. Behind his easy smile lies iron resolve. A doer, he proved himself with the Earthshot Prize,[245] launched in 2020 to tackle global sustainability, declaring, 'The next ten years will decide the planet's fate.' It has gained traction, not least with big business, and notable partners include Microsoft, Unilever, Walmart and Hitachi.

By 2024, life had tested William to breaking point, but he emerged stronger. He pressed on, proud of his family's strength and his work. Balancing his role as the Prince of Wales with being a devoted husband and hands-on father, he declared: 'I enjoy my work, and I enjoy pacing myself – and keeping sure that I have got time for my family too.' It was a clear line in the sand.

As the heir, the Prince of Wales remains resolute. With kingship looming, he has sharpened his focus, drawn firm lines, and reframed the role. In an interview with *Times* journalist Kate Mansey for the Royal Rota in November 2024, he said, 'I'm doing it with maybe a smaller "r" in the royal.' His model centres on 'impact, philanthropy, collaboration, convening, and helping people' – empathy, action, and results. Catherine, who shares his vision, is right beside him.

William, however, drew criticism over Homewards, his five-year plan to tackle homelessness. Detractors pointed to the irony: a prince with three homes and a £20 million recurring annual income fronting the cause. In the ITV documentary *Prince William: We Can End Homelessness*, he met the backlash head-on: 'Criticism drives you forward.' He added, 'We are pushing forward to deliver change and hope.' The documentary charted year one of the initiative, including a visit to Nansledan, where his Duchy of Cornwall is building twenty-four homes.[246]

LBC's James O'Brien and anti-monarchist Graham Smith, chief executive of Republic, slammed the royal gesture, insisting housing insecurity needs systemic reform, not symbolic charity. The national charity Crisis estimated just £1.9 billion could end homelessness – a drop in the royal fortune. One caller, Colette, called out William's double standards live on air: 'He steps out of a chauffeur-driven limo to discuss ending homelessness in five years. He could do it in five minutes by selling assets.' William, while acknowledging the criticism, defended his mission. responded to it, 'I'm not sitting here saying I'm going to solve the entire world's homelessness problems. But I am going to show people how to prevent homelessness. Ultimately, we are pushing forward to deliver change and hope and optimism…'[247]

In August 2025, Prince William drew criticism for disappearing behind the gates of Forest Lodge, his third home, which sources close to him said would be his 'forever home' even when he is King.[248] Choosing seclusion over Windsor Castle or a Buckingham Palace critics said raised uncomfortable questions about his commitment, especially after hundreds of millions of public pounds were spent refurbishing the Palace, now seemingly set to be sidelined when he is monarch.[249]

Columnist Amanda Platell, writing in the *Daily Mail*, was blunt: William is 'obsessed with privacy' and 'needs to man up' for the role he was born into. She said with a paltry number of public engagements compared to his late grandmother Queen Elizabeth II, his father King Charles III, and his aunt Princess Anne, William risks becoming a part-time King, invisible to a public increasingly sceptical of the monarchy's relevance. His sending a message not taking part in the 80th VJ Day commemorations like his father, still battling cancer, was noted too. It suggested, she said, he had forgotten everything the late Queen stood for. If he continues down this path, Platell argued, the Crown may face irrelevance under his reign. She makes a valid point; one the late Queen had made herself when she said she had to be seen to be believed. William's drive is for a leaner monarchy, aiming for just sixty-five staff for cost-efficiency when he is king. Privately it has unsettled senior royal aides who feel it is hypocritical.[250] They note that when he was the Duke of Cambridge and now as the Prince of Wales he often relies on staff from his late grandmother's and father's households, shifting their workload. Tensions flared in Christmas 2021 when Sandringham was opened for the annual shoot, forcing Charles and Camilla to detour to Norfolk after dining with the Queen at Windsor. Two days of tradition, with the Middleton family attending, left staff frustrated under the strain of William's convenience. So how will it work with only sixty-five staff when he is king, they argue?

William and Catherine now focus on a handful of serious causes; an effort shaped by criticism following their misjudged Caribbean tour. But is it enough? Plenty of billionaires run charities; wealth paired with compassion does not automatically justify taxpayer-funded perks – security, travel, or William's £25 million annual income from the Duchy of Cornwall estate, created in 1337 to bankroll the heir.[251]

He is thoughtful, channels Diana's empathy, and takes his duty seriously. But is that enough to justify the huge wealth and privilege? Royal biographer Tina Brown, the acclaimed journalist and former editor of *Vanity Fair*, did not think so – dismissing

William as a 'performative pinhead' peddling a hollow vision of a 'caring, sharing monarchy', undermining Charles's legacy, and floundering without Harry.[252]

The celebrated writer A.N. Wilson echoed concerns about the new-look monarchy, saying that without their links to the established Church of England and Armed Forces, the Royal Family are just 'a bunch of celebrities'. He went on, 'Sooner or later, that means the end of the monarchy. It seems to me that 2024 was an *annus horribilis* for the Royal Family – but, one hopes, not for the monarchy.'[253]

Supporters of the status quo can take comfort in the numbers – there is still little public appetite to scrap the monarchy. An August 2024 YouGov poll showed solid royal backing, even after a turbulent year. Charles III remains well-regarded with 63 per cent favourability (+34 net), but William and Catherine top the charts with 74–75 per cent approval. Princess Anne follows close behind at 71 per cent. Scandals, however, take a toll. Harry and Meghan sit at 30 per cent and 23 per cent approval. Prince Andrew, now toxic to the institution, hit a record low: just 5 per cent favourability, with a staggering 87 per cent disapproval.

In April 2025, an Ipsos poll had support for the monarchy at 55 per cent, with support for a republic at 28 per cent and 17 per cent still undecided. Even King Charles has acknowledged the monarchy's fragility, calling it a 'curious' institution whose future hinges on public will; famously telling his biographer Jonathan Dimbleby in 1994, 'If people don't want it, they won't have it.'

Yet even now, with his Scottish titles in hand, including the Duke of Rothesay, William refuses to wear the kilt. For Charles, it is more than tradition; it is a vital symbol of Scottish identity and the crown his son will one day inherit. Still, a senior source says, 'The King has repeatedly urged him, yet William won't budge.'

Charles, conscious of William's impetuousness, often delegates tough work issues to his senior aides. It has led to William clashing with the imperturbable Sir Clive Alderton, Charles's loyal private secretary, and others, echoing Charles's past tensions with the late Queen's aide, Lord Geidt. While Charles managed to ease Geidt out, William has failed to unsettle Alderton, a seasoned diplomat, reportedly becoming fixated on the senior courtier.[254]

William, indomitable, has clashed not only with his father's courtiers, but at times with Charles himself. In 2014, tensions flared over William's proposal to destroy the Royal Collection's 1,200 ivory artifacts, including Queen Victoria's 1851 Indian throne, as a bold stand against the illegal ivory trade. Charles rejected the move as 'naive', arguing that the cause could be championed without erasing history. He quietly removed ivory from display at Clarence House and Highgrove, but as king, he has gone further – securing the collection's ivory under legal protection. The episode underscored their diverging views on heritage, symbolism, and modern ethics.

The King, close sources say, believes William is occasionally hasty and can be too quick to dismiss sage, well-meaning advice. In early 2024, tensions rose when William flew his entire family in his helicopter, a habit that had already alarmed the late Queen. She had once warned him firmly to consider the line of succession, still haunted by Air Commodore John Blount's fatal crash in 1967. After his cancer diagnosis, Charles revisited the issue, instructing senior aide Sir Mike Stevens to obtain William's written acknowledgement of the risks. William refused, and his curt reply was sharp enough that Stevens reported it back to the King.[255]

Often Prince William lets slip his feelings through actions rather than words. By agreeing to appear in the Amazon television series *Clarkson's Farm*, he signals his awareness of farming struggles, including the threat inheritance tax poses to family farms. Engaging with farmer and TV personality Kaleb Cooper on mental health in March 2025, he also acknowledges broader challenges, perhaps silently aligning with Jeremy Clarkson's outspoken stance on government policies impacting agriculture and inheritance tax.

William is steadily evolving into the global statesman he must become, using soft power diplomacy on the world stage. In September 2023, he met with UN Secretary-General António Guterres and Ecuador's president Guillermo Lasso in New York, solidifying his role as an environmental advocate. In December 2024, he met President-elect Donald Trump in Paris for Notre-Dame's reopening, with Trump praising him as 'a good man doing a fantastic job'. Their warm exchange continued at the British ambassador's residence, where William shared updates on Catherine's health and the King's cancer battle, prompting Trump to call the situation 'sad', sparking further speculation about the King's condition.

King Charles has always had a curious relationship with Donald Trump. They get along well enough personally but clash on key issues, especially climate change. Back in 2019, as Prince of Wales, Charles played his part well. He welcomed Trump on a state visit with a firm handshake, his frail mother still the star of the show. Later, he seized his chance, steering the conversation towards saving the planet. Trump later admitted, 'He's really into climate change.' That day, Charles proved he could be both diplomatic and principled. But afterwards, he felt let down by Trump over his climate change stance.

Now, the road is rockier. Charles's warm meeting with Ukrainian president Volodymyr Zelenskyy at Sandringham in March 2025 sent a clear message of solidarity. But the timing was loaded. It was a few days after Trump had clashed with Zelenskyy and JD Vance in the Oval Office. Only 24 hours earlier, Prime Minister Keir Starmer had made a grand display of handing Trump an 'unprecedented' second state visit invitation, personally from the King. Washington insiders whispered that Trump had since 'gone cool' on the trip, angered by the optics of the Charles–Zelenskyy meeting.

The King's meeting with Zelenskyy was not just pageantry – it was a calculated show of solidarity with Ukraine, both for Britain and himself. But here lies the tension: an unelected monarch is meant to stay above party politics. Charles's actions raised eyebrows, and critics did not hold back. 'Spineless pawn,' one X user wrote, 'kissing Zelenskyy's boots, then begging Trump for tea.' Another called it 'pathetic hedging'; a monarch wedged between two charging bulls, praying neither gores him.

This is the tightrope Charles now walks. The Palace then announced that the King would fly to Canada in May 2025 – the first monarch to open Parliament there since 1957. A whistlestop visit, it came as Trump tested the patience of the sovereign realm, one of the Crown's most independent and mature dominions, referring to it as the US's '51st state'. While Trump imposed higher tariffs on his northern neighbour, the King stood firm, backing Canada with quiet steel.

King Charles today wields soft power diplomacy, but how far can he push it before the Crown itself is seen as overtly political? If neutrality wavers, so does the monarchy's legitimacy. In an era of strongmen and shifting alliances, the King's every move is under a microscope. The throne may be steady, but the ground beneath it is not. Charles's gamble may be calculated. He may want to make his mark in history, given his reign will be relatively short. It is a dangerous path; the margin for error is razor-thin.

Despite his ongoing cancer battle, King Charles has remained positive throughout, working hard, keeping his humour intact. At Waltham Forest Town Hall in December 2024, he quipped to Sikh leader Harvinder Rattan, 'I'm still alive, thank God,' showing his resilience. A spiritual man of purpose, he seeks to uplift others, challenge norms, and spark debate in an age where world leaders often fall short of true statesmanship. His hope is to inspire not divide, bridging his mother's legacy and William's future reign, though his sons' lingering feud still casts a long shadow over his short reign. For Charles, leadership is responsibility; being followed remains the people's choice.

Those close to the King are fully aware of his health balancing act. In late March 2025, it showed: the King was briefly hospitalised with cancer treatment side effects – a day after hosting 400 regional journalists in the Grand Ballroom at Buckingham Palace. Back at Clarence House, he continued light duties but scrapped a Birmingham trip and three ambassador meetings. The Palace called it 'a minor bump in a road heading the right way.'

The real danger to the British monarchy is not disgrace, sickness, or internal squabbling. It is silence. Indifference is the enemy now.

The Habsburgs once ruled a colossal empire spanning Europe – a patchwork of peoples and loyalties. For centuries from the late Middle Ages, they were defining figures. They held firm, but by 1918, they were gone. Undone by decay. Too rigid, too slow, and too fractured to survive. The First World War merely exposed what was already broken: military defeat, nationalist uprisings, financial ruin, and a refusal to change. As the world moved on, the monarchy stood still – and disappeared.

Charles I, the last Habsburg emperor, never officially abdicated. He went quietly, tried twice to claw back Hungary's crown, but failed, and died in obscurity and poverty in Madeira in 1922. His family scattered; some clinging to past glories, others vanishing from history altogether.

Outrage provokes a response. Apathy does not.

The Windsors remain; not by chance, but by adapting. They have learned to balance heritage with service, ceremony with relevance. The monarchy endures as part of Britain's political fabric – imperfect, yet vital.

But nothing is guaranteed. Today's royals face a shifting public mood. Younger Britons are not instinctive monarchists, they lean towards republicanism. Scandals take their toll. If the Crown ceases to connect, it will not collapse in chaos. It will fade gently, quietly – until one day it is no longer missed.

Legacy and spectacle are not enough. The monarchy's future hangs on something more fragile: the people's trust.

ACKNOWLEDGEMENTS

For over thirty-five years as a journalist, broadcaster and author I have chronicled the key royal characters of the modern-day House of Windsor up close. I have watched triumphs and trials at home and abroad. The royals, led by the King, do a solid job. Since 1990, I have followed the new king from the Prince of Wales to his reign. I have witnessed royal engagements and flown aboard the Royal Flight, seeing the inner workings of the Royal Household up close. I have even shared quiet talks with King Charles III and been granted two interviews with him on matters close to his heart. It has been a fascinating journey, one that granted me unique insight.

I met the late Queen, and the late Diana, Princess of Wales, reporting on her life and tragic end as a journalist and broadcaster. I watched her sons grow, met William and Harry, and even held baby Prince George at Kensington Palace. I have chatted with Queen Camilla many times and been formally introduced to her

– once when she became an honorary Stationer in July 2025, when I was an official witness to the ceremony, and again at the Foreign Press Association Awards dinner, where she sat at the top table as guest of honour.

My career has given me a front-row seat to history. I reported on overseas tours, coronations, jubilees, royal weddings, and funerals – of Diana, Queen Elizabeth II, the Queen Mother, Princess Margaret, and Prince Philip. I interviewed Prince Andrew, the Duke of York, and built a rapport with Sarah, Duchess of York, during her 1993 charity trek near Mount Everest. I co-chaired the London Press Club Ball on 9 October 2014 when Sophie, The Duchess of Edinburgh, then Countess of Wessex, graced the event as guest of honour. Conversations with Zara Tindall and Peter Phillips, the Queen's grandchildren living beyond the royal bubble, deepened my view even further.

In authoring this book, I set out to shine a light on the institution of monarchy and its central characters, past and present, during the 100 years since the late Queen Elizabeth II's birth. My unique perspective has given me the chance to spark reflection and debate. I have gone to great lengths to verify the stories by speaking to many inside sources. That said, any mistakes made in the transcript are mine alone and I will endeavour for them to be corrected at the earliest opportunity in later editions. To the best of my ability this book has been written freely, without fear or favour, and certainly without Buckingham Palace approval, control or interference.

Writing a book starts with passion, but it is always a team effort. My thanks to Bonnier Books UK – especially my publisher Ciara Lloyd, whose belief in this project began over a lively lunch and never wavered. I am deeply grateful to the entire publishing and export rights teams at Bonnier for their unwavering support.

Huge thanks to Barry Johnston, whose sharp editorial eye made every draft better – an absolute joy to work with you again. And to Perminder Mann, former CEO of Bonnier Books UK and now CEO of Simon & Schuster International – your friendship, vision, and trust have shaped my journey as a writer more than you know.

This book owes much to the many individuals who spoke to me with trust and candour, both on and off the record, though such is the nature of royal reporting that most must remain unnamed to protect their anonymity. I owe a special debt of gratitude to those anonymous sources whose insights and courage made this work possible. Your invaluable guidance illuminated truths that might otherwise have remained hidden. Thank you for trusting me to tell this story.

As a journalist and royal historian, I have thoroughly enjoyed the research process, studying royal speeches, poring over files and diaries, devouring biographies, and watching hours of footage and documentaries. Along the way, I have also drawn on the works of fellow authors like Tom Bower, Jonathan Dimbleby, Robert Hardman, Penny Junor, Alexander Larman, Angela Levin, Andrew Lownie, Valentine Low, Andrew Morton and my good friend Ingrid Seward. While I do not always agree with their conclusions, I respect their insights and the depth they bring to understanding the royal story. I would like to express my thanks to Prince Harry, the Duke of Sussex, whose memoir, *Spare*, offers a compelling, albeit subjective, perspective. I also greatly appreciated the memoirs of Paul Burrell and my friend Patrick Jephson.

My heartfelt thanks to those who have shared my journey as a writer. Your friendship means the world to me: Laura Collins, Dee Cayhill, Arthur Edwards MBE, Richard Freed, Kent Gavin,

Sinead Graham, Gary Goldsmith, Karen Jobson, Alan Jones, Richard Kay, Robin and Aasta Nunn, John Roslin, Ian and Annie Walker, Ken Wharfe MVO, chef Mervyn Wycherley RVM, and Shekhar and Milli Bhatia.

Gratitude also to my colleagues at US network ABC's *Good Morning America*: Almin Karamehmedovic, Andy Laurence, Dimitrije Stejic, Katie Den Daas, Victoria Murphy, Ailsa Anderson LVO, and Zoe Magee – and to the *Sunrise* team at Channel 7, Australia, especially Edwina Bartholomew, Natalie Barr, Mark Beretta, Jimmy Cannon, David 'Dougie' Walters, Sarah Stinson, Sam Armytage, Hugh Whitfield, and Kochie.

I am so grateful to my colleagues, past and present, who over the years made the job such fun and so many overseas jaunts and royal tours unforgettable: Harry Arnold, Ross Benson, Phil Dampier, Hugh Dougherty, Michael Dunlea, Rebecca English, Wayne Francis, Richard Freed, Geordie Greig, Alan Hamilton, Mike Howie, Duncan Larcombe, Jack Lefley, Kate Mansey, Ray Massey, Russell Myers, Emily Nash, Victoria Newton, Katie Nicholl, Charlie Rae, Chrissie Reeves, Mike Ridley, Lizzie Robinson, Jeremy Selwyn, Chris Ship, Camilla Tominey, Ted Verity, Ashley Walton, Mark Wilkinson, Matt Wilkinson, Doug Wills, Judy Wade and James Whitaker, to name just a few.

A big thank you too to my son Charlie for his love and kindness and making me proud of him every day, and of course to my late father Vic, who passed in 1999, but whose strength and guidance continues to inspire me. I would like to acknowledge my brothers Steve and Andy and sister Heather too.

Lastly, my eternal thanks to my beloved mother, Jean, who passed aged eighty-five in October 2024 during the writing of this book. A resilient, sharp-witted lady to the end, I had discussed the material at length with her and she was eagerly awaiting its completion. She inspired my love of learning and encouraged me to read Modern European History, jointly with English Literature, at university. Her vivid tales of the Second World War – evacuations, rationing, gas masks, and the eerie silence of Doodlebugs before devastating explosions – sparked my imagination and passion for journalism and witnessing history first-hand. My last memory of her was her tuning into a documentary on television about the Nuremberg Trials, absorbing every detail.

She often spoke of her parents, Bill and Edith Figg, listening intently to King George VI or Winston Churchill on the crackling wireless, and them telling her and her brothers to be quiet so they could take in every word. The King, she said, brought hope, while Churchill's words were an inspiration, a weapon, cutting through the darkness. This book is for you, Mum, with all my love.

In loving memory of Mrs Jean Edith Jobson, 11 May 1939–14 October 2024.

SELECT BIBLIOGRAPHY

Aldrich, Richard and Cormac, Rory, *The Secret Royals: Spying and the Crown, from Victoria to Diana*, Atlantic Books, 2021.

Aronson, Theo, *Princess Margaret: A Biography*, Michael O'Mara Books, 1997.

Bagehot, Walter, *The English Constitution*, first published by Trübner & Co., 1867; Fontana Press; New edition, 1993.

Bedell Smith, Sally, *Prince Charles: The Passions and Paradoxes of an Improbable Life*, Random House, 2017.

Bedell Smith, Sally, *Elizabeth the Queen: The Life of a Modern Monarch*, Random House, 2012.

Benson, Ross, *Charles: The Untold Story*, Gollancz, 1993.

Bloch, Michael, *The Duke of Windsor's War*, Weidenfeld & Nicolson, 1982.

Bolitho, Hector, *Edward VIII: His Life and Reign*, Eyre & Spottiswoode, 1937.

Bower, Tom, *Rebel Prince: The Power, Passion, and Defiance of Prince Charles*, William Collins, 2018.

Bower, Tom, *Revenge: Meghan, Harry, and the War Between the Windsors*, Blink, 2021.

Bradford, Sarah, *George VI: The Dutiful King*, Weidenfeld & Nicolson, 1989.

Bradford, Sarah, *Elizabeth II: Her Life in Our Times*, Penguin Books, 2011.

Brandreth, Gyles, *Philip and Elizabeth: Portrait of a Marriage*, Century, 2004.

Brandreth, Gyles, *Philip: The Final Portrait*, Coronet Books, 2021.

Brandreth, Gyles, *Elizabeth: An Intimate Portrait*, Michael Joseph, 2022.

Brown, Craig, *Ma'am Darling: Ninety-Nine Glimpses of Princess Margaret*, Fourth Estate, 2017.

Burrell, Paul, *A Royal Duty*, Penguin Books, 2003.

Catterall, Peter (ed.), *The Macmillan Diaries: Prime Minister and After, 1957–1966*, Macmillan, 2011.

Connors, Jane Holley, *The Glittering Thread*, University of Technology, Sydney, 1996.

Dimbleby, Jonathan, *The Prince of Wales: A Biography*, Little, Brown, 1994.

Gilbert, Martin, *Winston Churchill: A Life*, Heinemann, 1991.

Glenconner, Lady Anne, *Lady in Waiting: My Life in the Shadow of the Crown*, Hodder & Stoughton, 2019.

Hamilton, Alan, *The Real Charles*, Fontana, 1988.

Hardman, Robert, *Charles III: New King, New Court. The Inside Story*, Macmillan, 2024.

Heald, Tim, *Princess Margaret: A Life Unravelled*, Weidenfeld & Nicolson, 2007.

Hesse, Prince Georg, *Erinnerungen*, Fritz Knapp Verlag, 1980.

Hewitt, Gavin, *A Soul on Ice: A Life in News*, Macmillan, 2005.

Hicks, Lady Pamela, *Daughter of Empire: Life as a Mountbatten*, Weidenfeld & Nicolson, 2012.

Higham, Charles, *The Duchess of Windsor: The Secret Life*, McGraw-Hill, 1988.

Hoey, Brian, *Prince William*, The History Press, 2003.

Holden, Anthony, *Prince Charles: A Biography*, Bantam Press, 1998.

Irving, Clive, Hall, Ron, and Wallington, Jeremy, *Scandal '63: A Study of the Profumo Affair*, Heinemann, 1963.

Jenkins, Roy, *Churchill: A Biography*, Macmillan, 2001.

Jephson, P.D., *Shadows of a Princess*, HarperCollins, 2000.

Jobson, Robert, *Harry's War: The True Story of the Soldier Prince*, John Blake, 2008.

Jobson, Robert, *The New Royal Family*, John Blake, 2014.

Jobson, Robert, *Diana's Legacy: William and Harry*, MPressmedia, 2019.

Jobson, Robert, *Charles at 70: Our Future King*, John Blake, 2019.

Johnson, Boris, *Unleashed*, HarperCollins, 2024.

Junor, Penny, *The Firm*, Harper Nonfiction, 2011.

Junor, Penny, *Prince William: Born to be King: An Intimate Portrait*, Hodder & Stoughton, 2012.

Junor, Penny, *The Duchess: The Untold Story*, William Collins, 2017.

Lacey, Robert, *Battle of Brothers*, William Collins, 2020.

Larman, Alexander, *The Crown in Crisis: Countdown to the Abdication*, Weidenfeld & Nicolson, 2020.

Larman, Alexander, *The Windsors at War: The Nazi Threat to the Crown*, Weidenfeld & Nicolson, 2023.

Levin, Angela, *Camilla: Duchess of Cornwall – From Outcast to Future Queen Consort*, Simon & Schuster, 2022.

Logue, Mark & Conradi, Peter, *The King's Speech: How One Man Saved the British Monarchy*, Quercus, 2010.

Low, Valentine, *Courtiers: The Hidden Power Behind the Crown*, Headline, 2022.

Lownie, Andrew, *The Mountbattens, Their Lives and Loves*, Blink, 2019.

Lownie, Andrew, *Traitor King: The Scandalous Exile of the Duke and Duchess of Windsor*, Blink, 2021.

Mayer, Catherine, *Charles: The Heart of a King*, WH Allen, 2016.

Morton, Andrew, *Diana: Her True Story – In Her Own Words*, Michael O'Mara Books, 2017.

Morton, Andrew, *The Queen: 1926–2022*, Michael O'Mara Books, 2022.

Nicholl, Katie, *Kate: The Future Queen*, Hachette, 2015.

Orwell, George, *The Lion, and the Unicorn: Socialism and the English Genius*, Secker & Warburg, 1941.

Petropoulos, Jonathan, *Royals and the Reich: The Princes von Hessen in Nazi Germany*, Oxford University Press, 2006.

Robert, Andrew, *Churchill: Walking with Destiny*, Viking, 2018.

Röhl, John, *Kaiser Wilhelm II: A Life in Power*, Cambridge University Press, 2004.

Scobie, Omid and Durand, Carolyn, *Finding Freedom*, HQ, 2020.

Seward, Ingrid, *The Queen & Di: The Untold Story*, Arcade, 2001.

Seward, Ingrid, *William & Harry: A Portrait of Two Princes*, Arcade, 2003.

Seward, Ingrid, *William and Harry: The People's Princes*, Welbeck, 2008.

Seward, Ingrid, *My Husband, and I: The Inside Story of 70 Years of the Royal Marriage*, Simon & Schuster, 2017.

Shawcross, William, *Counting One's Blessings: The Collected Letters of Queen Elizabeth the Queen Mother*, Pan, 2013.

Simmons, Simone, *Diana: The Secret Years*, Michael O'Mara Books, 1998.

Simmons, Simone, *Diana: The Last Word*, Orion Publishing Group, 2005.

Stewart, Andrew, *The King's Private Army: Protecting the British Royal Family During the Second World War*, Helion and Company, 2016.

Sussex, Duke of, Prince Harry, *Spare*, Penguin Random House, 2023.

Thornton, Michael and Kirkwood, Pat, *The Time of My Life*, Quartet Books, 1983.

Townsend, Peter, *Time and Chance*, Collins Publishers, 1978.

Vickers, Hugo, *Behind Closed Doors: The Tragic, Untold, Story of the Duchess of Windsor*, Hutchinson/Random House, 2011.

Wallace, Richard, *The King's Loot: The Greatest Royal Jewellery Heist in History*, The History Press, 2024.

Warwick, Christopher, *Princess Margaret: A Life of Contrasts*, Carlton Publishing Group, 2000.

Wharfe, Ken & Jobson, Robert, *Diana: Closely Guarded Secret*, John Blake, 2016.

Wharfe, Ken & Jobson, Robert, *Guarding Diana*, John Blake, 2017.

Wheeler-Bennett, Sir John, *King George VI, The Official Biography*, Macmillan,1958.

Windsor, The Duke of, *A King's Story: The Memoirs of the Duke of Windsor*, first published by G.P. Putnam's Sons, 1947.

Ziegler, Philip, *King George VI: The Dutiful King*, HarperCollins, 2013.

SOURCE NOTES

Introduction

1 The last reigning English king to take charge of his men in combat was George II at the Battle of Dettingen in 1743, during the War of the Austrian Succession.

2 George I spoke mostly German. He understood some English but preferred to use German or French, making him unpopular.

3 The 1832 Reform Act under Queen Victoria's uncle William IV had expanded the vote to property-owning men. In 1867 it included many urban workers, and in 1884 rural labourers. Women gained the vote in 1918, with full equality in 1928.

4 In 1708, Queen Anne withheld Royal Assent from the Scottish Militia Bill, fearing the proposed militia might support a Jacobite uprising. It is the last time a British monarch vetoed a bill.

5 Recent polls show steady support for the monarchy: a 2023 British Social Attitudes survey found 54 per cent still back it, while only 25 per cent want it gone. An Ipsos poll in March 2024 echoed this, with just 24 per cent favouring abolition.

6 Sir Thomas Fairfax served as overall leader of the parliamentary forces and Oliver Cromwell as his formidable cavalry general during the civil war. Cromwell seized power after the war, driven by ambition and religious zeal, while Fairfax, though a brilliant general, stepped back – uneasy with the King's execution and radical change.

7 During the First World War, the British called Germans 'the Hun' – a derogatory term, likening them to ruthless barbarians and aimed at dehumanising the enemy to fuel anti-German feeling.

8 John Röhl, *Kaiser Wilhelm II: A Life in Power,* Cambridge University Press, 2014. Part of a trilogy on Wilhelm's life and reign.

9 The Campbell Case involved the prosecution of a communist newspaper editor for inciting mutiny, while the forged Zinoviev Letter falsely claimed Soviet plans to incite revolution in Britain, both fuelling fears of socialist subversion and contributing to the fall of Ramsay MacDonald's government in 1924.

10 Queen Elizabeth's comments were widely reported in BBC News and other major news outlets. After the vote, David Cameron apologised for saying she 'purred' on hearing Scotland chose to stay in the UK via a Sky News microphone, September 2014.

Chapter 1: Lilibet and Grandpa England

11 The General Strike lasted for ten days from 3–12 May 1926. It was called by the Trade Union Congress (TUC) in support of the coal miners, who were on strike over cuts in pay and longer hours. The miners themselves held out for nearly eight months.

12 Hector Bolitho, *Edward VIII: His Life and Reign*, Eyre & Spottiswoode, 1937.

Chapter 2: The 'Little Man' and 'That Woman'

13 Bolitho, *Edward VIII: His Life and Reign.*

14 From Lord Mountbatten's diaries and letters, compiled posthumously in works such as *Personal Diary of Admiral the Lord Louis Mountbatten: Supreme Allied Commander, South-East Asia, 1943–1946* published by William Collins Sons & Co and *From Shore to Shore: The Tour Diaries of Earl Mountbatten of*

Burma, 1953–1979, HarperCollins. Additionally, his life has been extensively chronicled in biographies, including Andrew Lownie's *The Mountbattens: Their Lives & Loves*, Blink Publishing, 2019.

15 Between 1931 and 1935 Baldwin was the Lord President of the Council, who is the presiding officer of the Privy Council, and the fourth of the Great Offices of State.

16 Published by Random House on 4 April 2023.

17 Known as the 'Runciman Mission', Lord Runciman was sent to mediate the Sudetenland crisis in 1938. The retired politician's report backed Sudeten German grievances, bolstering Hitler's position and leading to the annexation of the Sudetenland. It paved the way the way for the 'Munich Agreement' – a key step towards the Second World War.

18 Interview with Sir Steven Runciman on the four-part 1994 documentary series, *The Windsors: A Royal Family*, produced by Austin Hoyt.

19 The secret message revealed in *Royals and the Reich: The Princes von Hessen in Nazi Germany* by Jonathan Petropoulos, published by Oxford University Press, 2006. The book explores the Duke of Saxe-Coburg's deep involvement with the Nazi regime and how he became a significant figure to the Nazi leadership.

20 In 2013, declassified Cabinet Office files revealed that on or before 5 December 1936, Home Secretary Sir John Simon ordered the General Post Office to intercept telephone communications between Fort Belvedere, Buckingham Palace, and Europe.

21 In his September 1936 diary, Harold Nicolson recounts Sir Alan Lascelles' concerns about Edward VIII's neglect of duty during the *Nahlin* cruise with Mrs Simpson, foreshadowing the abdication crisis. His diaries were later published in three volumes by Collins between 1966 and 1968.

22 Baldwin seemed conveniently to ignore the fact that King Henry VIII founded the Church of England in 1534 after the Pope refused to annul his marriage to Catherine of Aragon. Seizing control of religion and church wealth, he secured his divorce, declared himself Supreme Head, and ignited the English Reformation.

23 Reported in the press at the time, during the visit to Dowlais Ironworks on 18 November 1936, King Edward VIII, moved by the workers' plight, remarked, 'These works brought all these people here. Something should be

done to get them at work again.' *The Times* headline read: 'The King Visits Distressed Areas: A Call for Action', emphasising his empathy towards the distressed communities. The *Daily Mail* headline read: 'Monarch's Plea: "Something Must Be Done" for the Unemployed'.

24 CAB 23/85 refers to a specific document from the UK National Archives' Cabinet Papers series, holding ministerial memoranda and reports, related to the 1936 abdication crisis. Number 23 shows a series of memoranda and reports presented to the Cabinet by ministers, known as the 'Cabinet Office: Cabinet Papers'. The number 85 refers to a particular document or volume within that series.

25 From a 1970 BBC interview with Kenneth Harris, as the Duke of Windsor, reflected on his view of the monarchy as outdated and his desire for reform.

26 CAB 24/85, UK National Archives' Cabinet Papers.

27 Interview with Sir Dudley Forward in the 1994 documentary *The Windsors: A Royal Family, Episode 2, Brothers at War*, produced by Glynn Christian and directed by Michael Waldman. Created by ITN Factual and aired on Channel 4.

28 The memo (CAB 24/263) refers to a specific document from the UK National Archives' Cabinet Papers series, holding ministerial memoranda and reports, related to the 1936 abdication crisis.

29 In English history, abdications are rare. Edward VIII's in 1936 is the most famous. Edward II was ousted in 1327 by his wife Isabella and her lover, Roger Mortimer. Richard II fell in 1399 under Henry Bolingbroke's pressure. James II, fleeing during the 1688 Glorious Revolution, left Parliament to label it an abdication.

30 Baldwin made this statement in the House of Commons on 10 December 1936, while announcing the King's intention to abdicate. Baldwin's speech detailed the events leading up to the abdication and expressed his personal reflections on the King's decision.

Chapter 3: This Ghastly Void

31 From *George VI: The Dutiful King* by Sarah Bradford, Weidenfeld & Nicolson, 1989.

32 From Sir John Wheeler-Bennett's *King George VI*, Macmillan & Co. Ltd. 1958.

33 The story of Bertie's relationship with speech therapist Lionel Logue is revealed in *The King's Speech: How One Man Saved the British Monarchy* by Mark Logue & Peter Conradi, published in 2010 by Quercus. The film *The King's Speech* starred Colin Firth as King George VI, earning him an Oscar, with the film winning Best Picture.

34 Sir John Wheeler-Bennett, *King George VI*. Sourced from a letter George VI wrote to his sister, Mary, the Princess Royal and Countess of Harewood, on 12 December 1936. The letter is part of the Royal Archives at Windsor.

35 Lionel Logue originally trained as an actor before becoming a renowned speech therapist. He was made a Member of the Victorian Order (MVO) in 1944 by King George VI for his dedicated service helping him to manage his stammer through pivotal speeches and public appearances.

36 *Elizabeth the Queen: The Life of a Modern Monarch* by Sally Bedell Smith, Random House, 2012.

37 *Young Elizabeth: The Making of the Queen*, Kate Williams, Weidenfeld & Nicolson, 2016.

38 Hugo Vickers, *Behind Closed Doors: The Tragic, Untold Story of the Duchess of Windsor*, Hutchinson, 2011.

39 In 1952 the Windsors sold Le Moulin de la Tuilerie and moved to Paris, where they took up residence at 2, rue de la Spontini. In June 1953, the Duke and Duchess of Windsor moved into 4, Route du Champ d'Entraînement, later known as Villa Windsor, which is in the 16th arrondissement of Paris, in the Parc de la Chambre de la Reine, a private section of the Bois de Boulogne Park. This became their primary residence.

40 Richard Wallace, *The King's Loot: The Greatest Royal Jewellery Heist in History*, The History Press, 2024.

41 *The Windsor Secret*, Charles Higham, McGraw-Hill, 1988 helped piece together the details of the Duke's financial affairs. While his will left much to Wallis Simpson, the full extent of his wealth, concealed through careful investments and international holdings, was gradually revealed by biographers and financial experts.

42 Interview with Sir Dudley Forward, *The Windsors: A Royal Family*, Channel 4, 1994.

43 Interview with Lady Alexandra Metcalfe in *The Windsors: A Royal Family*.

44 MI5 files KV 2/1363–1364. These MI5 files pertain to Lady Diana Mosley, née Mitford, covering the period from January 1934 to December 1946. These files are part of the Security Service's personal files (PF Series). The documents were part of a broader release of classified records from the UK National Archives on 30 January 2003.

45 The *Independent*, 4 December 1996, from an article by journalist John Crossland. It is further explored in Andrew Morton's book, *17 Carnations: The Windsors, the Nazis and the Cover-Up*, published by Michael O'Mara Books in 2015.

46 Others reported the number of flower stems that von Ribbentrop sent Wallis Simpson represented the number of letters of her name. The rumoured affair was said to have taken place in the 1930s, before she married Edward. Declassified FBI files in the late 1990s and early 2000s later revealed details of Wallis Simpson's 1936 affair with the Nazi ambassador Joachim von Ribbentrop. These files, part of US wartime intelligence on her, remained classified throughout the Second World War.

47 These sources have been explored in the books, *The Duchess of Windsor: The Secret Life* by Charles Higham, published by McGraw-Hill in 1988 and *The Duke of Windsor's War* by Michael Bloch, published in 1982 by Weidenfeld & Nicolson. The latter focuses on the activities and alleged sympathies of the Duke of Windsor during the Second World War, examining his controversial behaviour and relationships during the conflict. This also appears in various academic papers on Second World War intelligence and diplomacy.

48 Churchill made his famous statement about 'war and dishonour' in the House of Commons on 5 October 1938, during a debate following the Munich Agreement, which had been signed days earlier, allowing Nazi Germany to annex the Sudetenland region of Czechoslovakia in exchange for Hitler's promise of no further territorial demands.

49 The Norwegian Campaign of 1940 (April–June) was a disastrous Allied failure, as poor planning, inadequate coordination and German air superiority led to a swift Nazi victory, forcing British and French forces to retreat.

50 Caroline Erskine observed that King George VI and Churchill initially had a strained relationship. The King, who admired Churchill's confidence but found him intimidating, was uneasy in their early meetings, while

Churchill struggled to manage the dynamic with the monarch. Philip Ziegler, *King George VI: The Dutiful King*, HarperCollins, 2013; Martin Gilbert, *Winston Churchill: A Life*, Heinemann, 1991; *The Lascelles Papers*, Churchill Archives Centre, Cambridge.

51 The bombing of Buckingham Palace on Friday 13 September was reported contemporaneously in *The Times*, the *Daily Telegraph*, and royal biographies such as Sarah Bradford's *George VI* (1989) and Philip Ziegler's *The Dutiful King* (2013). It became a symbol of British resilience, widely covered in newsreels and on the radio.

52 Andrew Stewart, *The King's Private Army: Protecting the British Royal Family During the Second World War*, Helion and Company, 2016. The book unveils 'Operation Rocking Horse', a plan to evacuate the King and senior royals during a Nazi invasion to secure sites like Madresfield Court in Worcestershire, or fortified locations in western England and Scotland. If necessary, King George VI would be evacuated to Canada. Churchill viewed the monarchy as vital for national unity and any future resistance.

53 Richard Aldrich and Rory Cormac, *The Secret Royals: Spying and the Crown, from Victoria to Diana*, Atlantic Books, 2021. Professor Aldrich discussed related themes in documentaries such as *The King Who Fooled Hitler*, produced in 2020 by Brave New Media and directed by Paul Elston.

54 Andrew Roberts, *Churchill: Walking with Destiny*, Viking, 2018. The book examines Churchill's Second World War leadership; Michael Bloch, *The Duke of Windsor's War*, Weidenfeld & Nicolson, 1982, explores Edward's controversial wartime role.

55 On 20 August 1940, in the House of Commons, Winston Churchill delivered his renowned 'The Few' speech, honouring the RAF pilots engaged in the Battle of Britain. He famously said, 'Never in the field of human conflict was so much owed by so many to so few.'

56 On 18 June 1940, Churchill delivered his 'Finest Hour' speech in the House of Commons, declaring, 'If the British Empire and its Commonwealth last for a thousand years, men will still say, "This was their finest hour."'

57 In correspondence from King George VI expressing his concerns about Prime Minister Winston Churchill's desire to be present during the D-Day landings. In a letter dated 2 June 1944, the King wrote to Churchill: 'There is nothing I would like better than to go to sea, but I have agreed to stay at home; is it fair that you should then do exactly what I should have liked to do

myself? You said yesterday afternoon that it would be a fine thing for the King to lead his troops into battle, as in old days; if the King cannot do this, it does not seem to me right that his Prime Minister should take his place.' He signed it, 'Your very sincere friend, George R.I.'

58 From an interview with Hon. Margaret Rhodes and Jean Woodroffe, who were both with the princesses on that evening, *The Queen's Big Night Out*, Channel 4, 2015.

59 This diary entry of George VI has been shared during several commemorative events, including the 75th anniversary of VE Day, when the then Charles, the Prince of Wales read extracts from his grandfather's diary to mark the occasion on 8 May 2020.

60 Sarah Bradford, *George VI: The Dutiful King*, Weidenfeld & Nicolson, 1989.

Chapter 4: For Valour

61 Prince Philip first met Elizabeth in 1934 at the wedding of Prince George, Duke of Kent, and Princess Marina of Greece and Denmark. At the time, Elizabeth was just eight years old, and Philip, her distant cousin, was thirteen.

62 Gyles Brandreth, *Philip and Elizabeth: Portrait of a Marriage*, Century, 2004.

63 Prince Georg of Hesse, *Erinnerungen*, Fritz Knapp Verlag, 1980.

64 Prince Philip gave the interview to historian Jonathan Petropoulos in *Royals and the Reich: The Princes von Hessen in Nazi Germany*, Oxford University Press, 2006.

65 Andrew Lownie, *Traitor King: The Scandalous Exile of the Duke and Duchess of Windsor*, Blink Publishing, 2021.

66 The Cambridge Five were Soviet spies recruited at Cambridge University in the 1930s, driven by anti-fascist and communist ideals. Philby, Burgess, Maclean, Blunt and Cairncross infiltrated British intelligence, leaking secrets like D-Day plans and nuclear research to the Federal Security Service. Their betrayal, exposed over decades, deeply damaged British intelligence and strained Allied trust, marking them as infamous traitors.

67 Sally Bedell Smith, *Elizabeth the Queen: The Life of a Modern Monarch*, Random House, 2012.

68 The specific reference to Prince Philip being compared to Prince Albert is from Harold Macmillan's personal diaries, published in various editions. This remark is cited in multiple royal biographies, including *Philip and Elizabeth: Portrait of a Marriage* by Gyles Brandreth, Century, 2004.

69 Lady Pamela Hicks, *Daughter of Empire: Life as a Mountbatten*, Weidenfeld & Nicolson, 2012.

70 From BBC Television newsreel of King George VI's funeral.

71 From an interview by the author with a senior Royal Household source.

Chapter 5: Trouble in Paradise

72 Jane Holley Connors, *The Glittering Thread*, University of Technology, Sydney, 1996, on the post-coronation tour of Australia. Doctoral Thesis.

73 Lord Altrincham later renounced his inherited title in 1963 under the Peerage Act, choosing to be known simply as John Grigg.

74 The details of Pat Kirkwood's encounter with Prince Philip were documented in her memoir, *The Time of My Life*, Quartet Books, 1983. The book was co-written by Michael Thornton. Her husband, Peter Knight, confirmed her statements after her death in 2007.

Chapter 6: Forbidden Bonds

75 From *Time and Chance* by Peter Townsend, Collins Publishers, 1978.

76 Peter Townsend was part of Royal Air Force No. 85 Squadron, flying Hawker Hurricanes. A distinguished flying ace, he was awarded the Distinguished Flying Cross (DFC) and the Distinguished Service Order (DSO) for his bravery in combat, including his role in the Battle of Britain. Later, he became the commanding officer of No. 85 Squadron. Townsend's wife Rosemary later married and divorced John de László and, in 1978, wed the 5th Marquess Camden.

77 Peter Townsend, *Time and Chance*.

78 In 1967, George Lascelles, Queen Elizabeth II's cousin, divorced Marion Stein after an affair with Patricia Tuckwell. As the Princess Royal's son, he was not a royal prince or an HRH. Instead, he inherited his father's peerage, becoming Earl of Harewood.

79 Conversation between the author and Ken Wharfe, MVO.

80 Sir Martin (later Lord) Charteris, served as Private Secretary to Queen Elizabeth II from 1972 to 1977, following a distinguished military career and earlier roles within the Royal Household. Known for his candid opinions about the Royal Family, he once described the Duchess of York as 'vulgar' and King Charles, then Prince of Wales, as 'whiny'.

81 Lady Anne Glenconner, *Lady in Waiting: My Life in the Shadow of the Crown*, Hodder & Stoughton, 2019.

Chapter 7: A Buried File

82 From Richard Davenport-Hines, *An English Affair: Sex, Class, and Power in the Age of Profumo*, HarperCollins, 2013.

83 The diary entry was made in February 1960, from *The Macmillan Diaries: Prime Minister and After, 1957–1966*, edited by Peter Catterall and published by Macmillan, 2011. It coincided with the birth of Prince Andrew.

84 The 'Man in the Mask' scandal was a baseless *Private Eye* rumour linking Prince Philip to masked sex parties during the Profumo Affair.

85 Sir Joseph Simpson, Commissioner of the Metropolitan Police during the Profumo Affair, oversaw key investigations into the scandal's ties to espionage and national security. Appointed in 1958, Simpson played a pivotal role in managing the fallout, including confirming Ward's imminent arrest, which underscored the Affair's explosive political implications. He held the position until his death in 1968.

86 Clive Irving, Ron Hall, and Jeremy Wallington, *Scandal '63: A Study of the Profumo Affair*, Heinemann, 1963.

Chapter 8: Fair Game

87 In 1968, Prince Philip participated in his first network television interview on ITV's *Face the Press*, where he discussed topics such as the North-South divide, his role in modern society, and his views on contemporary Britain.

88 Walter Bagehot wrote about the concept of 'daylight' being let in on magic in his book, *The English Constitution*, 1867. In it, Bagehot discusses the role of the monarchy and the dangers of exposing the institution to public

scrutiny, suggesting that revealing too much could diminish its mystique and authority.

89 In the 1969 *Royal Family* documentary, Queen Elizabeth II humorously recalled a Home Secretary describing a visitor, widely believed to be the US ambassador Walter Annenberg, as resembling a 'gorilla' with 'a short body and long arms'.

90 John Grigg in an article published in the *Observer* on 29 June 1969.

91 Princess Anne called the *Royal Family* documentary a 'rotten idea' in an interview with Janet Street-Porter for the *Independent*, published on 5 February 2015, where she discussed the increased scrutiny faced by the Royal Family following the film.

92 Prince Philip became the first British royal to appear on NBC's *Meet the Press* on 9 November 1969, exploring the monarchy's evolving role and comparisons with European royals, in a bid to engage more openly with the public.

93 Jonathan Dimbleby, *The Prince of Wales: A Biography*, Little, Brown and Company, 1994.

94 Dimbleby, *The Prince of Wales: A Biography.*

95 Prince Harry, *Spare*, Random House, 2023.

96 Interview with the Princess Royal for the BBC TV documentary, *Queen & Country*, to mark the Queen's Golden Jubilee in 2002.

Chapter 9: The Camilla Dilemma

97 Letter by Prince Charles about Camilla to Lord Mountbatten.

98 As per Cambridge University tradition, his BA was later elevated to a Master of Arts (MA Cantab) degree without further study.

99 The letter to Prince Charles, dated 23 August 1974, comes from the Mountbatten diaries, and has been cited in many biographies about the British Royal Family. The diaries housed at the University of Southampton, became the centre of controversy when the UK Cabinet Office restricted access, citing sensitive content. Historian Dr Andrew Lownie fought for their release, leading to some being published online in 2021, though key entries, like those from 1947, remain withheld. Despite partial digitisation, the diaries are still not fully accessible to the public.

100 Rupert Murdoch triumphed over rivals to seize control of the *News of the World* in 1969. The same year he founded the *Sun* after buying the defunct *Daily Herald* and directed the editor Larry Lamb to transform it into a 'tearaway' tabloid.

101 James Beaton, GC, CVO, was appointed as the Queen's Personal Protection Officer (PPO) in 1982, a position he held until his retirement from the Metropolitan Police in 1992 with the rank of Chief Superintendent.

102 Andrew Lownie, *The Mountbattens: Their Lives & Loves*, Blink Publishing, 2019. It references multiple accounts of Mountbatten's alleged abuse of children and teenagers. Dr Lownie cites various sources, including testimonies and historical records, to substantiate his claims.

103 From the documentary *Diana: In Her Own Words*, Crown Productions in association with Channel 4, 2017.

Chapter 10: A Lamb to the Slaughter

104 Robert Jobson, *Our King, Charles III*, John Blake, 2023.

105 Jobson, *Our King, Charles III.*

106 Andrew Morton, *Diana: Her True Story – In Her Own Words,* Michael O'Mara Books, 1997. This edition includes transcripts from Diana's recorded interviews.

107 Jobson, *Our King, Charles III.*

108 Morton, *Diana: Her True Story – In Her Own Words*, 1997.

109 Jobson, *Our King, Charles III.*

110 Jobson, *Our King, Charles III.*

Chapter 11: Separate Lives

111 Morton, *Diana Her True Story – In Her Own Words.*

112 Morton, *Diana Her True Story – In Her Own Words.*

113 Robert Jobson, *Harry's War*, John Blake, 2008.

114 From an interview conducted by a ten-year-old Royal Marsden cancer patient called Alice for CBBC's *Newsround.*

Chapter 12: Special Friends

115 Sacha, Duchess of Abercorn spoke of her relationship to author Gyles Brandreth for his bestselling book, *Philip and Elizabeth: Portrait of a Marriage*, published by Century in 2004.

116 Sarah Bradford, *Elizabeth II: Her Life in Our Times,* Penguin Books, 2011.

117 Brandreth, *Philip & Elizabeth: Portrait of a Marriage*, 2004.

118 Gyles Brandreth, *Philip: The Final Portrait*, HarperCollins, 2021.

119 Brandreth, *Philip & Elizabeth: Portrait of a Marriage*. Brandreth claimed the newspapers and Fagan had got it wrong.

120 From Ingrid Seward's *Prince Philip Revealed*, Simon & Schuster UK, October 2020.

121 Interview by the author with a senior former member of the Royal Household.

Chapter 13: The People's Princess

122 In June 1997, Princess Diana collaborated with Christie's New York, and auctioned 79 of her dresses, including the 'Revenge Dress', raising $3.25 million for cancer and AIDS charities. Prince William inspired the idea. The Stambolian gown alone fetched £39,098.

123 Interview by the author with a royal source.

124 On 21 July, 2022, the BBC paid damages to Alexandra Pettifer (Tiggy) over false claims of an affair with Prince Charles and an abortion, fabricated to secure a 1995 Diana interview. A probe revealed journalist Martin Bashir had deceived Diana, damaging Mrs Pettifer and the Royal Family's image. The BBC apologised and paid a substantial settlement. In January 2025, William expressed being 'shocked and saddened' by the death of Tiggy's stepson, Edward Pettifer, thirty-one, who was among fourteen people killed on a New Year's Day terrorist attack when a truck hit crowds in New Orleans. King Charles also voiced deep sorrow, while the Pettifer family remembered Edward as a 'wonderful son, brother, and friend'. Harry made no public comment.

125 From two books by Simone Simmons, *Diana: The Secret Years*, Michael O'Mara Books, 1998, and *Diana: The Last Word*, Orion Publishing Group, 2005.

126 This statement came after Lord Dyson's independent report revealed BBC journalist Martin Bashir's use of forged documents to secure the interview, a move that deeply betrayed Diana's trust.

127 Simmons, *Diana: The Last Word*, 2005.

128 Richard Kay in 2017 documentary *Diana: The Woman Inside* produced by Sonia Anderson, who also directed the film. Entertain Me Productions Ltd created it.

129 The exact quote from Diana, Princess of Wales, in her 1995 BBC *Panorama* interview with Martin Bashir, was: 'I'd like to be a queen of people's hearts, in people's hearts, but I don't see myself being Queen of this country.'

130 Prince Harry, *Spare*, Penguin Random House, 2023.

131 From an interview with Alastair Campbell for *GQ* magazine, 2017.

132 Conversation by the author with Billy Tallon and confirmed by a second inside source.

133 In the 2017 BBC documentary *Diana, 7 Days*, William and Harry reflected on feeling overexposed and pressured by public expectations after their mother's death, highlighting the emotional toll and their sense of having let her down. William: 'I felt completely numb, disorientated, dizzy . . . you feel very, very confused. And you keep asking yourself, "Why me? What have I done? Why has this happened to us?"' Harry: 'I think it was a group effort to make us feel like this was normal. I was so young, I felt like I just wanted her back, but I was also being prepared for public life at the same time.'

134 From an interview with Prince Harry in a 2017 BBC documentary entitled *Diana, 7 Days.* In it he described walking behind his mother's coffin as a 'very long, lonely walk' and expressed that no child 'should be asked to do that, under any circumstances'.

135 Interview with Lord Charteris on the four-part documentary series *The Windsors: A Royal Family.*

Chapter 14: The Proud Meddler

136 Prince Philip's private secretary, Brigadier Sir Miles Hunt-Davis, testified at the Diana inquest, at the Royal Courts of Justice in London presenting letters exchanged between Philip and Diana in 1992 that showed a supportive relationship. Diana addressed him as 'Dearest Pa' and thanked him

for his understanding. Hunt-Davis denied any suggestion Philip wished harm upon her, emphasising the letters' cordial tone. The proceedings began on 2 October 2007 and concluded on 7 April 2008.

137 Toxicology reports revealed that Henri Paul, the driver of the Mercedes car in which Princess Diana and Dodi Fayed were killed, had a blood alcohol level over three times the French legal limit, which contributed to the reckless driving that led to the accident in the Pont d'Alma tunnel in Paris in 1997.

138 Prince Harry, *Spare*, 2023. Also an interview by the author with a royal source.

139 Paul Burrell, Princess Diana's former butler, went on record with the claims about Charles's pampered lifestyle on an Amazon Prime documentary *Serving the Royals: Inside the Firm*, in 2015.

140 From an interview with Prince Charles in a 2005 interview with CBS's *60 Minutes*. When interviewer Steve Kroft noted that becoming king would mean the death of his mother, Charles responded, 'Well, exactly. It's something that comes as a result of something awful happening to you.'

141 Paul Burrell, *A Royal Duty*, Penguin Books, 2003.

142 The Peat Inquiry, commissioned by Prince Charles in 2003 and led by his private secretary Sir Michael Peat, was an internal investigation into allegations of misconduct within the Prince's household, including the sale of royal gifts and claims of sexual assault.

143 Channel 4 Dispatches programme entitled *Charles: The Meddling Prince*, 12 March 2007. MP Brian Iddon tabled an Early Day Motion on the lack of transparency in the Duchy accounts in May 2007.

144 From an interview by the author with a senior royal source. In 2023, Bloomberg estimated his net worth at approximately £9.42 billion.

145 Interviews by the author with sources close to King Charles.

146 From conversations by the author with a former royal aide.

147 Interviews by the author with Royal Household sources in Charles's circle.

148 Interviews by the author with Royal Household sources in Charles's circle. Maurice Chevalier (1888–1972) was a celebrated French actor and singer, known for his signature boater hat and iconic songs like 'Louise' and 'Thank Heaven for Little Girls'.

149 From conversations with a source close to Charles.

150 From conversations with senior royal sources.

151 The documentary by John Bridcut entitled *Prince, Son, and Heir: Charles at 70* was aired on 8 November 2018, on BBC One. It was created to mark Prince Charles's seventieth birthday, offering an intimate look into his life, work, and thoughts on becoming king.

Chapter 15: Sacred Vows

152 The world exclusive scoop was by Robert Jobson, the author of this book.

153 In *Spare*, Harry confirmed that both he and his brother William had initially urged their father not to marry Camilla. Harry also damningly criticises her as 'dangerous', accusing her of trading private information with the press to bolster her image, leaving, as he put it rather sensationally, 'bodies in the street'.

154 In the Channel 4 documentary *Queen Camilla: The Wicked Stepmother*. Tom Quinn, author of several royal books including *Backstairs Billy: The Life of William Tallon, the Queen Mother's Most Devoted Servant*, Robson Press, 2015, recounted an alleged exchange he had with Harry. 'I met Harry at a polo match,' Quinn said. 'When I asked about Camilla, his face darkened, and he said, "Everyone treats her like a goddess, but in fact, she's the wicked stepmother."'

155 *Middle East Quarterly*, Fall 1997, Volume 4, No. 4.

156 From an interview by the author with Inspector Ken Wharfe MVO.

157 Interview by the author with a senior former royal aide.

158 Interview by the author with a senior royal source.

Chapter 16: The Epstein Connection

159 Interview by the author with a senior palace aide.

160 Interview by the author with a palace source.

161 From an interview with Geordie Greig in the *Evening Standard*, published on 8 March 2011.

162 Interview by the author with a senior royal aide.

163 Report by Ian Gallagher and Nick Constable for *Mail on Sunday*, 9 March 2025.

164 From an exclusive report by *Daily Mail* chief reporter Sam Greenhill on 14 December 2024: Prince Andrew was labelled a 'useful idiot' for aiding China's agenda by Mareike Ohlberg, co-author of *Hidden Hand: Exposing How the Chinese Communist Party is Reshaping the World,* Oneworld Publications, 2020, with Clive Hamilton.

165 *Daily Mail* report, 16 December 2024.

Chapter 17: Time's Up

166 Interview by the author with an anonymous senior Royal Household source.

167 Prince Harry, *Spare*, 2023.

168 Interview by the author with a former Royal Household source.

169 Prince Harry, *Spare.*

170 Rebekah Wade (now Rebekah Brooks) was editor of the *News of the World*, and in 2001 her then husband, actor Ross Kemp, went on holiday with Mark Bolland, Prince Charles's deputy private secretary, and his partner, Guy Black, director of the Press Complaints Commission (PCC). This close relationship drew criticism, with some accusing the PCC of being compromised. Wade served as editor from May 2000 to January 2003 before moving on to edit the *Sun.* She is currently the Chief Executive Officer of News UK, a position she has held since September 2015.

171 Prince Harry, *Spare.*

172 Prince Harry made this statement during a January 2023 interview with ITV's Tom Bradby, while promoting his book, *Spare.*

173 Priddy shared these insights in a December 2017 interview with the *Daily Mail*, where she also provided personal photos and videos from their thirty-year friendship.

174 Harry met Chelsy Davy in 2004 and had an on-off relationship that lasted until 2011.

175 In his memoir *Spare* and the ITV-aired interview *Harry: The Interview,*

Harry said William did not warn him against marrying Meghan but raised concerns about the relationship's pace, which Harry saw as scepticism of Meghan's role.

176 'Tiaragate' erupted when Prince Harry clashed with the Queen's dresser, Angela Kelly, over delays in Meghan accessing her wedding tiara, prompting Harry's outburst: 'What Meghan wants, Meghan gets!' Concerns over a tiara's Russian provenance led the Queen to select the Queen Mary Diamond Bandeau, highlighting growing tensions within the Royal Household in the build-up to the royal wedding. In his memoir *Spare*, Harry admitted tensions over Meghan's wedding tiara, blaming Kelly, for delays and unresponsiveness in arranging access to Queen Mary's Diamond Bandeau, causing pre-wedding frustration. He claims that she insisted he sign a formal agreement to release the tiara for Meghan's hair trial, which he refused.

177 Interview by the author with an anonymous senior royal source.

178 Prince Harry, *Spare*.

179 Sunninghill Park was a wedding gift from the Queen. Timur Kulibayev, the billionaire son-in-law of Kazakhstan's then-president Nursultan Nazarbayev, bought it for £15 million, £3 million above the asking price, under controversial circumstances. It fell into disrepair, was demolished in 2016, and replaced by a fourteen-bedroom mansion.

180 From an interview by the author with a former palace aide.

181 Interview by the author with a senior royal aide.

182 The Sussex children, Prince Archie and Princess Lilibet of Sussex, hold titles by birth but have no constitutional role. Though sixth and seventh in line to the throne, they perform no duties, live outside the UK and carry no official function, making their status symbolic, not constitutional.

183 From the 2022 Netflix documentary series *Harry & Meghan*. It was directed by Liz Garbus and produced by Archewell Productions, the company founded by the Sussexes.

Chapter 18: The Fallout

184 Interview by the author with a royal aide.

185 They did not own the cottage as the property belongs to the Crown Estate, and they held it on a long-term lease.

186 In March 2021, Buckingham Palace investigated Meghan's alleged bullying of staff. Around ten aides took part, leading to updates in Human Resources policies, though details are still private.

187 Valentine Low, *Courtiers: The Hidden Power Behind the Crown*, Headline, October 2022/ Paperback, 2023.

188 Interview by the author with an anonymous palace aide.

189 Prince Harry, *Spare*.

190 From an interview by the author with a senior royal aide.

191 Eva resigned as Director of Community Engagement in November 2024 to work in the private sector but remains an adviser to the King.

192 On 9 June 2021, respected BBC royal correspondent Jonny Dymond reported on Radio 4's *Today* programme that a palace source claimed that the Queen was 'never asked' by the Duke and Duchess of Sussex about naming their daughter Lilibet.

193 Interview by the author with a senior palace source.

Chapter 19: The Flights of Angels

194 From an interview by the author with a senior palace source.

195 Interview by the author with a royal source.

196 Interview by the author with a senior royal source.

197 George Strachan Ltd, a family grocer in Ballater and Aboyne, held royal warrants to the late Queen Mother, Queen Elizabeth II, and the Prince of Wales for supplying delicacies to the Balmoral Estate, reflecting years of trusted service to the Royal Household.

198 Interview by the author with a royal source.

199 Gyles Brandreth's *Elizabeth: An Intimate Portrait,* Michael Joseph, 2022, also published that the Queen suffered with multiple myeloma in 2022 within weeks of her death.

200 Robert Hardman, *Charles III: New King, New Court. The Inside Story*, Macmillan, 2023.

201 The Sovereign's Ring, also worn during coronations, symbolises the monarch's sacred bond with the nation and their duty to rule. It is usually placed on a monarch by senior aides and is removed and handed to the next

monarch on their death.

202 Princess Margaret met President Lyndon B. Johnson during her visit to America in 1965, when she represented her sister, Queen Elizabeth. The two reportedly got along well at the White House dinner he hosted in her honour.

203 The phrase 'flights of angels sing thee to thy rest' is a reference to William Shakespeare's play, *Hamlet*. In Act V, Scene 2, Horatio speaks the words, 'Now cracks a noble heart. Good night, sweet prince, and flights of angels sing thee to thy rest,' which were invoked by the new king, Charles III, to express his deep respect for his late mother through this classic literary reference.

204 Prince Harry, *Spare*.

205 From an interview by the author with a senior member of the Royal Household.

206 Prince Harry made this statement during an interview with Anderson Cooper on CBS's *60 Minutes*, which aired on 8 January 2023. The interview was part of the promotional tour for his memoir, *Spare*.

Chapter 20: Vivat Rex Carolus!

207 Notably, some members of the Ascension Choir had previously performed at the wedding of Prince Harry and Meghan Markle in 2018 as part of the Kingdom Choir.

208 Confirmed to the author by senior royal sources at the palace and the media, including the *Mail on Sunday*. When pressed, the palace press office claimed that the servant involved had suffered mental health issues due to loss of a parent. The newspaper ran the story in its entirety, but did not name either royal servant. Fortnum & Mason announced it had adopted a proactive approach to combating shoplifting. In response to rising thefts and a perceived lack of effective police action, the luxury department store decided to employ private detectives and initiate its own prosecutions against shoplifters, rather than relying solely on law enforcement.

209 *Mail on Sunday*, 15 September 2024.

210 Exclusive report by Matt Wilkinson, the royal editor of the *Sun*, 12 December 2024. The cocaine abuse story comes from a senior royal aide in an interview with the author.

211 The Cambridge Dictionary defines a 'grifter' as someone who gets money dishonestly by tricking others.

212 Robert Hardman, *Charles III: New King. New Court. The Inside Story*, updated edition, November 2024.

Chapter 21: Worryingly Decrepit

213 Interview by the author with a Royal Household source.

214 Based on interviews conducted by the author with individuals close to the King and the Royal Household.

215 In the past 250 years, Edward VIII's 326-day reign in 1936 remains the shortest; William IV reigned for seven years (1830–37), overseeing the pivotal Reform Act of 1832; while Edward VII's nine-year reign (1901–10) defined the Edwardian era and advanced diplomacy through initiatives such as the Entente Cordiale with France in 1904.

216 Conversation with the King and the author at Dumfries House, September 2018.

217 Interview by the author with a senior royal source.

218 Interview by the author with a senior royal source.

219 Interview by the author with a senior royal aide.

220 Interview by the author with a senior royal source.

221 Prince William made the comments in an interview with *The Times* journalist Kate Mansey in November 2024 in Cape Town for the UK royal rota.

222 Interview by the author with a senior royal source.

223 Interview by the author with a senior royal source.

Chapter 22: Royally Minted

224 From an article by former Liberal MP Norman Baker in the *Guardian* on 24 November 2023.

225 A royal source told the author.

226 From an article by Libby Purves, *The Times*, 4 November 2024.

227 From an article in the *Guardian* by journalists Felicity Lawrence, Rob

Evans and Henry Dyer on 5 April 2023.

228 From an article by Craig Prescott in the *Sunday Times*, 3 November 2024.

229 In Robert Hardman's book, *Queen of Our Times: The Life of Elizabeth II*, published in 2022. David Cameron approved the Sovereign Grant Bill and deal during his tenure as prime minister, acknowledging that on reflection the new arrangement was 'generous' to the monarchy.

230 Reporter Kate Mansey then of the *Mail on Sunday*, now Assistant Editor of *The Times* won the 2022 'Scoop of the Year' for uncovering Michael Fawcett's honours-for-donations scandal. Gabriel Pogrund of the *Sunday Times* earned 2023 Journalist of the Year for his work on the 'cash-for-honours' scheme, aided by colleague Dipesh Gadher.

231 Hauser & Wirth was founded in 1992 in Zurich by Iwan Wirth, Manuela Wirth and Ursula Hauser, who were joined by Partner and President Marc Payot in 2000. A family business, the firm represents over ninety artists and estates.

232 Interview by the author with a senior household source.

233 In response to a Freedom of Information request from Republic, the Ministry of Defence disclosed that it spent £506,681 on equerries, military aides serving the Royal Family, in 2023. The Ministry of Defence stated that 'the vast majority of costs come from fixed staff costs, which would still be incurred by the government department regardless of where these personnel were employed.' Graham Smith, CEO of Republic, criticised this expenditure, describing it as a 'disgraceful use of highly trained military personnel' and calling for an end to the practice.

234 Tom Bower, *Rebel Prince: The Power, Passion and Defiance of Prince Charles*, William Collins, 2018. Clarification on the toilet seat story from an interview by the author with a Royal Household source.

235 Interview by the author with a senior royal aide.

236 Interview by the author with a senior royal source.

237 Sir Malcom Ross was Master of the Household, and later Comptroller of the Lord Chamberlain's Office for Queen Elizabeth II from 1991–2005 responsible for the domestic affairs of the royal residences, including the management of staff and official events. He joined Prince Charles's staff as Master of the Household in 2006 and served in this position until 2008.

238 Information from an interview by the author with an anonymous inside palace source.

Chapter 23: The Silent Threat

239 From the documentary *Charles: The Private Man, the Public Role*, which aired on ITV on 29 June 1994.

240 From a speech to the House of Commons by Tony Benn on 16 November 1998.

241 Interview by the author with a royal source.

242 The Australian Voice referendum (2023) proposed enshrining an Indigenous advisory body, the Voice to Parliament, in the Constitution but was rejected by a majority of voters nationwide.

243 Prince Harry told Oprah Winfrey in the televised interview on a CBS special on 7 March 2021: 'My father and my brother, they are trapped. They don't get to leave. And I have huge compassion for that.'

244 Article by Richard Kay, *Daily Mail*, 27 March 2025.

245 Prince William's Earthshot Prize was founded in 2020 and funds innovative solutions to global environmental challenges. Five winners annually each receive £1 million to develop their projects. His Homewards initiative announced in 2023 targets homelessness in the UK with localised, sustainable strategies. Both reflect his commitment to tackling urgent social and environmental issues.

246 *Prince William: We Can End Homelessness* is a two-part documentary filmed over twelve months that aired on ITV1 and ITVX on 30 and 31 October 2024. Produced by Mindhouse, the series was directed by BAFTA-winning director Leo Burley and executive produced by Arron Fellows.

247 *Prince William: We Can End Homelessness*, ITV.

248 Matt Wilkinson revealed in *The Sun* that Prince William was moving his family from Adeliade Cottage to Forest Lodge, Windsor in an exclusive on 16 August 2025.

249 Amanda Platell, 19 August, *Daily Mail.*

250 Interview by the author with a senior royal source.

251 Prince William does not own the Duchy of Cornwall but controls it as

Duke of Cornwall and he is paid the profits annually during his tenure.

252 Tina Brown, *The Diana Chronicles* (2007) and *The Palace Papers* (2022), both published by Penguin Random House; also from columnist Richard Eden, 'Eden Confidential', *Daily Mail*, 12 November 2024.

253 A.N. Wilson, *Daily Mail*, 31 December 2024.

254 Prince Charles had a strained relationship with Lord Geidt, the Queen's former private secretary, whose attempts to unify royal households and streamline operations were seen by Charles as overreach that could limit his influence. In 2017, Geidt was reportedly forced out following concerns raised by Charles and the Duke of York, a move some described as a 'palace coup' that expanded Charles's control over the monarchy.

255 Interview by the author with a former member of the Royal Household.